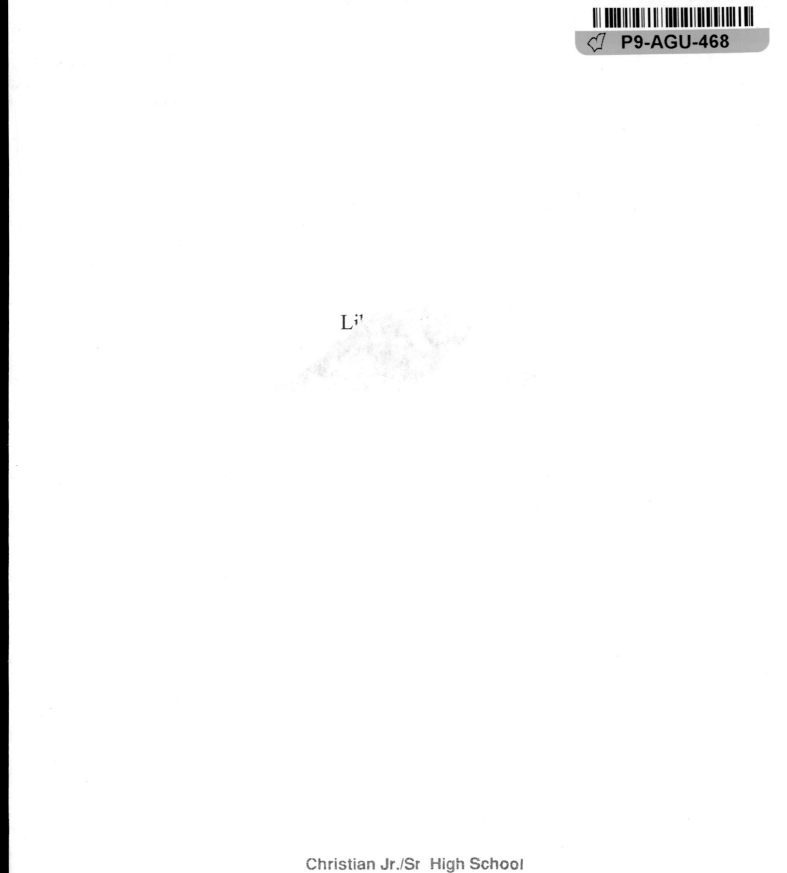

Li'

Library 101

A Handbook for the School Library Media Specialist

Claire Gatrell Stephens and Patricia Franklin

LIBRARIES UNLIMITED

A Member of the Greenwood Publishing Group

Westport, Connecticut • London

Library of Congress Cataloging-in-Publication Data

Stephens, Claire Gatrell.
  Library 101 : a handbook for the school library media specialist /
Claire Gatrell Stephens and Patricia Franklin.
     p. cm.
  Includes bibliographical references and index.
  ISBN 978–1–59158–324–0 (alk. paper)
  1. School libraries—United States—Handbooks, manuals, etc. 2. Instructional materials
centers—United States—Handbooks, manuals, etc. I. Franklin, Patricia, 1951–
II. Title. III. Title: Library one hundred and one.
  Z675.S3S77   2007
   027.80973—dc22   2007018420

British Library Cataloguing in Publication Data is available.

Library of Congress Catalog Card Number: 2007018420
ISBN: 978–1–59158–324–0

First published in 2007

Libraries Unlimited, 88 Post Road West, Westport, CT 06881
A Member of the Greenwood Publishing Group, Inc.
www.lu.com

Printed in the United States of America

∞

The paper used in this book complies with the
Permanent Paper Standard issued by the National
Information Standards Organization (Z39.48–1984).

10 9 8 7 6 5 4 3 2 1

*Thanks to my family who continually support me in my
professional endeavors.
Also, thank you to Lori Luther who taught me that there is so much
more to being a library media specialist than just reading books.*

Pat Franklin

*For Shirley Petit, who thought I would be a good media specialist.
Also, for Teanna and Kathy, you are wonderful new media specialists.
I've enjoyed working with you and watching you embrace the profession.
Finally, thanks to God for leading me to a career I love.*

Claire Stephens

Contents

Part I
Day-to-Day Basics

Part II
The Media Specialist as Teacher Collaborator

Part III
Long-term Vision—Managing Your Collection

Part IV
Equipping Your Library Media Center

Foreword

How We Got Started . . .

Pat—Career Discovery

I was never sure what I wanted to be when I grew up. With my husband in the U.S. Navy, we lived in big cities and little towns all over the world. I taught speech and English in junior high school, effective writing to military personnel, high school completion courses to soldiers, and every content area to pregnant teens. Along the way, I took graduate courses in reading and even considered becoming a guidance counselor. (This still makes my friends laugh because they know I would just tell kids with problems to "snap out of it!" and to "think about people with real problems!")

My first graduate course taught by Donna Baumbach at the University of Central Florida convinced me that I wanted to be a library media specialist. In that class were friendly colleagues with energy and ideas, people who were passionate about learning and making their media programs stimulating and motivating. Here was a career that combined the fun of teaching, the love of books, and the curiosity of emerging technologies all into one. I would never get bored! My first year was the best possible scenario imaginable. I was at Liberty Middle School, a large school (2,200 students) that had another full-time media specialist, Lori, and two media clerks. Lori taught me everything—from how collaborating with teachers can enhance instruction, to how weeding books can make a collection bigger and stronger. I learned that service is our top priority and that teachers and students who enjoy coming to the media center will promote your program for you. Even after I was asked to open the library media center for Discovery Middle School, the relief school for that large middle school, I continued to look to Lori as a mentor because of her expertise.

Six years after opening Discovery, we moved the entire school to a new building, so it was like opening another new school with the luxury of knowing your entire staff! Since then I have opened a new high school, Timber Creek High School, which now has 4,200 students. Every day I wake up and feel good about going to a job that is neither mundane nor trivial. What I do affects everyone in my school. As you read this book, remember that every day will be different, offering new challenges. Enjoy the challenges, and if you are stressed out, just check out a good book and relax!

Claire—The Accidental Librarian

I never intended to be a media specialist. I wanted to teach Television Production. In 1987, I was hired to teach at Dr. Phillips High School in Orlando, Florida. The school was brand new and boasted a state of the art television studio. The teachers in that program, Keith Kyker and Chris Curchy, were wonderful, and the program grew. My own creative tendencies naturally drew me to Chris and Keith's program and I began collaborating with them on video projects. Several years later, when the campus was about to expand, I saw the chance to segue into teaching one or two sections of the television class. Even though

I was certified to teach the TV course, my assistant principal told me they preferred teachers to be certified in "the primary area of certification," which was media specialist. I enrolled at the University of Central Florida, where I earned my media specialist certification and the opportunity to teach the course.

As it always does, time passed, and one day I got a phone call from the district Library Resource Specialist. "Don't hang up," she said, and then began to tell me about a middle school that needed a media specialist who knew how to do TV. I was not looking for a new position, but the time was right for me to make a change. I said yes. When I called my mother to tell her about the career change, her response was, "Oh, I'm not surprised to hear that at all. You worked in the school library all through elementary and junior high. I think you only stopped because they wouldn't let you do it in high school." She was right, and I had totally forgotten that I had been one of those kids we affectionately call a library nerd.

My first day on the job as a media specialist, I walked into my library and looked around. I didn't know where to begin, so I decorated a bulletin board. Looking back at that day, I laugh at myself for using my time that way, but I know when I left at the end of the day that I felt at home, like I was where I belonged, and I am there still. I've been a school media specialist for more than 11 years now, first at Walker Middle School, and for the past three years at another brand new school, Freedom High School. I can honestly say it is the best job in the world. I am always busy, never bored, always learning, and surrounded by books and students. What more could anyone want? I hope this book will help readers to enter into the field of school library media and find their home, too.

Acknowledgments

The American Association of School Librarians, a division of the American Library Association, Chicago, Illinois.

Clip art used by agreement with ClipArt.Com.

Dr. Donna Baumbach, Department of Educational Services, University of Central Florida, Orlando.

Follett Software Company.

Garrett Book Company.

Debbie Hall, Media Specialist, Trinity Lutheran Church and School, Orlando, Florida.

Keith Kyker.

Dr. Judy Lee, Program Coordinator, Online Masters of Education and Certificate Program in Educational Media, University of Central Florida, Orlando.

Sam Morris.

Nancy Pelser-Borowicz, Media Director, Orange County Public Schools, Orlando, Florida.

Doug Johnson photo courtesy of the author's Web site.

Judge "Rick" Roach, District 3 Representative, Orange County School Board, Orange County Public Schools, Orlando Florida.

Dylan Thomas, Director, Community Relations, Orange County Public Schools, Orlando, Florida.

School Board of Orange County, Orange County Public Schools, Orlando, Florida, for permission to use interior photos of district library media centers.

Jim Trelease photo courtesy of the author's Web site.

H. W. Wilson Company.

And a Special Acknowledgement to . . .

Our fellow media specialists working for Orange County Public Schools in Orlando, Florida, who warmly embraced our requests for ideas and information to include in this book. They unselfishly shared so many tips of the trade with us that we could not include them all. Thanks to all of you. You are the best!

Pat and Claire

Part I

Day-to-Day Basics

1

Your Role as a School Library Media Specialist

So, you wanted to be a school library media specialist because you love books and you love kids. Well, that's a good start! Being a library media specialist is one of the most rewarding professions available to teachers. It is also one of the most challenging. Your role is largely determined by your grade level, the mission of your school, and your clientele. More often than not, you are wearing many hats and devoting the bulk of your time to what is needed most in your school. In the day-to-day operation of a library media center, service is your most important job. You are employed to be of service to your students, teachers, administrators, and parents.

According to *Information Power: Building Partnerships for Learning*, prepared by the American Association of School Librarians (AASL), school library media specialists' job descriptions fall into three categories: teaching and learning, information access, and program administrator. In an ideal world, we would have sufficient staff, funding, and time to cover each of these areas thoroughly. In the real world, we work constantly in each of these areas, but how much time we devote to each area can vary greatly.

Teaching and Learning

Our first mission is to get to know our students. By learning about them, we will become better teachers. When we learn our school's demographic statistics, discover our student's religious beliefs and their socioeconomic level, we will have a better idea of the

3

Sidebar 1.01

In an ideal world, we have clerks help us with clerical tasks, but in the real world...

"Having a clerk let me devote more attention to work with classes and small groups without having to keep an eye on the circulation desk. Now, I am without a clerk. I have student assistants who can check out, but if there are problems, or if someone needs to pay for a lost book, I'm the only one who can do that. When I had a clerk, I could go to classrooms to assist teachers and do book talks. Now if I'm not in the library, it is closed."

Jennifer Dillon, NBCT Library Media Media Specialist, Williams Middle Magnet School Tampa, Florida

types of materials to purchase. But by getting to know students as individuals, we will be able to really teach them. We will know their interests and how these interests will lead them to the subject matter content and the higher level thinking skills we are teaching with each lesson.

Since any teacher's major concern is student achievement, we are another way a student finds success in the classroom. Whether we are teaching an entire class or giving one-on-one instruction, we are teaching library skills that connect to content areas. Before flexible scheduling, we taught library skills in isolation. Today, we know that students learn better when what they are doing matters to them. We collaborate with teachers by developing lessons that incorporate important research skills into their content area lessons.

Sometimes teachers may want us to teach an entire lesson on something like using an encyclopedia, or they may just want us to pull a cartload of books that will apply to the research their students are undertaking in the classroom. On other occasions, we teach in the library media center where we direct students to numerous resources; sometimes we teach in the computer lab where we show students how to find and present information. Often, we go to the classroom where we give book talks or teach units on plagiarism, intellectual freedom, or other issues relevant to the teacher.

No matter how or what we teach, the actual lessons must be a collaboration between the media specialist and the teacher. Whether it is the media specialist or the teacher who initiates the lesson and writes the lesson plan, it somehow must lead to greater learning for students. An elementary school media specialist might teach a lesson on what a call number is, or where to find the call number on a book, or how to look at the online catalog to find the call number and then how to find it on the shelves. Any of these lessons will further the knowledge of a little one trying to do a report on an animal for his teacher. A middle school media specialist may give a book talk on historical fiction that enhances a history unit on the Holocaust. With all of the many excellent historical fiction books available, the teacher could expand the unit to touch on how different countries were affected by the Holocaust, including the United States. A high school media specialist might teach a lesson on the advantages of using subscription online databases as opposed to search engines to find accurate, up-to-date information for a science report. No matter what the lesson, media specialists are teachers who develop lesson plans and teach critical skills to students.

We must also constantly update our own skills. When we buy new equipment, it is imperative that we become experts in that equipment because teachers will come to us for setup and use problems. It is imperative to attend conferences to learn about emerging technologies, as well as current teaching trends, so that we can support the needs of our teachers. Many times we learn on the go, but finding the answers to questions about equipment or about the latest educational trend is an essential part of our job. For example, a teacher asked recently if the professional section of the library media center had any

TABLE 1.01: Where Can I Find Library Lessons and Standards?

Web sites

http://www.wayne.k12.in.us/bdmedia/capture.htm—This site for Ben Davis High School in Indianapolis, Indiana, contains links to an online orientation designed by media specialist Pamela S. Bacon, author of *Creating Online Courses and Orientations*, published by Libraries Unlimited.

http://falcon.jmu.edu/~ramseyil/vasols.htm—This site contains links to standards for library studies in the state of Virginia.

http://www.libraryinstruction.com/lessons.html—Library Instruction.Com bills itself as the librarian's weapon of mass instruction! Check out this site for interesting lesson ideas.

Books

Collaborative Library Lessons for the Primary Grades: Linking Research Skills to Curriculum Standards by Brenda S. Copeland and Patricia A. Messner. Published by Libraries Unlimited.
Instant Library Lessons: 2nd Grade by Karen Wannamaker. Published by Upstart Books.
Stretchy Library Lessons: Library Skills: Grades K-5 by Pat Miller. Published by Upstart Books.
Stretchy Library Lessons: Reading Activities: Grades K-5 by Pat Miller. Published by Highsmith Inc.
Magical Library Lessons by Lynne Farrell Stover. Published by Upstart Books.
Stretchy Library Lessons: Seasons and Celebrations by Pat Miller. Published by Upstart Books.
Dewey & the Decimals: Learning Games & Activities by Paige Taylor. Published by Highsmith Press.

These Web sites and books are excellent sources for usable library lessons and standards information.

books on differentiated learning. Perusing books on that topic and others gives us insights as to what is important to teachers.

Information Access

The second important part of our job is to provide information access. We teach students how to use the online catalog so that they can find that one great book they need. We teach them where the index of a book is so they can find the information they need to finish their project. We teach them how to do Boolean searches so that they can get beyond the books and find relevant, accurate, up-to-date information on the Internet. We provide access by making wise purchases of books, audiovisual materials, and online databases. Using core collection lists from vendors often results in older, unappealing books. We look at each book or read reviews to purchase books just right for our clientele and for the units we know our teachers are teaching to incorporate state benchmarks.

We provide for all students by making sure our collection covers all areas of interest to teachers and students. Knowing that we have diverse populations in our schools, we make sure we have something that will appeal to everyone. Many of our students have learning or physical disabilities. Providing materials on all reading levels increases the number of students who will use your collection. Knowing your students and providing for those with physical and learning disabilities will open up your collection to more students. Audiobooks, large-print books, and adaptive computer screens are just a few ways to help students with disabilities.

Sometimes we provide access by talking to a class in the media center or computer lab. In some circumstances, we must take part of our collection into a classroom. We also provide access in students'

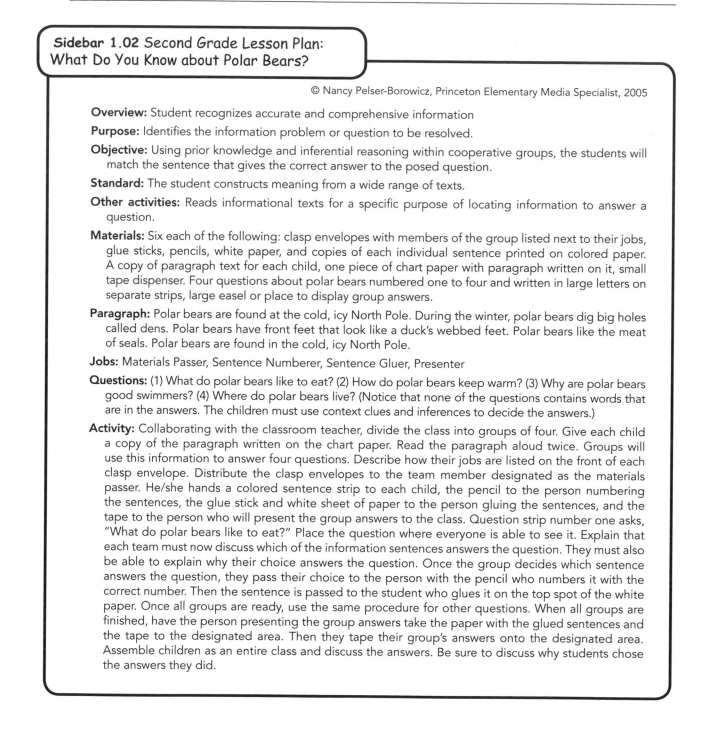

Sidebar 1.02 Second Grade Lesson Plan: What Do You Know about Polar Bears?

© Nancy Pelser-Borowicz, Princeton Elementary Media Specialist, 2005

Overview: Student recognizes accurate and comprehensive information

Purpose: Identifies the information problem or question to be resolved.

Objective: Using prior knowledge and inferential reasoning within cooperative groups, the students will match the sentence that gives the correct answer to the posed question.

Standard: The student constructs meaning from a wide range of texts.

Other activities: Reads informational texts for a specific purpose of locating information to answer a question.

Materials: Six each of the following: clasp envelopes with members of the group listed next to their jobs, glue sticks, pencils, white paper, and copies of each individual sentence printed on colored paper. A copy of paragraph text for each child, one piece of chart paper with paragraph written on it, small tape dispenser. Four questions about polar bears numbered one to four and written in large letters on separate strips, large easel or place to display group answers.

Paragraph: Polar bears are found at the cold, icy North Pole. During the winter, polar bears dig big holes called dens. Polar bears have front feet that look like a duck's webbed feet. Polar bears like the meat of seals. Polar bears are found in the cold, icy North Pole.

Jobs: Materials Passer, Sentence Numberer, Sentence Gluer, Presenter

Questions: (1) What do polar bears like to eat? (2) How do polar bears keep warm? (3) Why are polar bears good swimmers? (4) Where do polar bears live? (Notice that none of the questions contains words that are in the answers. The children must use context clues and inferences to decide the answers.)

Activity: Collaborating with the classroom teacher, divide the class into groups of four. Give each child a copy of the paragraph written on the chart paper. Read the paragraph aloud twice. Groups will use this information to answer four questions. Describe how their jobs are listed on the front of each clasp envelope. Distribute the clasp envelopes to the team member designated as the materials passer. He/she hands a colored sentence strip to each child, the pencil to the person numbering the sentences, the glue stick and white sheet of paper to the person gluing the sentences, and the tape to the person who will present the group answers to the class. Question strip number one asks, "What do polar bears like to eat?" Place the question where everyone is able to see it. Explain that each team must now discuss which of the information sentences answers the question. They must also be able to explain why their choice answers the question. Once the group decides which sentence answers the question, they pass their choice to the person with the pencil who numbers it with the correct number. Then the sentence is passed to the student who glues it on the top spot of the white paper. Once all groups are ready, use the same procedure for other questions. When all groups are finished, have the person presenting the group answers take the paper with the glued sentences and the tape to the designated area. Then they tape their group's answers onto the designated area. Assemble children as an entire class and discuss the answers. Be sure to discuss why students chose the answers they did.

homes by making sure parents are aware of our online databases or our summer reading lists by highlighting them in our school newsletter and on our school Web site.

Program Administrator

In order to truly make your school library media center the heart of the school, you must administer your program to benefit all stakeholders: students, teachers, administrators, and parents. Although you

TABLE 1.02: Student diversity in the same school district.

Knowing the students at your school helps you understand their background experiences and perspective on the world. This knowledge will guide you in materials selection, lesson planning, and program development. The table below shows how diverse school populations can be within one district.

Name of Middle School	Discovery	Liberty	Robbinswood	Southwest
Caucasian	55%	33%	12%	52%
African American	10%	8%	72%	19%
Hispanic	30%	56%	12%	18%
Asian	7%	3%	3%	10%

Source: Orange County Public Schools, June 2005. Available at: http://www.ocps.net.

Sidebar 1.03 Check Out the Media Center

©Patricia Franklin 2004

Newsletters are a great way to communicate with the parents of your students. The article below was included in the fall 2004 issue of the Timber Creek High School newsletter.

The media center has been a busy place since school started. If your student hasn't stopped by, make sure you mention that we have new books on display for checkout. In September, during Banned Books Week, September 27 to October 1, we spearheaded the "We Elect to Read" campaign and discussed the freedom to read we are so fortunate to have thanks to the First Amendment. In October, we are spotlighting Graphic Novels for Teen Read Week, which is October 17 to 23. In November, we display Hispanic books and culture, and in December, we showcase Holidays around the World. Ask your child to stop by and see what is new!

If you would like to know what books we have in our media center, just go to www.sunlink. ucf.edu. This Web site is a state database that shows you books from public school libraries in Florida. If you see a book that you'd like but we don't have it, check if another school in Orange County has it. Let us know, and we will borrow it for you.

Does your child have a report to write and you just don't feel like driving to the library? Can't find anything that is accurate and reliable by surfing the Web? That's why we have purchased online subscription services for your child to use at school and at home. The passwords for Timber Creek student use are published in this newsletter.

Don't forget our Timber Creek High School Book Club. Each month, we choose a book and ask students, teachers, and parents to read this book and attend a meeting to discuss it. In October, our book selection was *The Curious Incident of the Dog in the Night-time* by Mark Haddon. Our November selection is *Before Women Had Wings* by Connie May Fowler. We are excited about Ms. Fowler joining us at TCHS for a discussion of her book. Please join your child for that exciting discussion. (You won't get extra credit in your English class, but your child will!) Happy Reading!

may have teachers envy you because of the flexibility of working in the library media center, in reality, your day is longer and you probably have no planning period like other classroom teachers. You will undoubtedly take work home as you help plan lessons and programs or peruse professional journals for ideas or book reviews.

TABLE 1.03: Sample day in the life of a media specialist.

No day is ever the same for a busy library media specialist. Below is a sample of some of the things that you may encounter in a typical day.

6:50 A.M.	Arrive at school. Begin going through snail mail and e-mail.
7:00 A.M.	Open media center to students who need to print, research, read, and so forth.
7:45 A.M.	First period. Teach a class how to use your newest online database.
8:45 A.M.	Second period. Plan with teacher to teach PowerPoint for science project.
9:45 A.M.	Third period. Go to a classroom to troubleshoot an LCD projector problem.
10:00 A.M.	Work on book order list from reviews read last night.
10:45 A.M.	Fourth period. Go to a classroom to give a book talk on new books.
11:45 A.M.	Lunch (only interrupted a few times!)
12:15 A.M.	Meet with teacher about upcoming book club.
12:30 P.M.	Meet with bookkeeper about latest purchase order.
12:45 P.M.	Fifth period. Continue working on book list.
1:00 P.M.	Check in new books. Return e-mail from teachers, administration.
1:45 P.M.	Sixth period. Rearrange shelves to accommodate new books.
2:45 P.M.	End of school day. Students stop by the media center for reading or using the computer. You finish e-mail, tie up loose ends, meet with teachers, and finish going through snail mail.
3:30 P.M.	Gather periodicals and professional journals to read later and head home.

Never the Same

Whether you are teaching and learning, accessing information, or administering your program, you can be sure of one thing. Your day-to-day life as a media specialist will never be routine. The activities shown in Table 1.03 are those that happen in between helping students and teaching or facilitating classes, and are only possible if you have expert clerks who operate the circulation desk and help with cataloging and shelving books.

Understanding library organization is the first step to becoming an effective library media specialist.

Bibliography

American Association of School Librarians. *Information Power: Building Partnerships for Learning.* Chicago: American Library Association, 1998.

2

Understanding Library Organization

At a meeting a few years ago, a young teacher recently appointed to the position of media specialist at her school bragged about moving books around.

"There were books about cars everywhere," she said. "I moved them all together. Now all the car books are in the 300s!"

Librarians in the room gasped and attempted to explain to the young teacher why the car books belonged in different locations around the book stacks. The teacher in this story had no training or experience in the field of library media, so her actions were understandable. She did not know how and why libraries are organized. Unfortunately, experience over the past few years indicates that she is not alone. A lack of qualified candidates, staff cuts, and poor administrative awareness about the importance of library programs have caused school principals across the country to place inexperienced staff in charge of the school media center. Given this situation, we felt it important to provide a background on the hows and whys of library organization.

Effective organization allows everyone using the collection to locate individual things quickly, easily, and correctly. With even a small school library containing thousands of items, good organization is necessary in order to operate efficiently. Most school and public libraries in the world follow a similar pattern of organization popularized by Melvil Dewey.

Why the Dewey Decimal System?

Up until the late 1800s, library materials were not organized according to subject matter. Books were numbered according to their locations on the shelves. In other words, each book had a fixed location—a specific place on a specific shelf without regard to what was located around it. Melvil Dewey radically changed this approach to library organization with the development of what we call the Dewey Decimal System. While not perfect, Dewey's method of classification allows flexibility for librarians who can now rearrange

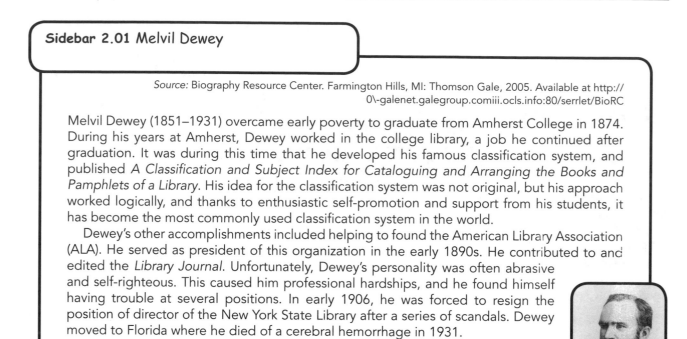

Sidebar 2.01 Melvil Dewey

Source: Biography Resource Center. Farmington Hills, MI: Thomson Gale, 2005. Available at http://0\-galenet.galegroup.comiii.ocls.info:80/serrlet/BioRC

Melvil Dewey (1851–1931) overcame early poverty to graduate from Amherst College in 1874. During his years at Amherst, Dewey worked in the college library, a job he continued after graduation. It was during this time that he developed his famous classification system, and published *A Classification and Subject Index for Cataloguing and Arranging the Books and Pamphlets of a Library*. His idea for the classification system was not original, but his approach worked logically, and thanks to enthusiastic self-promotion and support from his students, it has become the most commonly used classification system in the world.

Dewey's other accomplishments included helping to found the American Library Association (ALA). He served as president of this organization in the early 1890s. He contributed to and edited the *Library Journal*. Unfortunately, Dewey's personality was often abrasive and self-righteous. This caused him professional hardships, and he found himself having trouble at several positions. In early 1906, he was forced to resign the position of director of the New York State Library after a series of scandals. Dewey moved to Florida where he died of a cerebral hemorrhage in 1931.

Melvil Dewey

or move collections as needed without having to recatalog large numbers of items. It also allows library patrons to locate multiple resources while browsing the shelves since books with similar subject matter are grouped together.

How Does the Dewey Decimal System Work?

Dewey divided all areas of knowledge into 10 main categories, as illustrated in Table 2.01. Each of these 10 areas is further subdivided into specialized fields related to the overall topic. So, for example, the 500s are broadly called *Sciences*; however, as you begin to browse this area of your collection, you will notice a pattern emerging. Books falling between 510 and 519 relate to mathematics, 520 to 529 have astronomy as their common bond, 530 to 539 contains books about physics, and so on. Each section is further subdivided and divided again. Carried to the extreme, the Dewey Decimal System makes it possible to catalog a book with exacting precision based on its content.

Most school librarians do not push their Dewey numbers to the extreme. Depending on their level, most school collections use the basic Dewey number with only one to three numbers extended beyond the decimal point. Below is an example. Each call number is for the same book, *The Galveston Hurricane* by Kristine Brennan, published by Chelsea House in 2002. The first number comes from a middle school, the second and third come from high schools.

976.4—This number used for books about the history of Texas.

976.413—This number used for books about Matagorda and neighboring counties in southeast Texas. (Galveston is nearby.)

976.4139—This number used for books specific to Galveston County Texas in the twentieth century. (Sources: Sunlink, at http://www.sunlink.ucf.edu, and *Dewey Decimal Classification and Relative Index*, 22nd ed., 2003.)

Why would these numbers be different? Librarians make these decisions based on their school community and collections. Therefore, an elementary media specialist might decide to limit Dewey numbers to the whole number to the left of the decimal point, making it easier for younger students to understand. A middle school and high school might expand their numbers going one, two, or more places to the right of the decimal. As students gain a better understanding of decimals in general, their ability to locate books will increase. Finally, assuming a progression with the elementary collection being the smallest and the high school collection being the largest, increasing the places in the Dewey number allows for more effective grouping of the books according to subject matter.

As you become more familiar with the Dewey Decimal System, you will begin to understand why it is possible to find books about cars in several different locations of the Media Center. In the 300s, you might find books about the impact of the automobile on society or the business of making and selling cars. In the 600s, you will find books related to the mechanics and engineering of cars. Finally, in the 700s, the racing enthusiast will find books related to motor sports—race cars! The selection of the Dewey number depends on the emphasis of the book. Refer to section two, chapter 4 for more detailed information about cataloging your collection.

Special Collections

In addition to standard Dewey numbers, most libraries commonly pull groupings of books together in special collections. Many of these, such as a fiction section, are commonplace. In reality, fiction should be included with the 800s as literature. Most libraries now reserve the 800 section for works of classical literature, poetry, and plays, along with literary criticism, while novels of all sorts are shelved together in a separate section.

In a public library, special collections often include sections devoted to local history, genealogy, audio recordings, and more. College and university libraries often have special collections devoted to government documents, specialized areas of study, and archival works. Common special sections in schools might include a section dedicated to careers, award-winning books such as the Newbery Medal winners, or professional materials for teachers. Table 2.01 contains a list of special sections common to most libraries. When you are considering creating an unusual special section in your Media Center, it is important to take time and carefully consider the following things:

- How and why will this special collection meet the needs of my patrons?
- Does this collection fill a long-term need? If not, consider placing the items in question on reserve temporarily.
- Where will I house the items in this collection? Is there enough space in the area for the collection to grow?
- What existing resources are available for the collection? Will you need to weed or buy items for the new section?
- Will you have to change the cataloging for these items?
- Will this collection circulate? What will the checkout period be? Will there be a limit to the number of items a patron can borrow?
- Will the change require processing the books in some way? For example, you may add a special designation to the spine label or an identification sticker.
- How will patrons know where to find the items in this collection?

TABLE 2.01: Dewey decimal system.

000 Generalities

010 Bibliography
020 Library and Information Sciences
030 General Encyclopedic Works
040 Unassigned
050 General Serials and Their Indexes
060 General Organizations & Museology
070 News Media, Journalism, Publishing
080 General Collections
090 Manuscripts and Rare Books

200 Religion

210 Natural Theology
220 Bible
230 Christian Theology
240 Christian Moral and Devotional
     Theology
250 Christian Orders and Local Church
260 Christian Social Theology
270 Christian Church History
280 Christian Denominations and Sects
290 Other and Comparative Religions

400 Language

410 Linguistics
420 English and Old English
430 Germanic Languages—German
440 Romance Languages—French
450 Italian, Romanian Languages
460 Spanish, Portuguese Languages
470 Italic Languages, Latin
480 Hellenic Languages, Classical Greek
490 Other Languages

600 Technology (Applied Sciences)

600 General Technology
610 Medical Sciences and Medicine
620 Engineering and Allied Operations
630 Agriculture
640 Home Economics and Family Living
650 Management and Auxiliary Services
660 Chemical Engineering
670 Manufacturing
680 Manufacture for Specific Uses
690 Buildings

800 Literature and Rhetoric

810 American Literature
820 English and Old English Literature

100 Philosophy and Psychology

110 Metaphysics
120 Epistemology, Causation, Humankind
130 Paranormal Phenomena, Occult
140 Specific Philosophical Schools
150 Psychology
160 Logic
170 Ethics (Moral Philosophy)
180 Ancient, Medieval, Oriental Philosophy
190 Modern Western Philosophy

300 Social Science

300 Sociology and Anthropology
310 General Statistics
320 Political Science
330 Economics
340 Law
350 Public Administration
360 Social Services, Associations
370 Education
380 Commerce, Communications, Transport
390 Customs, Etiquette, Folklore

500 Sciences

510 Mathematics
520 Astronomy and Allied Sciences
530 Physics
540 Chemistry and Allied Sciences
550 Earth Sciences
560 Paleontology, Paleozoology
570 Life Sciences
580 Botanical Sciences
590 Zoological Sciences

700 The Arts and Sports

710 Civic and Landscape Art
720 Architecture
730 Plastic Arts, Sculpture
740 Drawing and Decorative Arts
750 Painting and Paintings (Museums)
760 Graphic Arts, Printmaking and Prints,
     Postage Stamps
770 Photography and Photographs
780 Music
790 Recreational and Performing Arts

900 Geography and History

900 World History
910 Geography and Travel

(continued)

TABLE 2.01: Dewey decimal system.   (*continued*)

830 Literatures of Germanic Languages
840 Literatures of Romance Languages
850 Italian, Romanian Literatures
860 Spanish and Portuguese Literatures
870 Italic Literatures, Latin
880 Hellenic Literatures, Classical Greek
890 Literatures of Other Languages

920 Biography, Genealogy, Insignia
930 History of the Ancient World
940 General History of Europe
950 General History of Asia, Far East
960 General History of Africa
970 General History of North America
980 General History of South America
990 General History of Other Areas

Sidebar 2.02 Library of Congress Classification System

Sources: Library of Congress Classification. World Book Online Reference Center. 2005. World Book, Inc. Available at http://0-www.worldbookonline.com (accessed March 24, 2005).

Library of Congress. *Library of Congress Classification Outline.* Available at: http://www.loc.gov/catdir/cpso/lcco/lcco. html (accessed May 5, 2005).

Another commonly used classification system was developed by the United States Library of Congress (LOC) in the early 1900s, specifically for its large collection of books. It is now used by many large research and university libraries. The LOC system is even more precise than the Dewey approach, establishing 21 major areas of knowledge. Letters are used to distinguish the classifications, as seen below. For more information about the LOC system, refer to the Web site, http://www.loc.gov.

A—General Works
B—Philosophy, Psychology, Religion
C—Auxiliary Sciences of History
D—History (General) and History of Europe, Asia, Africa, Australia, and so forth.
E—History of the Americas
F—History of the Americas
G—Geography, Anthropology, Recreation
H—Social Sciences
J—Political Science
K—Law
L—Education
M—Music and Books on Music
N—Fine Arts
P—Language and Literature
Q—Science
R—Medicine
S—Agriculture
T—Technology
U—Military Science
V—Naval Science
Z—Bibliography, Library Science, Information Resources (General)

TABLE 2.02: Common special sections.

Type	Call Number Designation
Reference	R or REF above Dewey number and cutter
Fiction	F or FIC above the cutter
Individual biography	B above the cutter
Collective biography	920 above the cutter
Easy	E above the cutter
Professional	Pro or Prof above Dewey number and cutter
Audiovisual Materials	This varies. AV above the Dewey and cutter is common, but some prefer to identify the type of media using CD, for example, to indicate a compact disk.
Story collection	SC above the cutter. Note: many libraries are phasing out special story collection sections. These books are increasingly being blended into the collection as appropriate, nonfiction, fiction and so forth.

This special collection of children's books is included in the Freedom High School library to support curriculum in child development, parenting, and fine arts/illustration.

A special section can make your library collection unique and be an important asset to your patrons. With careful planning and execution, establishing a special collection is easy to do and will enhance your library media center for years to come.

Bibliography

Holzberlein, Deanne B. *Dewey Decimal Classification.* World Book Online Reference Center, 2005. World Book, Inc. Available at http://www.worldbookonline.com (accessed March 24, 2005).

Mitchell, Joan S., ed. *Dewey Decimal Classification and Relative Index,* 22nd ed. Dublin, OH: Online Computer Library Center, Inc., 2003.

Near North District School Board Library Services. *Dewey Decimal System Classification System, 13th Abridged.* Available at: http://www-lib.nearnorth.edu.on.ca/dewey/ddc.htm#900 (accessed April 24, 2006).

The University of Illinois at Urbana-Champaign. *Dewey Decimal in the UIUC Bookstacks: Biography of Melvil Dewey.* Available at: http://www.library.uiuc.edu/circ/tutorial/biography.html (accessed May 7, 2005).

Recommended Resources for Elementary Students on Library Organization

Fowler, Allan. *The Dewey Decimal System. A True Book.* New York: Children's Press/Grolier, 1996. ISBN 0–516–20132–8.

Library Skills for Children: Using the Dewey Decimal System. DVD/Video available from Schlessinger Media, a division of Library Video Company, copyright 2003, 2004. ISBN 1–57225–915–9.

3

Circulation Policies and Mechanics

Establishing Circulation Policies

Circulation policies are guidelines used by staff and patrons when checking out materials. These policies usually address issues such as the number of items a patron may borrow, the length of time items may be kept, and if there will be consequences for not returning materials. As with any policy, your circulation guidelines should be in alignment with your school mission goal and objective statements, and it should be in writing. Professional ethics require us to frequently review and update our policies to ensure our media centers keep up with the changes taking place in our schools. Because they directly affect each patron, circulation policies are a logical first choice for evaluation.

Often circulation guidelines are controversial because, once established, these policies can become a roadblock for some patrons who desire to use your collection. For example, in many school districts, secondary students are required to have a school identification card. Commonly, students are required to present this card when checking out library materials. Students and library staff frequently find themselves backed into a corner—no card means no checkout. Students who do not want to read also use the identification card as an excuse. "I don't have my ID card" is a frequently used justification for not checking out a book. So, when establishing circulation policies, be sure to consider all the implications of the rule you are about to implement.

It is a good idea to examine the circulation policies at your school at least once each year. Summer break is a great time to do this so that new policies can be checked, approved, and advertised before the fall term. This also insures that the rules do not change in the middle of the school year, causing confusion for students and staff. Carefully weigh the pros and cons for each rule. Ask yourself: is there wiggle room in the policies for times that require flexibility? How do you determine that a particular situation merits breaking with the standard policy? Does the media center staff understand how to deal with situations that require breaking the rules?

Before deciding circulation policies, you may want to consider the following points:

- Does my school district offer circulation guidelines in their library handbook? Most districts have some sort of school library policies and procedures manual in place. If you do not have access to a district library handbook, consult your district level supervisor or resource teacher.
- What are the current circulation policies in my school? When examining these policies, ask students and teachers what they like and dislike about the policies.
- What circulation policies are common in my school district? If your district does not have a published book of guidelines, survey other school library staff to determine what they are doing in their schools. While each school is unique, you may want to establish similar policies to nearby schools for consistency.
- Should all patrons be treated equally when borrowing materials? Most schools treat students and teachers differently when checking out materials. Some schools have different classes of patrons with different borrowing privileges. For example, a child in kindergarten may not take out as many items as a fifth grade student and teachers may have extended checkout privileges.
- Should all materials be available to all patrons? Due to curriculum needs and cost factors, most school libraries limit checkouts depending on patron type. For example, students are not allowed to check out DVDs in many schools.
- Should materials have different checkout periods? In most school libraries, reference books are usually required to be returned the next day; however, novels are usually checked out for a week or longer. This is just one example of varying checkout periods; other items that might not warrant extended checkout include magazines, picture books, and graphic novels.
- What district and state guidelines and/or laws exist for recovering lost or damaged items? Unfortunately, students and teachers lose or damage many library materials each year. It is important to know and follow your district guidelines and state laws in this area. Consult your school principal before setting up a policy that may be impossible to enforce.
- Do you want to establish overdue fines? Again, consult your district guidelines and state laws regarding fines. Many media specialists enthusiastically support fines; others feel they discourage students from using the collection. Whatever your feelings, be sure you set and publicize your policy so that all your students and staff understand it.
- How many books should each type of patron be allowed to check out? For example, students may be allowed to check out one or two reference books, but a larger number of regular circulation materials. Some schools limit teacher checkout, others do not.

TABLE 3.01: Sample circulation checkout periods.

Magazines	No checkout, overnight only, two days
Picture books	One to two weeks
Chapter books	One to two weeks
YA novels	Two weeks to one month
Graphic novels	Two days to two weeks
Reference books	Overnight only, two days
Audio books	No checkout, two weeks

This table shows the results of a random survey in the authors' school district. The results indicate a variety of checkout periods for individual items. In this district, library personnel are able to determine checkout periods at each school site based on school community needs.

- What about audiovisual materials such as videos, DVDs (digital video discs), audio books, and software? Will you restrict who can check them out and for how long? How many of these more expensive items are you willing to allow a patron to take at one time?
- How will you handle circulation of audiovisual equipment? Will it be for teacher checkout only? Will the checkout period be limited or for the entire school year? Will you treat DVD players differently than overhead projectors?
- In an ideal world, what would your circulation policies be? Why are your ideals not the current policy? How could you change things to bring them closer to your ideal? Of course, none of us lives in an ideal world, but creative thinking like this allows you to visualize things differently. Once you have this vision of how things could be, reach for it. Design a plan to build your collection, alter your facility, and obtain funding, whatever is needed to make your dream real for your students and school community. You may be surprised how easily and quickly you are able to improve the situation for all your patrons.

Easy patron access of the collection is one of the primary goals for any media specialist. We want the books, videos, and other materials in the hands of our customers, not gathering dust on the shelf. Your circulation policies are the door your patrons must pass through to get the things they need. Take time to consider these important guidelines. Develop a fair plan for circulating your library's collection that your school community can enthusiastically support. "We've always done it that way," is not a good enough reason to continue down the same path. Examine your alternatives and carefully consider the options available to you and your patrons. You may decide to change some rules and keep others. The payoff

TABLE 3.02: Sample circulation policy statement from Canal Winchester High School in Canal Winchester, Ohio.

Fiction and nonfiction books	**Reference**
* - May check out up to three items * - Length of loan is 10 school days * - Can renew infividual items as long as there are no holds on that item	* - Reference materials are not available for checkout. Ask the Media Center staff for possible copies.
Magazines	**Video/audio tapes**
* - Same loan period as fiction and nonfiction materials * - Only one magazine can be checked out at a time. * - Renewals are not available.	* - These materials check out to students only with teacher permission.

Fines will be charged for lost or damaged items. If materials are overdue, no other item can be checked out until they are returned.

Anyone wishing to check material out from the Media Center must have a "Media Center Use Agreement" signed and turned into the Media Center Office

Courtesy of Shari Phillips, Media Specialist. Visit Canal Winchester on the Internet at: http://www.canalwin.k12.oh.us/HS/Departments/MediaCenter/hsmcmain.htm.

TABLE 3.03: Circulation policies, Potowmack Elementary School.

*All students visit the library once each week for a half hour class session.
*Teachers may sign up for additional library time when they are working on a special project.
*Classes that miss their regular library time because of a holiday, snow day, or special event will be rescheduled whenever possible.
*Books may be checked out for two weeks before they are considered overdue.
*Students are welcome to renew books for a maximum of four times, with the exception of books that are in high demand.
*Reference materials may be checked out for one day, used at school, and returned at the end of the day.
*Students, teachers, and staff can place a hold on a requested item.
*Lost or damaged items must be paid for.
*Students are always welcome in the library between 7:30 and 3:10 to exchange books, even if their class isn't scheduled to visit the library that day.

These policies are courtesy of Potowmack Elementary School in Sterling, Virginia. Michelle Rzewski, Media Specialist. Visit Potowmack on the Internet at: http://cmsweb2.loudoun.k12.va.us/potowmack/site/default.asp.

will come when you see the smiling face of the student who just found the right resource for their report, personal information quest, or pleasure reading.

Circulation Mechanics—How to Check It Out!

Once your circulation policies are in place, you can begin to check out items from your collection. Here, again, the new library media specialist will need to consider many things.

First, is your circulation system manual or automated? Increasingly, automated systems are the norm, but there are still schools using the traditional signature card method of circulating materials. Schools using automated systems are wise to be aware of old-fashioned checkout methods. Computer systems sometimes fail, rendering automated circulation impossible and effectively ending a patron's ability to check out items until the computer system is reestablished. The wise media specialist will be aware of traditional checkout methods and be prepared with backup plans in the event of technology failure. This does not mean you will want to automatically fall back on the old-fashioned methods for checking out books, but being knowledgeable about their workings will enable you to develop your own approaches for handling computer failure.

Traditional Checkout Methods

Many adults will be familiar with the old-fashioned signature checkout card. When using the card system, each book had a pocket, usually located on the inside back cover, that contained a signature card with the book's identifying information typed on the card's top left corner. The patron signed his or her name on the card and indicated a location such as a homeroom where he or she could be contacted. The card and date due slip were stamped with the return date. The date due slip was placed in the book pocket or an attached date due slip was stamped with the due date and the patron's part of the checkout procedure was complete.

The media specialist then placed the book card in a file tray. Typically, the cards were organized by the due date, and then within each date group, the cards were sorted into Dewey order. Finally, within each Dewey grouping, they were alphabetically organized by the cutter letters under the call number.

Checking in an item involved locating the correct date in the file, then matching the Dewey and cutter information on the signature cards to the book at hand. Once the correct card was located and returned to the pocket, the book was considered checked in and returned to the shelves for future use.

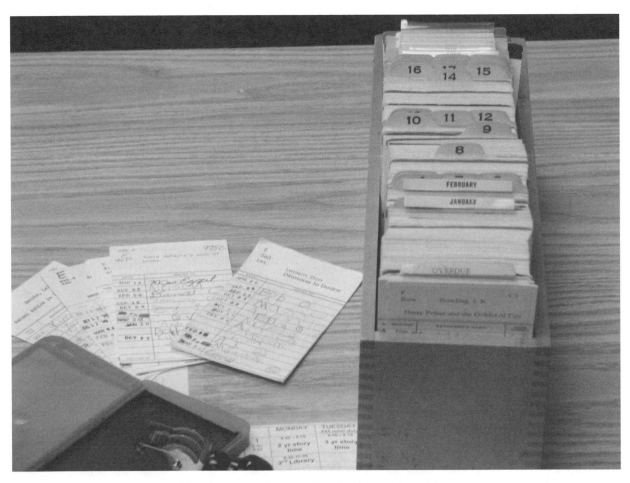

Before automation systems, library materials were checked out using this common manual system.

In the event of multiple copies, a copy number was added to the card. This was usually done by using a small letter 'c' followed by the number of the copy, for example, c2 or c3. Note, with modern automation systems, the copy number designation is no longer necessary as the unique bar code number assigned to each book separates one copy from another.

Checking Out with Automated Circulation Systems

Checking out with computerized systems is easy because the circulation software will keep track of each item, who it is assigned to, and when it is due. When checking out materials, identify the patron in the database. Then the book's bar code is scanned assigning it to the patron. The computer calculates the return date based on the circulation policies programmed into the software. Depending on your system, you may use a date due card, slip, or printout to let patrons know when their materials are to be brought back to the media center. When returned, the book is scanned again using the check-in mode of the management system. The computer will record any overdue fines to the patron's record, and the book can be returned to the shelf.

Your circulation policies are even more important with computerized management systems because all the information related to circulation must be entered into the software program before you begin using it. A computerized system also allows for faster transactions between staff and patrons, so it becomes

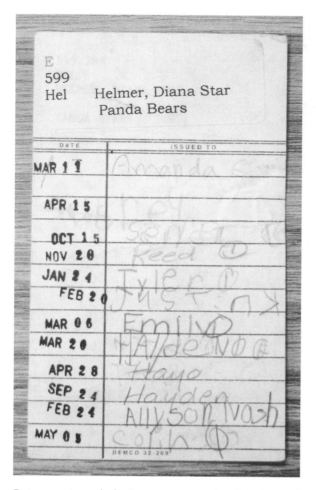

Patrons signed their names on the book card which was then stamped with the due date.

Book cards were filed in Dewey order behind the corresponding due date.

essential that the system knows how many books a student can check out or what fine level you are willing to tolerate before a patron loses checkout privileges. Consult your software manual for information about what is needed to set up the circulation part of your program.

Perhaps the biggest issue in checking out with computer systems is identifying the patron. In most cases, it is easy to search out a patron in the database by name; however, this takes longer and slows down the checkout process. Media specialists in smaller schools who are able to get to know their student body will not find the issue of manually looking up students to be difficult. However, in larger schools, the media center staff does not see students on a daily basis and are not able to identify individuals by name. In a perfect world, this would not be an issue; the patron would simply provide his or her name to the library staff for checkout. Unfortunately, most staff members have many stories illustrating why this is not a good idea. For whatever reason, students of all age levels do not identify themselves correctly. This misidentification leaves staff holding innocent patrons responsible for returning items they never checked out. Therefore, the issue of identifying students is important.

Increasingly, secondary students receive school identification cards. These cards contain a photo of the student and their identification number in bar code form that can be scanned by the media management system software. The use of this photo ID card allows positive identification for those checking out books.

For young children, the use of identification cards is not practical. Elementary media staffs have developed a variety of ways to deal with this problem. Some simply require the teacher to be present at the circulation desk to verify student names during checkout. Others have created rolodex cards with each student's name, a scannable bar code, and a photo. One media specialist in our district makes a class file using manila folders. She attaches student pictures to the folder; underneath each student's photo is a label with their name, student number, and a scannable bar code. In most cases, a whole class easily fits onto one file folder. These folders are kept at the circulation desk for use whenever the class visits the media center during the year. Students independently visiting the media center identify their teacher, and the media staff pulls the file to locate the student's photo and bar code for checkout.

Handling Overdue, Lost, or Damaged Materials

Make sure you have clear circulation policies in place for overdue materials so that you are able to handle both students and staff with late items consistently. Depending on the size of your school and library staff, you should make an effort to notify patrons regularly about overdue materials. Most management softwares contain a prewritten notice for this purpose. Check your software manual, it is often possible to edit the notice, customizing it for your school.

If you charge fines, notifying students about overdue materials is particularly important so that they do not run up a large charge that they cannot pay. Traditionally, most schools send weekly notices. This may be difficult with large schools or if you are a running your media center single-handedly. However, make every attempt to send out notices at least once a month at a minimum.

If your school is not automated, overdue notices will have to be hand generated. You can do this using a variety of predesigned forms available from library supply stores. It is also easy to generate a form of your own using basic word-processing software. However you generate the notice, it is important to do them consistently.

Teachers are usually involved in distributing overdue notices. Make sure they understand the process, how the notice is written, and their delivery role. Another reason to involve teachers in distributing overdue notices is the valuable information you can gain from them. Because teachers are on the front lines each day, they are aware of student attendance patterns and can notify the librarian when students are not coming to school, withdrawn, or transferred to other classes. Depending on the situation, the media center records will need to be updated and possible additional steps will need to be taken for students who are no longer attending. One note: be aware of the rules in your district regarding the privacy of student information. Many schools have policies recognizing library circulation records as private. If this is the case in your district, then you will need to take special care to hide title information on notices or find an alternative delivery method such as mailing notices home.

When deciding your circulation policies, you must determine at what point you will consider an overdue item to be lost. For some school libraries, an item is considered lost when it is not returned after a month, but others use two months or longer. Your media management software will probably not automatically set a long-term overdue book to lost. It may also be too time consuming for library staff to set long-term overdues to lost status. Many media specialists find dealing with reclassifying long-term overdues is best left to summer breaks; others address the issue immediately and establish a replacement fine for the missing item. It is also advisable to consult your district office about charging students for the replacement of lost materials, since the policy about this type of fee can vary widely from state to state and district to district.

When collecting overdue fines and lost book fees, be sure you know what paperwork you are expected to fill in by your district and school. Commonly, some monies must be receipted while other funds do

When using automated circulation systems, locate the patron record, then scan the book's bar code to check it out.

not require a written record. The first step in collecting fees and fines is to be sure your school community understands all the policies you have put in place. Advertise them using all possible means—school newsletters, Web sites, open house nights, the Parent Teacher Association (PTA), and school advisory council meetings, and so forth. Be prepared to answer any questions about the policies that may come from the community.

Most students will return items and pay fines without any problem. Students who do not return materials after receiving repeated notices will need to be contacted. Common steps for handling long-term overdues are listed below:

- Contact the student directly. Most students respond positively to direct contact. Sometimes you may be willing to negotiate a reduction in the fine in exchange for return of the missing item.
- Consider asking a teacher, club sponsor, or coach to intervene with the student. In the case of secondary school students, coaches and club sponsors have considerable influence. One word from a coach is usually enough to settle the situation. However, before involving an outside teacher or coach, check your district's privacy of student records policy. If involving a coach violates the privacy of student records, don't do it.

As media specialists, we are concerned about issues like censorship and free access to information. Library staffs are frequently in the forefront helping to maintain important civil liberties in this area. However, many times we are uninformed about another equally important civil liberty—the right to privacy. This issue involves more than adults; our students also have privacy rights. Often our education or library science courses either did not cover this area or glossed quickly over it in the rush to cover all the course content. A wise media specialist will investigate the national, state, and local laws governing the privacy of student information and then bone up on school district policy that applies these laws in their area.

The Family Educational Rights and Privacy Act of 1974 (FERPA) governs student privacy rights. The act gives parents rights over the educational records of their minor children. Although library records are not clearly defined as educational records, FERPA does clearly bar schools from publicly releasing student information without written parental consent. Some states have passed laws allowing parental access of their children's library records.

The library community also has a strong commitment to patron privacy rights. ALA's Library Bill of Rights requires free and open access to information. AASL affirms that children and youth are entitled to the same privacy rights as adults in their *Position Statement on the Confidentiality of Library Records*. In general, students should expect to use media center collections and seek information without scrutiny. Secondly, students should expect their library records will remain confidential.

Media specialists must investigate their district policies and the laws regarding student privacy. Establish policies and train staff to support patron privacy rights. This might mean not revealing who checked out an item or not posting overdue notices where others can see them. In their teaching capacity, media specialists might include lessons on privacy and help educate students about the importance of keeping personal information confidential. Ultimately providing student patrons with the maximum privacy available according to your district policy, ALA guidelines and FERPA will enhance the ability of students to pursue information and pleasure reading, thereby increasing student learning.

Refer to these resources to start learning more about FERPA and school library programs:

General Information:

LibraryLaw Blog: Are student library records protected by federal law (FERPA)? A surprising analysis. Information from Helen Adams explaining FERPA's impact on school libraries. Available at: http://blog. librarylaw.com/librarylaw/2005/07/are_student_lib.html.

Family Educational Rights and Privacy Act. Information from ALA. Available at: http://www.ala.org/ala/ washoff/oitp/emailtutorials/privacya/10.htm.

Family Educational Rights and Privacy Act (FERPA). Information from the U.S. Department of Education. Available at: http://www.ed.gov/policy/gen/guid/fpco/ferpa/index.html.

Resources from the American Library Association:

Position Statement on the Confidentiality of Library Records. Available at: http://www.ala.org/ala/aasl/ aaslproftools/positionstatements/aaslpositionstatementconfidentiality.htm.

Privacy: An Interpretation of the Library Bill of Rights. Available at: http://www.ala.org/Template.cfm?Sect ion=interpretations&Template=/ContentManagement/ContentDisplay.cfm&ContentID=103219.

Privacy Tool Kit. Available at: http://www.ala.org/ala/oif/iftoolkits/toolkitsprivacy/privacypolicy/privacypolicy. htm.

Recommended Resources:

Adams, Helen R., Robert F. Bocher, Carol A. Gordon, and Elizabeth Barry Kesler. *Privacy in the 21st Century: Issues for Public, School, and Academic Libraries.* Westport, CT: Libraries Unlimited, 2005. ISBN 978-159158209-0.

Sidebar 3.02 Voice of Experience from Claire Stephens

If your management system has a note feature, use it to keep track of various actions taken by the media center staff. This can help you track events and cut down on document storage. Below are some sample notes you might find in our system.

4/15/2005—Spoke with student about *The Call of the Wild*, bar code #T01234, this book is 2 months overdue. Student says she has book and will return it.—tt

4/30/2005—Student still has not returned above book, letter sent to parents.—sm

5/7/2005—Parent called and said book was chewed up by family dog, will send check to cover cost.—sm

5/9/2005—Paid for damaged book, *The Call of the Wild*, bar code #T01234, $6.98, receipt #5678.—cs

As you can see, we record the date, action taken, and our initials to let others know who made the entry in case there are questions. Keeping these types of notes on the computer has saved us time in the long-run since we can quickly call up information to verify what has happened and how we handled the situation

- Be prepared with alternatives. If a student tells you they cannot afford to pay a fine or replacement cost, provide them with options. Perhaps the student can pay a small amount each week or work off the debt. A caution: before agreeing to allow students to work off a debt, it is best to contact the student's parents about the situation so they are informed about what types of work their child will be doing and the length of time involved.
- Parent contact is recommended after other attempts to get materials returned have failed. At elementary school, parents can be a great help from the beginning. You may try a quick phone call to solicit help. Many media management software systems will print a letter that can be mailed for this purpose as well. When contacting parents, remember to keep records of each attempt. This can be easily done by maintaining a parent contact log. Another easy way to keep a record of parent contact attempts can be to record each attempt in your media management system software. Check your manual—many of these systems allow you to record and save notes under each student's record. When we use this facet of our software at our school, we record the date, action taken, and initials of the person making the note. This allows us to review when, what, and who took action regarding a situation.

One final note regarding circulation mechanics: train your staff well. The media specialist is responsible for establishing policies and routines for circulating the collection, but if your staff does not understand your expectations, confusion will reign. Seemingly insignificant things can sidetrack circulation procedures, so it is important to cultivate an attention to detail on the part of all staff. For example, in schools with some types of theft prevention systems, leaving a date due card in the book pocket after check-in will mask the sensor and make it easy for another student to steal the book. Staff must be trained to remove the date due card at check-in. Another example: not watching the computer monitor during checkout and check-in procedures can cause a staff member to miss an important error message. This lack of awareness could lead the staff member to believe that an item was checked out or in when it really was not. Be sure that all staff and volunteers know and understand your expectations when it comes to circulating materials. Work with them to be sure that everyone understands and enforces the policies. Each person must also follow all procedures with the same care, so that all patrons are handled consistently and professionally. Keeping track of all these details can seem overwhelming at times, but in the end, your patrons will appreciate the efforts of you and your staff because they will always be able to find and use the materials they need.

Bibliography

Adams, Helen R. "Privacy Matters: Confidentiality." *School Library Media Activities Monthly*, http://www.schoollibrarymedia.com/columns/privacy/index.html (accessed January 4, 2007).

Wasman, Ann M. *New Steps to Service: Common-Sense Advice for the School Library Media Specialist.* Chicago: American Library Association, 1998.

Woolls, Blanche. *The School Library Media Manager*, 2nd ed. Englewood, CO: Libraries Unlimited, 1999.

4

Media Management Systems

Planning

In order to run a library media center effectively in the twenty-first century, circulation, cataloging, and inventory must be done electronically. This entails planning for, choosing, and implementing a library media management software system.

Not that long ago, we didn't have media management software. Instead, we had large pieces of furniture called the card catalog that were a mainstay of every library. The catalog's alphabetical drawers contained numerous cards for all items in the collection, identifying each piece by author, title, and subject. Librarians had a separate large piece of furniture with drawers that held catalog cards arranged by Dewey number. This was our all-important shelf list, essential during our yearly inventory. Library information cards were kept on file for each patron at the circulation desk. When checking out a book, students wrote their name on the card in the pocket of the book and we interfiled that book card with other cards due on the same date. When the student returned the book, we found the book's card by checking the date the book was due which was stamped in the back of the book and put the card back in the book's pocket. How time consuming! Those good old days were really not that good.

And don't even talk about inventory! Entire drawers from the shelf list were carried to each bookshelf. Workers matched the cards to the books. The cards of missing items were marked with paper clips. The margin of error was huge and the time element was incredible!

Today we are fortunate to have media management software that takes care of these processes. There are many media management software programs available for schools. Some are school based and some are district managed. They vary by price and appearance, but, essentially, they were all created to help you manage your collection.

You might be opening a new school and need to evaluate different systems to decide which is most appropriate for your unique library media center. You might be changing

Sidebar 4.01 Library Automation Software Companies

Note: this is not a comprehensive listing of library automation companies, nor are we recommending any of the companies. If you are shopping for a media management system, take the time to search the Internet for additional vendors. A quick general search using your favorite search engine will yield a lengthy listing of management software vendors.

Alexandria (COMPanion Corporation)—http://www.goalexandria.com/

Book Systems—http://www.booksys.com

CASPR Library Systems, Inc.—http://www.libraryworld.net

Follett Software Corporation—http://www.fsc.follett.com/

Some questions to ask when considering a library automation software purchase:

What is the history of the software company? Do they have experience in the field of school libraries? Are there any nearby schools or districts using their products that you can visit?

What programs and services do they offer? Are they user-friendly for students, teachers, and library staff? Are they visually appealing? Are they suitable for your school size, budget, and student body? Can you network the software or is it stand-alone? What type of training is available? What type of tech support do they provide?

Exactly what will you need to purchase to begin using their product? Be sure to ask about hardware and software, for example, you may need to purchase one software module for your on-site OPAC (Online Public Access Catalog) stations and a separate one to allow students to access your OPAC on the Internet from home. You may also need bar code scanners or portable handheld inventory scanners. What about the computer requirements? Will you need to purchase a new computer system or can you use an existing machine?

Will you have to do some sort of retrospective conversion to input your existing collection into the system? If so, what will be involved in that process, and how much help will the software company provide? How much will it cost?

How committed is the company to the software? How frequently do they upgrade the program? How will you get the software upgrades? If they have a major new product in development, you may want to wait to purchase the newer software if it means the company will only be supporting their existing program for another year or two.

What are the costs of maintaining the system once you install it? You will probably need to pay for annual tech support, and some companies also supply things like bar codes that you may wish to purchase.

software because you are dissatisfied with your current program or it is no longer viable. No matter what your reason for examining management software programs, you must ask many questions in order to compare the systems you are considering.

If you have a library that has never been automated, you have a much bigger job. You must learn about the conversion process. All the information on each of those card catalog cards must be converted to digital data. How will the conversion be accomplished? You may have to send the cards in your shelf list to the company so that they can convert the data. Choosing the right time during the school year to implement the conversion is crucial. No matter what your situation, form a planning committee to consider all aspects of the conversion process and to formulate questions for the software companies you are evaluating.

Carefully select committee members who will constitute your planning committee. Professional library colleagues are great consultants, as they discuss the pros and cons of various systems. Consult with your technology specialist to make sure school computers and networks are in place to support your chosen system. Your principal is an integral part of the decision-making process. He will provide the funds for your purchase, so he must be convinced that your purchase is functional and necessary. Your staff should also have input into your decision, as they will be using the software on a daily basis.

When looking for software, analyze your needs. Consider all the aspects of processing and circulating materials. Will this software meet those needs and make your job easier? Also, consider the software's reputation for technical support. You are looking for technical support that is fast and friendly, no matter what your technology expertise. You may have to wait at peak times, but support personnel should take your concerns seriously and help you no matter how big or small your problem.

Ask about the cost of annual support and what the plan covers. Technical support may seem like an expensive and unnecessary option, but it is really an essential program that you will use consistently. Whenever you have a question, you are free to get expert answers to make your job easier. Plus, this annual fee should allow you to download upgrades, as they are available. Sometimes larger districts have an employee whose job includes interfacing with media management software technical support. In these situations, the district may deal entirely with the costs of technical support; media specialists would not need to budget for this service. A user-friendly software management program will allow you to access the Web site and make suggestions for future upgrades. Do pay for technical support; include its cost in your budget each year.

Investigate what type of training is available for your software. Attend training sessions before you implement your new management system, after setup, and again when you feel somewhat comfortable with your system. Make sure that your principal understands the importance of attending initial trainings and future advanced trainings as the software is upgraded. These programs are very powerful, but that power is lost if you do not understand all the program's intricacies.

Media management software is used to perform operations that were traditionally done by hand. While automation saves time, it is important that the software completes the tasks you did manually and makes your media center more efficient. The library must function as it always has, but your behind the scenes activities should be easier and more complete. Learn all you can about your media management system and use it to your advantage.

Using Your Media Management Software

Media centers today depend on their media management software to keep track of materials and patrons. Many companies specialize in media management software. Library professionals choose software that is user friendly and that has excellent technical support. Keep your user ID or customer number and technical support phone number handy for questions when they arise. No matter how often you call, expect experienced technical support representatives who are willing to help. Be prepared for a wait at peak times, but look for competent and friendly support.

Each book or other item to be cataloged must be processed using bar codes that are compatible with your software. For a small fee, vendors will process books to your specifications to integrate with your software system. This service is worth the money! If your district has centrally catalogued materials, you may not be involved in this process, but if you are, have the vendor do the work and you upload the information into your system from a data disk. Vendors will ask you specific questions before they begin to process your books, so you need to think about how you will organize your media center. For example, will you have a Reference section; a separate section for Story Collections or Easy books? You also need to think about how books and audiovisual materials will look after they are processed. For example, should fiction books have an F on the spine label and then the first three digits of the author's last name in capital letters? Or, should they have an FIC and the first three letters of the author's last name in lowercase letters?

Where would you like the bar code on the book? Top? Middle? How should it be placed on the material? Horizontally? Vertically? Most vendors provide specification sheets for you to stipulate

Library management software helps you keep track of patrons and their checkouts. This screen from the Follett Destiny system shows a sample patron record made up by a media specialist. She uses this record (with her dog's name) to practice procedures when training staff. (Image reprinted with permission of Follett Software Company. © 2000–2006 Follett Software Company.)

your wishes. Most important is to be consistent so that users will have an easier time accessing your collection.

Most software programs come with various components.

- The system setup allows you to customize the program for your school library media center. This is where you tell the software what passwords you want to use, what type of bar codes you will use, what types of materials you will have in the media center, and so forth. Here is where you set up a calendar for the year so that the program can adjust due dates for vacations and special events. This is also where you differentiate between patron types. You set the maximum due date for each patron type and tell the software how many days a patron can check out a book. For example, kindergarteners may be allowed to check out a book for one week, fourth graders may get two weeks, and teachers may have six weeks before they must return items.

- The cataloging component is most important. You should be able to access a record of each book or other item in the media center as well as a Machine-Readable Cataloging (MARC) record for each item. Entering MARC records correctly is crucial. The MARC record takes the place of the numerous catalog cards that stuffed that old large wooden card catalog. Complete MARC records make it easier for patrons to find the information they need. The more subject headings you enter into the record, the better. Each of these subjects can be accessed with a key word or subject search and makes the material more valuable to your clientele. Most media specialists attend classes teaching them to create MARC records and continually update that knowledge with refresher courses. This is where you enter the call number of an item. You might also mark the item in a bibliographic category so that it is easily searchable. Many vendors will provide you with a data disk of your purchase that you can easily upload. Beware: many times these vendor records are too brief or not cataloged where you would like them. Check records often in case you want to enhance the record so your patrons can access it more easily.

This screenshot from the cataloging module of Follett's Destiny software program allows library staff to access basic information about specific titles and make changes as needed. (Image reprinted with permission of Follett Software Company. © 2000–2006 Follett Software Company.)

- The patron database should be easy to access. It should allow you to update or delete patrons globally. Using the global feature allows you to perform the same function on a group of patrons that are similar in one way. For instance, you may want to delete all of your eighth graders at the end of the school year since they are moving on to high school. By globally deleting all students with the same graduation date, you have eliminated the tedious task of deleting patrons individually. Adding one new patron should also be easy, so that when new students arrive, it is a quick process. This is where you tell the software what types of patrons you have (teacher, student, etc.), and enter any personal information you need, such as a phone number and address. Usually this information is accessible through a download from your school attendance program or your district. You may also set the maximum due date for each patron type.
- The circulation component should be easy to use. The patron should be accessible by name or student number. This is where you check in or check out books or just look at the status of a book. Is it checked out? When was it checked out last? Books should be able to be reserved for patrons easily. Fines should be accessed and paid in this module. Patron data can be accessed from here. Also books can be marked as lost in this component.

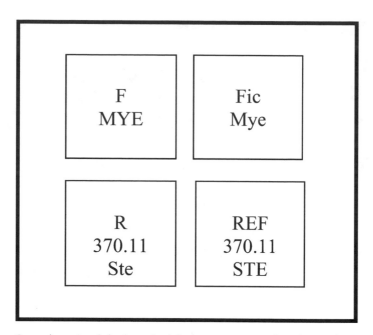

Sample spine labels—decide how you want book vendors to print them when ordering processed books for your collection.

- The inventory component is necessary in order to maintain your collection. Each year, all books and other cataloged materials are scanned with a remote scanner and then uploaded into the software. Inventory is best done while most of the books are circulating. Since all circulating books are considered found in the inventory, this allows you to scan fewer books. Completing an accurate inventory allows you and your administration to monitor your collection and plan for future purchases.
- The reports component allows you to run reports in order to learn more about your collection. You can gather all sorts of data that will help you evaluate your collection. For example, you can find out the age of certain parts of your collection or you can find out if any call numbers have been entered incorrectly. You can also find out all sorts of circulation data. For example, you can see how many fiction books have been checked out in the last year or how many students have books on reserve. This is also where you print overdue notices to send out to students. Students should receive notices at least once a month. Enlist the help of teachers to make students responsible for materials borrowed. Teaching responsibility is another way you can teach character education.
- The most important component for your students is the online public access catalog or OPAC (formerly known as the card catalog). This online catalog should be easy to use and should allow students and teachers to search by title, author, subject, or key words. This is the module that will teach students how to find call numbers, do Boolean searches and tell whether a book is on the shelf or checked out.
- The backup feature is one of the most important parts of the program for the library media specialist. Back up your data frequently and keep the disk at home or away from your library media center. Everyone has heard horror stories of servers crashing and data having to be restored by hand. A few years ago, a middle school library media center in our area burned down. Wouldn't it be great just to upload your data from a disk if that happened to you?

gbc
garrett book company
ORDER FORM & PROCESSING SPECIFICATIONS
GARRETT BOOK COMPANY   130 EAST 13TH STREET   P.O. BOX 1588   ADA, OK 74821
Phone: 800-475-6884 or 580-332-6884 FAX: 888-525-1560 or 580-332-1560
email: mail@garrettbooks.com   web site: www.garrettbooks.com

PROCESSING AND AUTOMATION ARE UNCONDITIONALLY GUARANTEED WHEN THE INFORMATION BELOW IS COMPLETE

___Data Disk & MARC Records (includes disk and one unattached
    barcode label) @ $.35 per book. $15.00 minimum charge
    ___Fee to attach above barcode @ $.10 each
___Additional Barcode Label @ $.15 each.
___Unattached Spine Label @ $.10 each.
    ___Attached Spine Label with protector @ $.20 each
    (Standard placement is 1.5" from btm. of bk.)
___Shelf List Card @ $.10 each.
___Circulation Card @ $.10 each.
___Unattached Book Pocket @ $.10 each. ___Attached @ $.20 each.
___Unattached Date Due Slip @ $.05 each. ___Attached @ $.15 each.
___Unattached Theft Detectors @ $.20 each.___ Attached @ $.40 each.
    Type: ___3M ___Checkpoint 9.5 ___other(specify) _____
___Accelerated Reader Labels @ $.15 each.
    (Standard Location is above spine label.)
___Unattached Processing Kit @ $.69 each.
    (includes shelf list, circulation, and catalog cards,
    pocket & spine label)
    ___Attached Processing Kit with protectors @ $.89 each.

Pocket or Date Due Slip Location: (If ordering both
    please specify location for each.)
    ___Front Inside Cover   ___Front Fly Leaf
    ___Back Inside Cover   ___Back Fly Leaf
    Write location for additional barcode
    or barcode located inside the book.
    Be specific please. _____

Circle Barcode Outside
Location Below

1	4	S P I N E	7	10
2	5		8	11
3	6		9	12
Back			Front	

Barcode Direction:
    ___Horizontal
    ___Vertical; Top of barcode
    aligns with spine
    ___Vertical; Btm of barcode
    aligns with spine
    ___Do Not cover book
    title with barcode.

CATALOGING OPTIONS:
*If no options are checked, standard options
(indicated by solid blocks) will be used.*

Subject Headings:
■ Sears
□ Library of Congress
□ Children's Library of Congress

Fiction:
■ Fic
□ FIC
□ F

Biography
■ 92
□ B
□ 921

Easy Fiction:
■ E
□ Treat as fiction

Easy Nonfiction:
■ Treat as nonfiction
□ E over dewey
□ E

Collective Biography:
■ 920
□ Other _____

Main Entry Letters Under Call Number (Excluding Biographies):
■ Three Letters
□ Two Letters
□ One Letter
    ■ Upper & Lower Case
    □ All Caps
Number of Letters of Biographees Surname:
■ Three Letters
□ Two Letters
□ One Letter
□ Entire Name up to 12 Letters

SPANISH LANGUAGE OPTIONS
PREFIX		CLASSIFICATION
■ NONE		■ 468
___SP	___Sp	■ 468
___SPA	___Spa	___Dewey by subject

AUTOMATION REQUIREMENTS:
Software System: _____   Version (if known) _____
Computer Type: ___IBM Compatible ___Macintosh   ___Zip disk ___email ___3.5" Disk ___CD Rom
MARC Record Format: ___1991 USMARC MicroLIF 852 holdings ___1987 USMARC MicroLIF ___USMARC 949 holdings

(correction of format, check the label or a data disk has been loaded successfully)

Barcode Symbology:
___Code 3 of 9 no check digit
___Code 3 of 9 Mod 10 check digit
___Code 3 of 9 Mod 43 check digit

Location Code: _____
___Interleaved 2 of 5 Follett check digit (Follett Classic)
___Codabar Mod 10 check digit
___Unsure-please attach a copy of your barcode label.

STARTING BARCODE NUMBER: _____
    [ ] Please continue barcode range on file.

School/Library Name as it will appear on barcode labels (maximum 30 characters).

___ ___

E-mail address for marc record download: _____

*PLEASE NOTE: WHEN AUTOMATION MATERIALS ARE ORDERED UNATTACHED, THEY WILL BE SHIPPED DIRECTLY FROM OUR
CATALOGER. MATERIALS WILL GENERALLY ARRIVE WITHIN 10-14 DAYS OF RECEIVING YOUR BOOKS.

PROCESSING INFO CONTACT:
NAME: _____

PHONE NUMBER: _____

Book processing specification sheet, courtesy of Garrett Book Company.

Textbooks

Many schools, especially on the secondary level, are asking their library media specialist to be responsible for textbook circulation using software that integrates with their media management system. It is important to purchase separate software for your textbooks, but look for one that integrates with your media management system. Most software companies now make programs for both textbook and library management. It is not advisable to add textbooks into your media management software. A textbook collection is managed differently from a library collection. For example, depending on the size of your school, you may have hundreds of copies of a single textbook. Most library collections only contain a few copies of individual titles. Most textbooks are circulated for the entire school year. Most library materials are not. This creates a problem if you circulate both types of books with the same system. Inventory is also a huge problem if both types of books are on the same system. Textbook software provides for the specific needs of your textbook collection. You can check out books to individual students or to classes of students. Textbook management software provides statistics on the status of your textbooks.

Circulating textbooks is a task that is time consuming for the media staff, but a great help for teachers and school administration. Find a room large enough to house all of your textbooks during the summer. Forge a close relationship with department chairs, team leaders or grade level chairpersons, or those in charge of choosing and purchasing textbooks. When books arrive, stamp them with your school name and label each textbook with bar codes that are compatible with your textbook software system. You must devise a plan at the beginning of the school year for students to check out textbooks and sign printouts that show which books were assigned to them. Distributing textbooks is more difficult than it sounds. Teachers all want their students to have books the first week of school, but with large student populations, this is impossible. You will undoubtedly give out books the first week of school, but to make those lines shorter, determine other days when students can receive textbooks. A good time may be in the late summer when students attend orientations to get their schedules or meet their teachers. We have a special day at our high school the Saturday before school starts where students can buy parking passes, choose lockers, and get textbooks. These extra days are more work for you, but will lessen your stress the first week of school. You must also devise an end of year plan to ensure that all textbooks are returned.

Like the media management software, textbook software also comes with various components.

- The system setup is similar to the media management system setup. It will allow you to set due dates for textbooks.
- The cataloging component is again most important. Titles should be added as completely as possible. You should be able to add, delete, or edit textbooks individually or globally with a bar code range.
- The patron database should be easy to access. It should integrate with the media management software so that you can edit and update from either database.
- The circulation component is the one used most often. The patron should be accessible by name or student number. Patron data can be accessed from here. You should be able to print student checkouts from this location.
- The inventory component is important because data is needed to purchase sufficient textbooks for upcoming years. Each year, textbooks are scanned with a remote scanner and then uploaded into the software. Numbers of textbooks are reported to department chairs before the end of the school year so that books can be purchased well ahead of time for the fall semester.
- The reports component allows you to run reports in order to keep accurate records on your textbooks. For example, you can run a report that will give you statistics on a particular title, letting you know how many books are available, circulating, or lost. Here you can also print overdue notices for textbooks that have not been returned. One report may even allow you to print a combined overdue notice to students so they know what textbooks as well as which library books they must return.

Increasingly, media specialists around the country are asked to manage their school's textbook collections along with their traditional library holdings. While managing the textbook collection makes sense in many ways, it represents a lot of extra work for the media staff.

Bibliography

Breeding, Marshall. *Library Technology Guides: Automation Companies.* Available at: http://www.librarytechnology.org/vend-search.pl.

Library Automation Resources. Available at: http://www.libraryhq.com/automation.html.

Osborne, *Andrew. Library Automation Systems and Vendors on the WWW.* Available at: http://libinfo.com/vendors-systems.html.

Stueart, Robert, and Barbara Moran. *Library and Information Center Management.* Englewood, CO: Libraries Unlimited, 2002.

Van Order, Phyllis, and Kay Bishop. *The Collection Program in Schools.* Englewood, CO: Libraries Unlimited, 2001.

5

Scheduling: Philosophy and Practicality

First the Philosophy

Before addressing the mechanics of scheduling the media center, it is important to determine what sort of program calendar your patrons are used to experiencing. There are two approaches to scheduling school media centers: fixed scheduling or flexible access scheduling.

Fixed Scheduling

Many elementary schools use fixed scheduling; it is less common on the secondary level, but some higher-level schools also use the format. In this approach, the school's administration usually creates the media center schedule. The library schedule is based on a rotation with other elective subjects such as art, music, or physical education. The rotation typically allows release time for the classroom teacher after dropping students off at the prescribed class. The time frame for the visit is also predetermined as a part of the rotation. The number of classes in the schedule rotation determines the number of days between visits, with one week being most common. In this scenario, the media specialist may teach a curriculum of research skills, but they do not necessarily coordinate with what is happening in the classroom.

The advantages of fixed scheduling:

- The media center is always full.
- The media specialist will see each child in the school.
- The media specialist can set up a schedule of lessons that will reach every student by the end of the school year.
- There is less need to mount a promotional program for your media center, since all classes routinely come to the facility.
- Each teacher in the school is assured of planning time.

The disadvantages of fixed scheduling:

- Unless there is a clerk to help them, students can only come to the library during their scheduled library time. Since the media center is constantly in use by classes, the media specialist cannot work with individual students or small groups.
- The time for the lessons is fixed, no matter what the need or grade level. The time between lessons is also set because of the schedule rotation. It is impossible to bring the same class to the media center two days in a row, even if it would benefit student learning.
- Lessons may not correlate with the classroom curriculum, making them less relevant, and research shows that skills taught in isolation are not likely to be retained or transferred to other learning.
- This format does not promote collaboration between the classroom teacher and media specialist since time in the media center is relief time for the teacher.

Flexible Access Scheduling

Many media specialists, on all grade levels, favor the flexible access scheduling approach. It reflects an entirely different philosophy for the library media center, since the emphasis is on cooperatively planned lessons that relate directly to the classroom curriculum. The teaching of information skills becomes an integral part of the curriculum, elevating the position of both the media center and the media specialist.

You never know what you might find when you walk into a flexible access media center. There might be multiple classes using the facility at the same time. A small group of students may work collaboratively on a project in one corner, while individuals browse for reading materials nearby. Classroom teachers will be in the media center team teaching with the media specialist to provide well-rounded instruction for their students.

Advantages of flexible access programs:

- Research indicates that being able to use the library when it directly correlates with a curriculum need is best for student learning (van Deusen and Tallman 1994).
- Information skill lessons take on meaning for the student, since they are presented in a way that directly ties them with the curriculum and addresses student needs.
- Because the teaching of research skills is tied to the curriculum, students develop into independent users of resources. This provides a firm foundation for becoming lifelong learners.
- Flexible scheduling allows teachers and students to explore subjects spontaneously when the teachable moment arises by coming to the media center.
- Time scheduling can be set to meet student-learning needs. If a library visit needs to take place two or more days in a row, the teacher simply reserves the time.

Disadvantages of flexible access programs:

- Since the media center is not on a regular schedule, the media specialist will have to work to promote the program and convince teachers to bring classes for instruction.
- There is no guarantee that each student will come to the media center for instruction. In fact, no matter how much promotional work the media specialist does, there will always be some teachers who will not bring their classes to the library. In extreme cases, the media specialist will have to carefully weigh the options available to him or her. It may be necessary to ask an administrator to recommend bringing a class in to the teacher who will not sign up for library lessons. This should be a last resort, however, as such a move would also probably create ill will.

There is much written about flexible and fixed access programs. In the November 2001 issue of *School Library Journal*, Doug Johnson very succinctly stated his reasons for supporting traditional fixed schedule programs. You can read the entire article online at http://www.schoollibraryjournal.com/article/CA179495.html.

A SUMMARY OF: MAKE YOUR POINT—IT'S GOOD TO BE INFLEXIBLE

Are flexible library schedules better than fixed ones? Not necessarily.

By Doug Johnson
Director of media and technology for the Mankato Area Public Schools in Minnesota

Doug Johnson feels that the American Association of School Librarians (AASL), through its position papers, standards, and policies, clearly states that flexibly scheduled library programs are superior to fixed schedule programs. Offering a different perspective, Mr. Johnson wonders if AASL has room for both the flexible and fixed scheduling options. Doug offers the following fixed scheduling strengths that he feels are not being addressed in the ongoing scheduling debate.

1. *If you can't see them, you can't teach them.* Not every teacher will collaborate with the media specialist to bring students to the media center for research. Some won't even bring students for book checkout. Flexible scheduling creates a situation that allows students of cooperative teachers to receive instruction while students in classes with noncollaborative teachers receive none. Is this really what we want? Perhaps it is better to give all students the ability to learn some skills even if the situation is not ideal.

2. *We make it possible for teachers to depart from the curriculum.* An advantage of testing has been the standardization of curriculum. Teachers must actually teach the skills they are required to teach. Research and information skills are an important part of the curriculum, but if flexible scheduling is not required for all classes, it allows teachers to approach these subjects in a potentially haphazard way. We must consider which scheduling style works better with a set curriculum.

3. *Reading matters, too.* By emphasizing independent reading, school library programs help improve essential reading skills. Each student deserves to experience story times, book talks, and library checkout! Should we stop encouraging children to be lifelong readers with regular library visits, to concentrate on teaching information literacy skills in flexibly scheduled programs?

4. *In truth, we conduct research every day.* Flexible scheduling encourages teachers and media specialists to collaborate on projects. Typically, these end up being large projects done at isolated points in the school year. In reality, most of us do small research projects each day. Regularly scheduled library visits that supply lessons focusing on the research process and tied to a class topic may well provide better practice in real problem solving.

5. *Our role includes teaching and caring for students.* Society asks schools to educate, socialize, and take care of the community's young people while their parents work. When media specialists in a fixed schedule host classes, they are not just providing prep time for teachers, they are helping hold up part of the school's obligation to teach and care for children. There is a practical bottom line here— it's hard to fire prep-time providers. We must ask if we want a more secure fixed schedule or a flexible schedule that makes us vulnerable to cuts. Effective media specialists recognize that a fixed schedule does not mean an inferior program and do their best to provide meaningful instruction and experiences for their students no matter what type of schedule they have.

Doug Johnson

Sidebar 5.02 Flexible Scheduling Is the Best!

Gail Przeclawski, NBCT Library Media
Media Specialist, Grand Avenue Elementary School
Orange County Public Schools, Orlando, Florida

I've learned from personal experience that flexible scheduling works best for me and my students. The reasons I prefer it fall into three categories: instructional, student related, and media center administration.

Flexible scheduling promotes collaboration with the teachers at your school and ensures relevant content for all library lessons based on what is happening in the classroom. The lessons are developmentally appropriate and the scheduling gives you the flexibility to time the length and frequency of lessons. Teachers love it when you help them with lessons and activities supporting their curriculum, and the student learning gains verify the advantages of the partnership between you and the classroom teacher.

Under flexible scheduling, my one-on-one time with students increases. I am able to approach them directly in the book stacks, at the catalog, or on the computer to take advantage of teachable moments. This results not only in stronger independent library users, but also in the formation of more personal relationships between me and the students—something I cherish!

Finally, flexible scheduling allows me to arrange my week so that I have time for the administrative functions of my job. Running my media program requires time to arrange for special programs to promote reading, providing teacher in-service, working with my clerical staff, and so forth. By carefully structuring my time, I am able to provide spaces in the week to address these day-to-day operational concerns as well—something I could not do on a fixed schedule.

So for me, Flexible Scheduling is the only way to go!

Gail Przeclawski

- The approach puts more pressure on the media specialist to be a knowledgeable, competent teacher across the curriculum, since lessons will come from all academic disciplines. Consequently, the media specialist must be familiar with standards from all curriculum areas.
- Because the media specialist's schedule varies daily, administering the business of the media center sometimes falls behind.
- Flexible scheduling costs schools more money since they must provide additional electives to take the place of the media center on the schedule rotation. They will also need to hire clerical staff to support the program while the media specialist is working with students and staff.

Fixed or Flex? What Schedule Is Best for Your Media Center?

There is an ongoing debate in schools over the issue of library scheduling. The AASL (a division of the ALA) issued a position paper supporting flexible scheduling in 1991. Citing the importance of integrating the library media program into the total educational program, the paper calls for support on all levels of the educational establishment for this philosophy of library scheduling. Many schools have embraced this approach and many have not. For some schools, the idea of flexible scheduling is impossible. It costs more since additional teachers will have to be hired and classes developed to take the place of the library in the schedule rotation. Some school districts are able to work around the cost by using

TABLE 5.01: Sample blended schedule.

Flexible access—Teachers may send a small group of five to six students for book selection. Or send small groups between 9:20 and 10:10 or after 1:20.

	Monday	Tuesday	Wednesday	Thursday	Friday
8:30 to 9:10	News crew team 2	News crew team 2	News crew team 2	News crew team 2	News crew team 2
9:15 to 9:40	Flexible access	Flexible access	Casey	Flex Walsh (K) story time in classroom	Flexible access
9:40 to 10:10	Flexible access	Flexible access	Flexible access	Gold	Harvey
10:10 to 10:40	Flexible access (Edwina lunch till 11:00)	Beavin (Edwina lunch 10:30 to 11:00)	Flexible access (Edwina lunch till 11:00)	Flexible access (Edwina lunch till 11:00)	Flexible access (Edwina lunch 10:30 to 11:00)
10:40 to 11:10	Flexible access	Flexible access to 11:00	Flexible access (11:00–11:30 Ann lunch)	Flexible access	Flexible access
11:20 to 11:55	First grade story time	First grade story time	11:30 to 12:00 First grade story time	First grade story time	First grade story time
11:10 to 11:40	Flexible access	11:00 to 11:25 Schoppe	Hauser	Greene	Mitchell
12:00 to 12:30	Ann lunch	Ann lunch	12:05 to 12:35 Kindergarten story time	Ann lunch	Ann lunch
11:40 to 12:10	Ruhle	May	Dee/Buchheister	Wood	Flexible access
12:10 to 12:40	Warford	Rector	Roffman	Ronat	Shannon
12:35 to 1:10	Kindergarten story time	Kindergarten story time	N/A	Kindergarten story time	Kindergarten story time
12:40 to 1:10	Vila	Castro	Grant	Simms	Fischer
1:10 to 1:40	O'Neale	Schultes	Flexible access	Turk	Kennedy
1:40 to 2:10	Bonnin	DuBose	N/A	Reese	Flexible access
2:10 to 2:40	Bromhead	Clark and Clinton (first in room)	N/A	Ogren	Gufford

Sample blended schedule from Windermere Elementary, Orange County Public Schools, Orlando, Florida. Ann Carmine, Media Specialist.

paraprofessionals to lead special programs under the direction of the media specialist or another teacher. Since the solutions to the problems presented by costs and staffing are varied, ask other media specialists in your area how the situation is handled in their work locations and districts. Many school administrators simply find it hard to understand the idea of flexible scheduling since it represents a philosophical shift in thinking about school libraries.

As a new media specialist, your schedule will probably be predetermined by the school's history and your principal. Take time to get to know your school and examine how they handle scheduling. In trying to meet the needs of students and teachers, many schools have developed blended schedule approaches to solve the scheduling problem. In these learning communities, some grades have regularly scheduled library times, while others operate on a flexible access plan. So, a kindergarten class may come each week for story time and checkout, while third, fourth, and fifth grade students may operate on an as needed basis. After getting to know your school and your role as its library media specialist, you will be in a better position to evaluate the scheduling approach.

School cultures are difficult to change. If you find yourself in a rigid fixed schedule and wish to move your school in the direction of flexible access, recognize that it will take time. Begin by working with your teachers. Find out what they are teaching, and try to support their curriculum during student library time. Encourage them to stay with their class and get involved in the lessons and activities you present to their students. When the teachers begin to see you as a partner in teaching students, the door for change will open.

In addition, you will need to arm yourself with background information to present to your school administration, parent groups, and community supporting the need for flexible scheduling. The resources list at the end of this chapter provides a great starting point for your search.

As you seek to alter the traditions of your school, be prepared to move slowly. It may take a year or longer to convince the administration to try your ideas. You may have to compromise by using a modified flexible access plan as described above for the first year or two while you build collaborative relationships with your faculty and staff. The important thing is to work within the established structure of your school, while at the same time gently nudging your learning community towards doing what is best for student learning and achievement. Keep in mind that your attitude toward the present schedule does affect learning. So no matter what schedule you have, focus your time and energy on meeting the needs of your learning community in the best way possible. As your school community sees what you can do for them, you may be surprised to find them demanding the changes you want so that they can make fuller use of your knowledge and expertise.

Practicalities of Scheduling

Regardless of the scheduling philosophy used in your school, you will need to address the day-to-day routines of scheduling your media center space. Even in a small school, this can become a daunting task. It requires establishing a scheduling calendar and procedure based on analysis of your facility, school calendar, daily bell schedule, and the needs of your faculty and students. New media specialists will learn quickly that certain times of year book up quickly, while there may be other times when few classes come to the media center for several days. However, it is always important to be organized in your approach to scheduling the media center space; your entire school depends on you to make things run smoothly in this important area. Here are some things to consider when planning a daily schedule calendar for your media center.

First, spend time in the media center. Since you can't change the arrangement of the entire room and collection overnight, note where everything is and how the space is currently used. It may help to make a map of the room identifying the general location of books by Dewey number, computers, tables, reading areas, and so forth. Ask faculty and staff who have used the facility for input about the current layout for ease of use. Examine old schedule books or calendars to see how the previous media specialist organized the room. Consider all the input you have gathered, and decide if you need to make any quick but simple changes. For example, if your class seating is on the opposite side of the room from the nonfiction and reference sections that are commonly used for student projects, you may decide to move tables closer to these areas. This would cut down on traffic and make it easier for students to find the materials they need.

Remember, the use of media center space is something that constantly changes. As a new media specialist in a school, you may not want to shake up the status quo too much, but after some time has passed, you can begin to instigate changes and work toward your vision for the space. Always keep in mind, your

Sidebar 5.03 Voice of Experience from Claire Gatrell Stephens: For New Media Specialists, a Word about Changing Established Policies

When I got my first job as a media specialist, the library had an upstairs loft area. All the nonfiction books were located there. The previous media specialist had a rule limiting student access to the loft. She only allowed two students at a time up there. I thought this was terrible and immediately lifted this "silly" rule. The clerk, who had been there through three different media specialists, advised me against changing the policy, but I didn't listen.

One day of my new policy showed me why access to the upstairs loft had been so tightly controlled. Poor visibility from the media center's downstairs area made student supervision in the loft very difficult. All sorts of mischief took place up there. Within one week, I admitted I was wrong and sought advice from the clerk and several long-time teachers at the school. Regretfully, I reestablished the two-person rule, but over the next few months, we reorganized the collection. We moved the most frequently used nonfiction materials to a more accessible location on the first floor, increasing student access to the books.

The moral of the story—don't discount the voices of experience in your school. Teachers, administrators, and staff who have been there for many years can help you gain insight into the hows and whys of your existing media center's policies and procedures. All you have to do is ask, and listen!

Claire Stephens

ultimate goal is to accommodate as many student groups as possible so that your media center can be the instructional hub of the school.

After you have your room arrangement settled, it is time to organize your daily scheduling calendar. Before starting this, you will want to do the following:

- Investigate how scheduling has been handled in the past at your school. Ask teachers and clerical staff to point out advantages and disadvantages with the existing system. Listen to and consider their input.
- Some schools have policies limiting teacher use of some spaces within the media center. For example, in order to create a fair use situation, a teacher may be allowed to sign up for a computer lab for only two or three days in a row. You need to know if your school has any procedures like this and develop an understanding of why the policy exists. If you want to alter the policy, consult with your administration before advertising your change.
- Get a copy of your school district's master calendar for the school year. You need to know all the holidays, workdays, and so forth before establishing your schedule book.
- Consult with your principal for any regulations he or she may have about scheduling spaces in the school. Most administrators are willing to allow you to take care of the scheduling during the school day. However, they may want you to block out certain times for specific events, such as testing or faculty meetings. Ask about policies regarding scheduling before and after school hours since the media center is a frequently requested space by many community groups who need a place to meet. This is important information to know before setting up your calendar; you will need to block out these times to be sure conflicts do not arise. Do not leave this meeting with your administrator until you agree about how the media center space will be scheduled.

Does the principal want to control community access through his or her office? How will you and the administrator communicate about the scheduling of the space to avoid conflicts?

- Obtain a copy of your school's hourly bell schedule.
- List the spaces that can be used by classes in your media center. Perhaps you have one or two class spaces. Most modern school media centers also have a computer lab area for class use; be sure to include it on your list. Would you also allow a class to come down for book checkout? If so, you will need to set up a space in your schedule for this so you can keep track of how many groups are in the media center at any given time and avoid overbooking the space.

Now you are ready to set up your daily calendar. There are as many different ways to do this as there are media specialists and media centers. You may try several different approaches before settling on the one that works best for you and your school community. Some people keep a simple wall calendar with the schedule information written on it. Others use a notebook style calendar that breaks each day down

Media specialist Teanna Manley of Westridge Middle School in Orlando, Florida, keeps her schedule manually in a calendar book.

TABLE 5.02: Media center signup sheet.

Date: Friday, September 26, 2006

	Blue Seating	Green Seating	Main Floor Computers	Target Asst. Lab. 213	Computer Lab 211	Prof. Resource Room 212	Small Conf. Room 203
First Period 7:20 to 8:13 Wed 7:20 to 8:01	Smith–research Am. Rev.–need book cart			Finnen–SRI tsting	Guidance–online career exp.–Ninth grade		Hershaw–IT teach. class
Second Period 8:19 to 9:12 Wed 8:07 to 8:48		Pristera –Ninth gr. Eng. Proj. Lesson using ref. books	Jones–FCAT exp.			ESOL Testing	
Third Period 9:18 to 10:11 Wed 8:54 to 9:35							Reynolds–Sch. Soc. Wkr, apts.
Fourth Period A 10:11 to 10:41 Wed 9:35 to 10:05						Staff in-service makeup sessions	
Fourth Period B 10:41 to 11:11 Wed 10:05 to 10:35							
Fourth Period C 11:23 to 11:53 Wed 10:47 to 11:17	Smith as above	Torres–marine sci, ecosystems–needs overhead & screen	Lettman–online dbase lesson–current events				
Fourth Period D 11:47 to 12:17 Wed 11:11 to 11:41							
Fifth Period 12:25 to 1:16 Wed 11:47 to 12:28							
Sixth Period 1:23 to 2:15 Wed 12:34 to 1:15		Pristera–Ninth gr. Eng. Proj.–as above		Finnen–SRI tsting			
After School	Beta Club Tutoring			Homer–teacher gradebook update		Staff in-service makeup sessions	Literacy team meeting
Evening		ESOL Parent Leadership Group meeting				SAC–6:30 Need MM proj.	

This schedule table is used at Freedom High School in Orlando, Florida.

into hourly blocks. Word processing software allows for the creation of tables that can be duplicated for each day of the year and show all the spaces and class periods. When using these tables, the teacher signs up in the block for the space and time they need.

Here are some other tips you may want to consider when setting up and using your daily schedule calendar for the media center.

- Always keep several pencils and a big eraser nearby. Plans change on a daily basis, so you don't want to write in ink on the pages.
- Some media specialists use laminated calendar pages and overhead markers that can be easily wiped off to deal with schedule changes.

Pat Franklin uses a white board positioned near the entrance of her media center to communicate with teachers and students. Each day she posts the teachers and the areas in the media center they are signed up to use. This information helps everyone move to the appropriate space in the room and get started quickly with their class.

- Keep a pad of sticky notes handy so teachers can write down the times and locations they reserve.
- Keep the schedule in your office so that teachers have to see you to sign up. This facilitates a discussion about the purpose of bringing the class to the media center and opens the door for collaboration between you and the classroom teacher.
- Make copies of the daily schedule each morning and put one at your circulation desk. Share the others with staff members such as your clerk or other school staff who might need to know who is signed up for the media center that day. This will increase communication and help everyone with his or her job preparations for the day.
- If possible, contact teachers the day before they are signed up to come to the media center. Review any plans you made to collaborate on a lesson.
- How far in advance should you schedule your media center? The answer depends on you and your school. There are some things, such as testing dates, that are predetermined, and your principal may want you to reserve those dates from the beginning of the school year. If you are new and aren't comfortable committing to a schedule form for the entire year, start with a desk calendar or print out enough pages of the form you create to cover the first grading period. Keep a blank page or legal pad at the end of your schedule notebook to reserve important dates beyond those covered in your existing planner. This will allow you time to make changes and revise your form. By the end of the first grading period, you should be able to set up your calendar for the remainder of the school year.

Everyone has to find a scheduling procedure that works for their school community. Keep in mind that you want your media center to be a full and active facility. Advertise your scheduling procedures and encourage teachers to bring classes for research or checkout. Even if you are not doing a lesson with a particular class, be sure to greet the students and their teacher. Let them know you appreciate them coming to the media center, and offer to be of service during their visit. This kind of customer service will earn you return visits, and before long, your media center calendar will be overflowing—which is a good problem to have.

Bibliography

American Association of School Librarians. *Position Statement on Flexible Scheduling.* Available at: http://www. ala.org/aaslTemplate.cfm?Section+positionstatements&template+/ContentManagement (accessed September 8, 2005).

Buchanan, Jan. *Flexible Access Library Media Programs.* Englewood, CO: Libraries Unlimited, 1991.

Lamb, Annette, and Larry Johnson. *IUPUI School of Library and Information Science The School Library Media Specialist: Scheduling.* Available at: http://eduscapes.com/sms/flexible.html (accessed September 8, 2005).

Needham, Joyce. "From Fixed to Flexible: Making the Journey." *Teacher Librarian* 30, no. 5 (2003): 8–13.

Public Education Network/American Association of School Librarians. *The Information-Powered School.* Edited by Sandra Huges-Hassell and Anne Wheelock. Chicago: American Library Association, 2001.

Przeclawski, Gail. Personal interview with a National Board certified teacher in early childhood/young adult library media, August 27, 2005.

van Deusen, Jean Donham, and Julie I Tallman. "The Impact of Scheduling on Curriculum Consultation and Information Skills Instruction: Part One The 1993–94 AASL/Highsmith Research Award Study." *School Library Media Quarterly* 23, no. 1 (1994), http://oldweb.ala.org/aasl/SLMR/slmr_resources/select_vandeusen21. html.

Wasman, Ann M. *New Steps to Service: Common-Sense Advice for the School Library Media Specialist.* Chicago: American Library Association, 1998.

6

Staffing Your Library Media Center

In the ideal world, the media center has a large staff which works diligently to implement all of the many and varied programs necessary for student achievement. However, in the real world, we make do with whatever staff the budget allows. An effective school library media center is staffed with one or more certified library media specialists, depending on the school population. Each school library media center should have at least one full-time media clerk or more, again, depending on the school population. Most schools look at staffing requirements set forth by the organization that gives them accreditation. For example, the Southern Association for Colleges and Secondary Schools bases its staffing requirements on school population.

School Library Media Specialist

The media specialist is the manager of the media center. Your duties are many and varied. They ultimately depend on what your principal expects and how well you articulate your vision of a best practice library media program. The media specialist is a:

- *Teacher*—Because of a thorough knowledge of curriculum, you collaborate with classroom teachers and teach library skills, research skills, and higher-level thinking skills in all content areas.
- *Manager*—You organize and manage materials and people.
- *Administrator*—You develop policies and procedures that fulfill the mission of the library media center.
- *Visionary*—You create a program that provides access to materials for all patrons and envision future growth to accommodate new technologies, curriculum, and educational challenges.
- *Caretaker*—You create an atmosphere that invites stakeholders to become part of the media program.

Source: SACS/CASI Public School Standards. Available at: http://www.sacscasi.org/region/standards/index.html (accessed April 30, 2006). (Link to accreditation standards 2005 for K-12 public schools.) Used with permission.

The excerpt below comes from the Southern Association for Colleges and Secondary Schools Web site. It identifies staffing guidelines for school library media centers for schools that subscribe to the association's standards.

640

Membership	1–249	250–499	500–749	750–999	1000–1249	1250–1499	1500–up
Administrative head	1	1	1	1	1	1	1
Administrative or supervisory assistants	0	.5 0 (elem)	1 .5 (elem)	1.5 1 (elem)	2 1.5 (elem)	2.5 2 (elem)	One (full-time equivalent) staff member shall be added *where needed* for each additional 250 students over 1,500.
Guidance professionals	.5	1 .5 (elem)	1.5 1 (elem)	2 1.5 (elem)	2.5 2 (elem)	3 2.5 (elem)	
Library or media specialists	.5	1	1	1	2* (secondary)	2* (secondary) 1 (middle–elem)	
Support staff for administration, library/media, or technology	1 .5 (elem)	2.5 1 (elem)	4 1.5 (elem)	4.5 2.5 (elem)	5 3 (elem)	5.5 3 (elem)	6 3 (elem)

* After employing one professionally qualified librarian or media specialist, the school may employ a professionally qualified technology or information specialist assigned to the library media center to meet the requirement.

STANDARD 6 RESOURCES

The school has sufficient human, financial, physical, and material resources to support its vision, mission, and goals.

Human Resources

In fulfillment of this standard, the school:

6.1 Employs an administrative head and administrative or supervisory assistants who have an earned graduate degree with 18 semester hours in administration or supervision (as a part of, or in addition to the degree) from an institution recognized by a U.S. regional accrediting agency**; (see note 1, 2, and 4)

6.2 Provides and assigns staff that is sufficient to meet the vision, mission, and goals of the school:

6.3 Employs instructional personnel who have an earned bachelor's degree that includes 12 semester hours of professional education (as part of, or in addition to, the degree) from an institution recognized by a U.S. regional accrediting agency**; (see note 2 and 4)

(continued)

6.4 Employs instructional personnel who have a college major (at least 24 semester hours) in their assigned field; (see note 1 and 2)

6.5 Employs counselors and media specialists who have an earned graduate degree in their assigned field from an institution recognized by a U.S. regional accrediting agency**; (see note 1 and 2)

6.6 Requires all professional personnel to earn at least six semester hours of credit or the equivalent during each five years of employment; (see note 3)

---

[1] Professional personnel that meet the qualifications for certification or licensing by the state in which employed are in compliance.

[2] Professional personnel who do not hold the required degree or have not earned the specified credits must be actively enrolled in a program that leads to meeting the requirement within three years. Active enrollment means earning at least six semester hours of credit per academic year.

[3] Six semester hours of credit is equivalent to 120 clock hours of participation in professional development activities, e.g., workshops, seminars, conferences, and peer review team visits (see page 17, Appendix D)

[4] Professional personnel who have training or experience that might be equivalent to the specified credits may request with justification that the State Council accept such training or experience in lieu of all or part of the requirement. (See page 15, Appendix B and page 16, Appendix C)

** *U.S. Regional Accrediting Agencies: Southern Association Colleges and Schools; North Central Association of Schools and Colleges; Middle States Association of Colleges and Schools; Western Association of Schools and Colleges; New England Association of Colleges and Schools; and the Northwest Association of Accredited Schools.*

- *Organizer*—You continually inventory and evaluate the collection, both print and nonprint.
- *Comptroller*—You make sure the library media center is run efficiently by formulating and implementing an effective budget.
- *Collaborator*—You work with other library media specialists, parents, and administrators in providing leadership for the betterment of your school and the profession.
- *Personnel manager*—You select and manage the library staff so that the library media program can grow.
- *Leader*—You continually lead by both providing and attending professional development opportunities.

School Library Media Clerk

When looking for an effective clerk, remember that service is the number one mission of the media center. Look for someone who is organized and truly likes children. Look for an energetic person, because there is always much to do. A good clerk makes your life easier by being a self-starter and is someone you can lean on. The clerk needs to look around the media center, see what needs to be done, and then do it. Actually, you are looking for a superwoman or superman who is smart, friendly, and loves

Sidebar 6.02 Media Clerk Job Description

Source: Orange County Public Schools, Noninstructional Job Descriptions. Available at: http://www.ocps.net/˜hrd/classified/cjd/mediaclerk1.htm (accessed April 30, 2006).

This excerpt from the media clerk I job description in the author's school district lists some of the expectations for district library staff. Your school district probably has a similar job listing. It is a good idea to become familiar with the job descriptions for media staff in your school. You also need to know the rules for work hours and days, breaks, lunches, and so forth. If you are not familiar with this information, try asking your school secretary or principal. They probably have a copy of the job descriptions and contract requirements for your district located somewhere in the school office.

POSITION TITLE: MEDIA CLERK I

General Description of Duties

Under direct supervision, the purpose of the position is to perform school-based duties associated with the daily operation of the media center. Employees in this classification function at an entry-level capacity and perform basic clerical/bookkeeping duties associated with the retrieval of information, stocking and maintenance of materials, and the assisting of patrons. Performs related work as directed.

Specific Duties and Responsibilities

Examples of Essential Functions

Processes new books and materials and adds to collection via computer; bar codes new materials.

Inventories all media center equipment; repairs and mends library materials; wraps books.

Maintains paperback, periodical, and video collections; organizes collections on an hourly and daily basis; stores outdated materials; maintains vertical file.

Performs customer service functions; provides assistance and information related to library policies and procedures; assists all students and teachers in their needs.

Shelves books and other materials in the reading room; keeps collection in proper order; stocks and restocks bookshelves.

Facilitates orientations for English classes.

Assists students at circulation desk with checking library materials in and out via computer-automated system.

Responsible for processing and maintaining all audio/visual materials and equipment; instructs users in the use and adjustment of audio/visual equipment.

Assists students with research questions and other school related projects; sets up workshops.

Creates and maintains student database; maintains student identification cards.

Creates and maintains book displays; coordinates book fair.

Removes books from book drop.

Laminates materials.

Answers the telephone; provides information and assistance to the staff; sorts and distributes incoming mail.

her or his job. These people are hard to find, so treasure your clerk! In reality, your clerk's job description will depend on the grade level of your school and your media program. However, most media clerks perform the following duties:

- Clerks help teachers and students locate information.
- Clerks use the media management system to check in and out books and run overdue notices for students and teachers.
- Clerks process and shelve books and audiovisual materials to your specifications.
- Clerks may learn to catalog and help with entering new books onto your database.
- Clerks learn to operate and maintain audiovisual equipment.
- Clerks supervise students and train student assistants.
- Clerks assist with inventories and maintain records.
- Clerks perform clerical duties, for example checking in magazines, filing catalogs, and helping with displays.

Volunteers

Never turn down a volunteer! Whether it is a mom who wants to be at school a few hours once a week or a retired community member who wants to help more often, become friends with your volunteers and keep them busy! Volunteers can do much of the work your staff does, freeing your clerk to help students and assist with media center activities. Volunteers can help with special events such as a book fair or a paperback book exchange. Ask your PTA to add your library media center to their list of volunteer opportunities. Ask for help in your school newsletter. Volunteers helping at your school on a regular basis will learn to know your library media center, and will be able to perform routine media tasks and

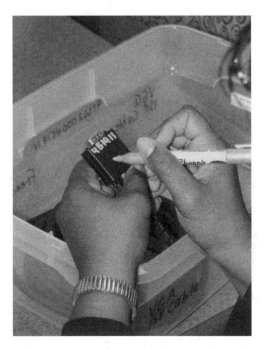

Volunteers can be trained to assist with many tasks, such as processing books and equipment.

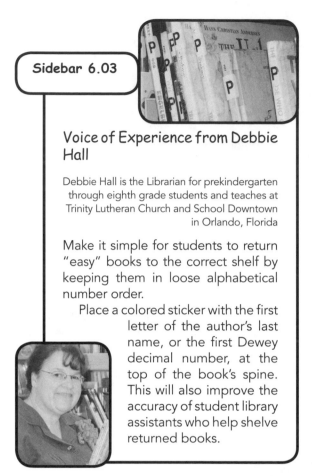

Sidebar 6.03

Voice of Experience from Debbie Hall

Debbie Hall is the Librarian for prekindergarten through eighth grade students and teaches at Trinity Lutheran Church and School Downtown in Orlando, Florida

Make it simple for students to return "easy" books to the correct shelf by keeping them in loose alphabetical number order.

Place a colored sticker with the first letter of the author's last name, or the first Dewey decimal number, at the top of the book's spine. This will also improve the accuracy of student library assistants who help shelve returned books.

even help students find materials and become personal advocates for your program in the community. At the end of the year, you may want to thank your volunteers with something small, such as a token gift or something more elaborate such as a luncheon to show them how grateful you are for their support and dedication.

Duty Teachers

Many schools send duty and substitute teachers to the library media center during their free periods. These people are a great resource. They are knowledgeable and can help clerks with quick jobs such as filing, checking in books, or labeling videos. There is always a job that someone with a few minutes can do to keep your media center running smoothly.

Student Assistants

Good student assistants can help your library media center stay in top condition and teach students skills that range from customer service to locating information in the media center or on the Internet. Whether you have students in an after school library club, or students each period of the day who get credit for your class, student

With proper training, student assistants of all ages can help with many library tasks. Here, Mandy, an elementary student assistant at Sunrise Elementary school in Orlando, Florida, helps shelve books after school.

assistants can help you in numerous ways. They can shelve books, create displays, perform clerical tasks, set up and even fix equipment and computers. They can run your closed circuit TV news show and create posters on computers to advertise library media center events. Our students are given a remote scanner during inventory and help us scan all of our books and equipment. They inspire us with ideas to promote our collection and help other students find information. They run errands and keep us current on school news and the latest trends!

Bibliography

American Library Association. *Position Statement on Appropriate Staffing for School Library Media Centers.* Available at: http://www.ala.org/aasl.

Scholastic, Inc. *School Libraries Work!* New York: Scholastic Library Publishing, 2006. Available at http://www.scholastic.com/libraries/printables/downloads/slw_2006.pdf

U.S. Department of Labor Bureau of Labor Statistics. *Occupational Outlook Handbook (OOH) 2006–07 Edition.* Available at: http://www.bls.gov/oco/.

Washington Library Media Association. *Qualities and Competencies for Staffing an Effective Library Media Program.* Available at: http://www.wlma.org/Professional/jobdescriptions.htm.

7

Arranging Your Media Center

The arrangement of your media center says quite a bit about your program. It is so important that when you apply for National Board Certification in Library Media, you must videotape your media center to show its layout and organization. Arrange your media center for efficiency, but it is just as important that you create a welcoming environment.

The constraints of the room often dictate the physical arrangement of the media center. Your circulation desk is probably built in and cannot be moved. Shelves may be massive and can't be rearranged. However, it is important to take a hard look at your space and decide what you can do to improve it.

One area you can improve is lighting. Usually lighting is built into the ceiling; however, many times that lighting can be updated to create a new, exciting look in your library media center. Make sure your circulation desk is bright and well lit so that you and your library clerks are able to work efficiently. Teachers want ample lighting in class areas for their students to read and write their assignments. It is important to have lighting around the book stacks to ensure effective student supervision throughout the school day. Some media centers use accent lighting in their leisure areas to create a warm and inviting atmosphere. No matter how you decorate, pay special attention to lighting in order to create the type of space where all students and teachers feel welcome.

Your media center must have room for classes to meet as well as room for students to work independently or in groups. Create leisure areas where students can relax and enjoy your merchandise. How much room you devote to each of these areas is dependent on the size of your school and your library media center. A common thought in the past was that the media center should accommodate 10 percent of your school population. Today we think differently—instead of trying to create enough room for an arbitrary number of students, focus on creating areas for classes and individual study that will benefit your clientele.

Table lamps like this one create an inviting space for patrons to work.

Many elementary schools have one large area for classes and another area featuring computers for drop in students.

High schools may have two or three large class areas, as well as enough computers for another class to use for research. These separate areas make it easier for teachers to schedule their classes. One class may be doing research while another class is checking out fiction books. A third class may be using your die cut machines to create projects for their class.

Remember that besides your students and teachers, members of the community will also use your media center. Local groups may use your media center for neighborhood meetings or community events. Arrange your media center to be conducive to a variety of activities and to be flexible enough to accommodate any type of gathering that may be scheduled in your space.

Circulation Desk

Your circulation desk is usually a permanent fixture that cannot be moved. Therefore, you must evaluate it and decide how to make it most effective. Place media management equipment, including printers,

The circulation desk is your home base; be sure to arrange it so you can work easily and efficiently.

where they are least intrusive. Make sure your book return is in a convenient location. Your checkout pattern should be efficient and still allow you to supervise the library media center. You should have at least one drawer that locks for fine money or important papers. A phone is a necessity at your circulation desk for convenience and safety.

Furniture

Your choice of furniture is dependent on the age level of your students, the size of the space, and your budget. Furniture comes in all shapes, sizes, and colors. Consider function and form; the furniture must be sturdy, provide comfort, and wear well. Quality furniture lasts years, maybe decades, so choose wisely. Students will be sitting and squirming in chairs and near tables, so they need to be sturdy and stain resistant. Form is also important. It is unwise to choose trendy furniture that will look out of date in a few years. A beautiful fabric may seem lovely, but what looks charming today may look ugly and old next year. The shape and color of the furniture should be pleasing to the eye and classic enough to last many years in the media center. Make sure you do not order too much furniture. You want enough furniture to accommodate classes, but too many tables and chairs make the room feel cramped and look smaller than it actually is.

Elementary school media centers often feature lower shelving designed for small children. This picture is from Tangelo Park Elementary, Orange County Public Schools, Orlando, Florida.

Many high schools place die cut machines out in the open where students can use them for projects and club activities.

To help prevent theft, these security system towers detect sensors located in library materials.

Security Systems

Along with your furniture, you may be considering purchasing a security system. There are many brands to choose from, and each system is designed to detect a sensor that you put in your books. This stops students from removing library materials without checking them out. Make sure you evaluate each system to decide what is best for your school. Don't just consider the price of the system, be sure to take into account the cost of the supplies needed to utilize the system. Also, investigate the cost of maintenance service and the reputation of the service department. It is imperative that you purchase the maintenance agreement, because once the system is in place, it must provide consistent security.

Shelves

The arrangement of shelves is dependent upon the shape of your room. The height of the shelves is dependent on the age of your students.

When you are considering both shelving and furniture, don't forget the Americans with Disabilities Act. This legislation guarantees access for all patrons to all resources. Shelves should be far enough apart for wheelchairs to move easily up and down the aisles. Space between tables and chairs should be easily accessible to all patrons. Since furnishings in elementary media centers are often lower for smaller students, there may be a need to purchase higher tables and work stations suitable for wheelchair access. Elementary media specialists facing this situation must consult their school and district experts on Americans with Disabilities Act compliance and be sure to select appropriate furnishings for their students.

Computers, including those that are used to access the online catalog, should be accessible to all. Consider purchasing computers with large screens for your visually impaired students. Study carrels can be used for the many Exceptional Education students who benefit from tapes, CDs, and MP3s of recorded library books or textbooks.

The wide, raised desktop of this computer workstation is designed for wheelchair access.

Teaching Areas

When you create an area for classes to meet, it must be a functional area for teaching. Arrange the space so that the teacher, whether it is you as the library media specialist or the classroom teacher, can see all of the students and so that they can see the teacher. Students must be able to hear the teacher without distractions from other areas of the room. If you have the opportunity to purchase an audio enhancement system or a microphone with an amplifier, do so. Voice amplification is an excellent tool for teachers to use to help focus their classes when they are teaching.

Organize the teaching area so that there is space for an overhead projector, a multimedia projector, or an easel with chart paper, depending on the tools the teacher needs to teach the lesson. This space may include enough computers for the entire class so that students can use the computers for research. There may be tables and chairs in order for the students to work in cooperative groups on projects. This space is a flexible work area where students have the ability to move from books to computers to their tables in groups or individually to effectively complete assignments.

Leisure Areas

In every library media center, students must have a special area to relax. If arranged in an engaging fashion, students will gravitate to this area. Soft chairs or sofas make this area attractive to patrons. Depending on your grade level, make this area one that will attract patrons. Many libraries center this area around periodicals or special collections that students will want to browse in a relaxing manner. Beanbag chairs, decorations, and bright carpets can all be used to create an area that makes students want to stop, drop, and read.

Many high school media centers are trying to emulate large bookstores that attract large numbers of customers. Some high schools are forming partnerships with businesses to make their space as appealing as businesses do. Cafes are becoming popular with high school students as they drink lattes and peruse books and magazines.

Some high schools are featuring cafes to help encourage independent student reading.

A rocking chair is frequently located in elementary school leisure seating areas. Teachers use the chair for story time and students use it for independent reading.

Decorations

It is important to create a warm and inviting atmosphere in your media center. Appealing decorations are one way to attract customers. Many companies produce posters, bookmarks, displays, banners, and other promotional materials that can turn your media center into an exciting vibrant area. Many of these resources are educational and can review some of the library skills you teach in lessons. Holiday-based exhibits give a seasonal feel to your space. Student-made decorations are a wonderful addition to the media center. When students see their own work displayed in the media center, they are excited and

Older students enjoy sitting in comfortable chairs and couches to relax and read their favorite book or magazine.

cannot wait to show their friends. Students are encouraged to visit the media center and feel a part of your collection when they see their artwork prominently displayed. When your school has a contest or festival, display the winning projects or trophies to signal to students your pride in good work and your willingness to help students achieve.

Technology Areas

At an increasing rate, library media centers are expected to house and maintain computer labs. Look at this as an opportunity, not as extra work. Scheduling computer lab time creates a pathway allowing you to learn more about your teachers and their curriculum. This may be a chance for you to collaborate with the teacher by helping her create the lesson, by teaching computer skills to her class, or by introducing print resources that could augment online resources. The optimal arrangement is to have computer labs that you schedule, but are separate from the media center for classes who need no direction, as well as a bank of computers for classes who wish to use computers along with print materials for research. What a perfect opportunity to teach a lesson on evaluating Web resources, on the difference between search engines and online databases, or on ethics and plagiarism. Students on every grade level who have computers at home still need guidance as to the most efficient way to use those computers to save time and to get optimal results.

When contemplating adding computers to the media center, consider electrical needs. Most old media centers do not have electrical outlets or network connections available for a bank of computers large enough for an entire class. Even new schools sometimes do not plan for sufficient electrical needs. When you are in the planning stages of updating or creating a space to house computers, make sure you choose the most up-to-date network options available. Do not scrimp on wiring and networking. Even if you choose the latest and greatest, it will be old hat soon. It is important to get connections that can be upgraded as technology evolves.

Computer Lab Layout

When you design your computer lab, you will probably be limited by the placement of electrical outlets and network connections. However, if you are designing the space, your first concern should be ease of supervision. Computers should be arranged so that the teacher has direct line of vision of all the computer screens. Computers in circular clusters are not conducive to this. U-shaped tables or rows may be the best arrangement. The teacher must be able to get to student computers quickly to give individual help to struggling students. The ability to observe all screens from one area of the room is important but difficult. Flat

Computer labs are a part of most modern media centers.

screens make it easier because they take up so much less room. If it is possible, have a teacher computer equipped with software so that that you can monitor student screens from your computer.

TV and Multimedia Production

Many library media specialists are asked to teach a TV production course and to produce the daily announcements watched on closed circuit TV. Organizing and broadcasting the morning announcements may be the job of a class that the media specialist teaches or may be a group of student volunteers that rotates by the week. However you structure the class, these students must be taught the fundamentals of broadcasting as well as the technical aspects of TV production. The media center must have a room stocked with equipment that allows students to broadcast to the entire school. Some media centers will be outfitted with state of the art equipment, and students will be exposed to high-tech methods of constructing a news show. Other schools will broadcast their announcements using the bare essentials. No matter the quality or quantity of the equipment used, an outstanding show can be produced using creativity and organization. See chapter 11 for more information about television production facilities.

Workroom

Every library media center needs a workroom for processing books and audiovisual materials. This is where supplies and decorations are kept. Orders are delivered to this room, and materials are handled according to your policies and procedures manual so that they are shelf-ready. Your library media clerk may have her office in this room. This room may serve as a room for teachers to meet to plan collaboratively with you or each other. Because of this, your workroom may be a good place to house professional resources. These materials help teachers who need ideas for teaching, help with classroom management, or need to keep current on new trends and ideas in education. Professional materials also benefit teachers writing grants and administrators looking for information. Materials in your professional collection help teachers in all subject areas with their content curriculum as well as with other issues important to the teaching profession. Materials can also include practice test books for teachers pursuing advanced degrees who need to take the Graduate Record Exam (GRE). Include anything in your professional collection that will benefit teachers as they strive to increase their level of professionalism.

Storage Room

The more storage the better! If you have extra rooms, use them. Unused equipment, today, may be just what you are looking for tomorrow. With that said, do weed equipment just as you do books. Filmstrip projectors are no longer needed. If you are saving your slide projectors in case a speaker needs one, it is fine to save one, but saving numerous machines just takes up much needed space. A storage area is needed to place equipment waiting to be checked out or repaired or that is only used occasionally. It also houses seasonal decorations. Many schools use their media center storage areas to house class sets of books for English classes. This area can also be used to house manipulatives or materials used by the exceptional education or ESL (English as a Second Language) departments. The advantage to housing these materials in the media center is that all teachers, no matter what their content area, are able to access the materials. Since the library media specialist is an expert at cataloging and tracking materials, this arrangement benefits the entire school.

The arrangement of your library media center is not arbitrary. When someone walks through your front door, they know nothing about you or your program except what they see. You want them to see a vibrant efficient space that encourages students, teachers, parents, administrators, and community members to use your space effectively. Teachers must see the media center as an extension of their classroom, a place where learning can continually take place. The practical arrangement of the media center encourages the pursuit of knowledge and positively affects student achievement.

Bibliography

Baule, Steve. "Planning Considerations for Library Media Center Facilities." *Library Media Connection* (Nov–Dec 2005): 14–15.

Dolan, Thomas G. *Library or Media Center.* Available at: http://www.peterli.com/archive/spm/655.shtm.

Hart, Thomas L. "Do You Really Want Your Library Media Center Used?" *Library Media Connection* (Nov–Dec 2005): 16–19.

Kinney, Robert. *Teaching TV Production in a Digital World.* Westport, CT: Libraries Unlimited, 2004.

Kyker, Keith, and Chris Curchy. *Television Production: A Classroom Approach.* Westport, CT: Libraries Unlimited, 2004.

Lamb, Annette, and Larry Johnson. "Program Administration: Elements of Facilities." *The School Library Media Specialist.* Available at: http://eduscapes.com/sms/adminstration/elements.html.

Wilson, Lisa. "Bringing Vision to Practice: Planning and Provisioning the New Library Resource Center." *Teacher Librarian* 32, no. 1 (2004): 23–27.

Part II

The Media Specialist as
Teacher Collaborator

8

Standards—State, National, and Your Own

Standards! Standards! Standards! They are everywhere in education these days, and, honestly, it's a good thing. While some cry about the loss of academic freedom, many recognize the need to identify basic educational requirements and to be sure we, as educators, are meeting those needs. So, where does that leave us as media specialists? Are there standards out there for us? Absolutely, there are standards that affect us in terms of the curriculum we teach. There are also standards to help us define our professional positions in our schools, districts, and community. Finally, we should consider developing our own standards. These standards will serve our media centers and provide guidelines for staff, teachers, and students to help them navigate our libraries. On a day-to-day basis, these may be the most important standards of all.

It is important to become familiar with the standards that affect you and your media program. In the current era of accountability, you will be asked to demonstrate your compliance with these guidelines. Be sure to document them in your lesson plans. Standards can also become planks on which you can stand when asking for funding or permission to establish special programs. Use them to demonstrate needs to your principal and show how your request will help you meet the standard's requirements.

Academic Standards

In a book like this, we cannot address the individual standards of each state and school district. It is important that you locate these standards for your state and district. If you are new in your district or state, you may need to become familiar with the vocabulary of standards in your area. A variety of terms are used across the country for standards, including words and phrases such as objectives, benchmarks, grade level expectations, indicators, and so forth. If you do not know how standards are labeled in your community, ask! Learning this important language will help you communicate with your teachers and administrators in a way that they understand and will increase their confidence in your professionalism.

Often you must look beyond standards that are obviously titled for curriculum that applies to the media center. For example, in our state, there are recognized standards for library media. There are also standards imbedded in other curriculum areas that require the use of the media center (see sidebar 8.03). As professionals, we need to be sure we are providing materials and programs to meet those standards as well as our own. We must also be sure we are working with our teachers to teach these vital skills to students. Meeting these standards is not a them or me situation, it is an us situation. In a good library media program, there is collaboration with classroom teachers. Become familiar with all the curriculum

Sidebar 8.01 Locating Standards for Your State and Local District

We cannot identify all the individual places for you to look for standards in a book of this sort, but here is a list of some places to look if you are just starting out:

- Your state department of education Web site
- Your district-level media supervisor
- Your school principal
- Your school curriculum resource specialist or classroom resource teacher
- Your state or local professional organization

The important thing is not to feel intimidated! Ask questions; don't stop until you find the information you need. If you are new to the profession, you cannot be expected to know everything, so keep searching until you find the standards that apply to your state and school district.

Sidebar 8.02 Sample State Library Standards

Source: Alaska Association of School Librarians. *Library/Information Literacy Standards, Student Content Standards for School Libraries.* Available at: http://www.akla.org/akasl/lib/studentstandards.html (accessed May 26, 2007).

Most states have adapted standards applying to school libraries. Since we are obligated to teach in accordance with the requirements of the standards in our area, it is important to be familiar with the standards in your state. The mission statement and standards below were developed through a collaborative process in the state of Alaska during the 1998/99 school year and approved by the State Board of Education on December 10, 1999. They were incorporated into *Alaska Standards: Content and Performance Standards for Alaska Students* in February 2000.

ALASKA LIBRARY/INFORMATION LITERACY STANDARDS

Mission Statement

The school library is a primary source for information and curriculum support. The school library program functions as the information center for the school by providing access to a full range of

(*continued*)

information resources, in both traditional and electronic format, and opportunities to acquire information literacy skills and integrated and interdisciplinary learning activities which support the curriculum. The mission of the school library program is to ensure that all students and staff become literate, life-long learners and effective and responsible users of ideas and information.

A. A student should understand how information and resources are organized.
A student who meets the content standard should:

1) recognize that libraries use classification systems to organize, store and provide access to information and resources;
2) understand how information in print, non-print and electronic formats are organized and accessed;
3) understand how library classification and subject heading systems work;
4) search for information and resources by author, title, subject or keyword, as appropriate; and
5) identify and use search strategies and terms that will produce appropriate results.

B. A student should understand and use the research processes necessary to locate, evaluate and communicate information and ideas.
A student who meets the content standard should:

1) state a problem, question or information need;
2) consider the variety of available resources and determine the best ones to use;
3) access information;
4) evaluate the validity, relevancy, currency and accuracy of information;
5) organize and use information to create a product; and
6) evaluate the effectiveness of the product in conveying the intended message.

C. A student should recognize that being an independent reader, listener, and viewer of material in print, non-print, and electronic formats will contribute to personal enjoyment and lifelong learning.
A student who meets the content standard should:

1) read for pleasure and information;
2) read, listen to, and view a wide variety of literature and other creative expressions; and
3) recognize and select materials appropriate to personal abilities and interests.

D. A student should be aware of the freedom to seek information and possess the confidence to pursue information needs beyond immediately available sources.
A student who meets the content standard should:

1) know how to access information through local, national and international sources in printed and electronic formats;
2) recognize the importance of access to information and ideas in a democratic society;
3) access information on local, state, national and world cultures and issues;
4) evaluate information representing diverse views in order to make informed decisions; and
5) assimilate and understand how newly acquired information relates to oneself and others.

E. A student should understand ethical, legal and social behavior with respect to information resources.
A student who meets the content standard should:

1) use library materials and information resources responsibly;
2) understand and respect for the principles of intellectual freedom;
3) understand and respect for intellectual property rights and copyright laws; and
4) develop and use citations and bibliographies.

Sidebar 8.03 Check Other Curriculum Areas for Information Skill Standards!

Source: Sunshine State Standards Language Arts Grades 3–5. Available at: http://www.firn.edu/doe/curric/prek12/pdf/langart3.pdf (accessed April 30, 2006).

Some media center standards can be found in other academic listings. The following example comes from the Florida Sunshine State Standards. Note the inclusion of information literacy skills in the examples cited.

FLORIDA SUNSHINE STATE STANDARDS FOR LANGUAGE ARTS/READING GRADES 3–5

Standard 1: The student uses the reading process effectively. (LA.A.1.2)

1. Uses a table of contents, index, headings, captions, illustrations, and major words to anticipate or predict content and purpose of a reading selection.
2. Selects from a variety of simple strategies, including the use of phonics, word structure, context clues, self-questioning, confirming simple predictions, retelling, and using visual cues, to identify words and construct meaning from various texts, illustrations, graphics, and charts.
3. Uses simple strategies to determine meaning and increase vocabulary for reading, including the use of prefixes, suffixes, root words, multiple meanings, antonyms, synonyms, and word relationships.
4. Clarifies understanding by rereading, self-correction, summarizing, checking other sources, and class or group discussion.

Standard 2: The student constructs meaning from a wide range of texts. (LA.A.2.2)

1. Reads text and determines the main idea or essential message, identifies relevant supporting details and facts, and arranges events in chronological order.
2. Identifies the author's purpose in a simple text.
3. Recognizes when a text is primarily intended to persuade.
4. Identifies specific personal preferences relative to fiction and nonfiction reading.
5. Reads and organizes information for a variety of purposes, including making a report, conducting interviews, taking a test, and performing an authentic task.

standards that apply to your school. Ask yourself how you can assist your teachers in meeting the needs of their individual courses and reach out to them providing opportunities for interaction between the media center and their curricula. The more teachers you can bring into the media center, the better.

National Standards for Teaching

AASL and the Association for Educational Communications and Technology (AECT) collaborated to provide standards for student learning related to library information skill studies. Their standards are divided into three categories, nine standards, and 29 indicators of student performance. The AASL/AECT standards are written broadly to provide a conceptual framework and to support local efforts. It is expected that school library professionals will work on the local level to adapt these standards to meet their local needs.

> ### Sidebar 8.04 National Standards for Information Literacy
>
> Excerpted with permission from chapter 2, "Information Literacy Standards for Student Learning," in *Information Power: Building Partnerships for Learning.* © 1998 American Library Association and Association for Educational Communications and Technology. ISBN 0-8389-3470-6. Order by phone at 1-866-SHOP-ALA (1-866-746-7252).
>
> The following categories and standards are from *Information Power* by AASL and AECT. To see the entire document including student indicators, read *Information Power* or refer to the AASL Web site: http://www.ala.org/ala/aasl/aaslprottools/informationpower/informationliteracy.htm.
>
> ## INFORMATION POWER: BUILDING PARTNERSHIPS FOR LEARNING
>
> ### The Nine Information Literacy Standards for Student Learning
>
> #### Information Literacy
>
> **Standard 1:** The student who is information literate accesses information efficiently and effectively.
>
> **Standard 2:** The student who is information literate evaluates information critically and competently.
>
> **Standard 3:** The student who is information literate uses information accurately and creatively.
>
> #### Independent Learning
>
> **Standard 4:** The student who is an independent learner is information literate and pursues information related to personal interests.
>
> **Standard 5:** The student who is an independent learner is information literate and appreciates literature and other creative expressions of information.
>
> **Standard 6:** The student who is an independent learner is information literate and strives for excellence in information seeking and knowledge generation.
>
> #### Social Responsibility
>
> **Standard 7:** The student who contributes positively to the learning community and to society is information literate and recognizes the importance of information to a democratic society.
>
> **Standard 8:** The student who contributes positively to the learning community and to society is information literate and practices ethical behavior in regard to information and information technology.
>
> **Standard 9:** The student who contributes positively to the learning community and to society is information literate and participates effectively in groups to pursue and generate information.

Professional Standards

There are certification standards in each state that certified media specialists must meet to enter the profession. Districts may have professional standards for media specialists as well. Check with your district level supervisor or professional organization to find out if media specialist standards exist in your district. You might also check your district's policies and procedures manual for this information. In addition to the certification standards required by each state and district, several organizations identify professional standards for media specialists. These standards don't exist to limit our profession, but to provide a framework we can use to launch our many exciting programs.

The National Board for Professional Teaching Standards formed in 1987 to promote high levels of professional practice in all areas of the education field. Persons desiring national board certification participate in a rigorous application process to document and reflect on their educational processes. The field of Early Childhood/Young Adult Library Media was added to the potential certification fields early this

Sidebar 8.05 NBPTS Media Specialist Certification Standards

The National Board for Professional Teaching Standards (NBPTS) certification process for media specialists recognizes three broad categories of professional competence: what media specialists know, what media specialists do, and how library media specialists grow as professionals. Each category is further divided into strands reflecting the professional practices of good media specialists. The NBPTS standards for library media are listed below. For additional information about National Board standards and the application process, refer to their Web site: http://www. nbpts.org.

What Library Media Specialists Know

I. *Knowledge of Learners*—Accomplished library media specialists have knowledge of learning styles and of human growth and development.
II. *Knowledge of Teaching and Learning*—Accomplished library media specialists know the principles of teaching and learning that contribute to an active learning environment.
III. *Knowledge of Library and Information Studies*—Accomplished library media specialists know the principles of library and information studies needed to create effective, integrated library media programs.

What Library Media Specialists Do

IV. *Integrating Instruction*—Accomplished library media specialists integrate information literacy through collaboration, planning, implementation, and assessment of learning.
V. *Leading Innovation through the Library Media Program*—Accomplished library media specialists lead in providing equitable access to and effective use of technologies and innovations.
VI. *Administering the Library Media Program*—Accomplished library media specialists plan, develop, implement, manage, and evaluate library media programs to ensure that students and staff use ideas and information effectively.

How Library Media Specialists Grow as Professionals

VII. *Reflective Practice*—Accomplished library media specialists engage in reflective practice to increase their effectiveness.
VIII. *Professional Growth*—Accomplished library media specialists model a strong commitment to lifelong learning and to their profession.
IX. *Ethics, Equity, and Diversity*—Accomplished library media specialists uphold professional ethics and promote equity and diversity.
X. *Leadership, Advocacy, and Community Partnerships*—Accomplished library media specialists advocate for the library media program, involving the greater community.

decade. Media specialists desiring this certification seek to document their performance on the standards listed in sidebar 8.05.

Personal Standards for Your Media Center

Establishing standards for your media center is an idea that can be very helpful in terms of communicating your vision to your students, faculty, and school community. It also helps clarify your expectations for clerical staff and volunteers and provides guidelines that can be used for staff and program evaluations. Creating school specific standards can touch on a variety of things. They can establish criteria for the day-to-day operation of your media center. Other standards might address the ideals you have for your media program. You might also create standards to address the interaction between your media center and the community.

Some people might feel that making individual school standards is just creating extra work for themselves. But this reflective practice does not take long and is worth the time. As media specialists, we often work in isolation at our schools. We may have a clerk or two that we supervise, but we do not have a department to mull things over with and decide policies. As a result, the overworked media specialist often finds that the vision is in his or her head and nowhere else. This creates frustration for our coworkers and clerical staff; they can't read our minds. Committing your standards to writing provides you with a way to communicate your vision with the school community. Once articulated and shared, they provide a starting point for discussion and common program development. Share the written standards with your principal for feedback and approval. Provide copies to your faculty, PTA, and school advisory council. You may find you need to alter your program standards annually based on feedback from your faculty, staff, and administration.

Writing Your Standards

Consider writing standards in three categories for your media program.

1. Media center operations
2. Media center program
3. The media center and community

Standards for Media Center Operations

These guidelines will help your clerical staff understand your expectations and vision of how the media center should function. These standards should be brief and to the point, but should also make clear the needs of media center operations.

For a sample of these standards, refer to sidebar 8.06. Be sure to share these standards with your principal and any administrator involved with performance evaluations for your staff. Be sure your staff has a copy and refer to it during staff meetings when addressing problems. This document can be a valuable resource for communicating effective performance expectations to staff. Be sure to review it and update it annually.

Standards for Your Media Program

This document should define your vision for the media center program. It should contain a statement aligning the school media center goals with national, state, and local standards as used by your district. Additional standards should delineate program requirements that are specific to your school. For example, perhaps your school serves a low-income area with struggling students. You might state a program goal delineating services designed to increase parent involvement in student reading. An example of a

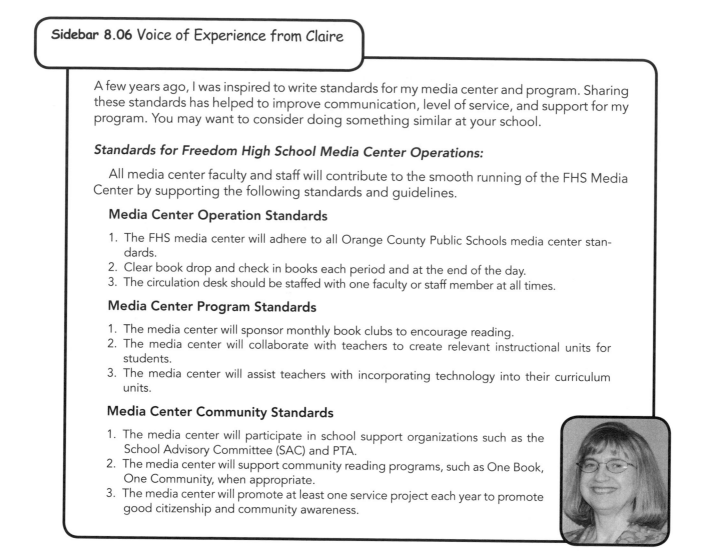

Sidebar 8.06 Voice of Experience from Claire

A few years ago, I was inspired to write standards for my media center and program. Sharing these standards has helped to improve communication, level of service, and support for my program. You may want to consider doing something similar at your school.

Standards for Freedom High School Media Center Operations:

All media center faculty and staff will contribute to the smooth running of the FHS Media Center by supporting the following standards and guidelines.

Media Center Operation Standards

1. The FHS media center will adhere to all Orange County Public Schools media center standards.
2. Clear book drop and check in books each period and at the end of the day.
3. The circulation desk should be staffed with one faculty or staff member at all times.

Media Center Program Standards

1. The media center will sponsor monthly book clubs to encourage reading.
2. The media center will collaborate with teachers to create relevant instructional units for students.
3. The media center will assist teachers with incorporating technology into their curriculum units.

Media Center Community Standards

1. The media center will participate in school support organizations such as the School Advisory Committee (SAC) and PTA.
2. The media center will support community reading programs, such as One Book, One Community, when appropriate.
3. The media center will promote at least one service project each year to promote good citizenship and community awareness.

media program standard might be: *The media center will facilitate family reading initiatives on a regular basis to encourage parents and students to read together.*

Standards for the Media Center and Community

No media program operates in isolation. We depend on parents and community organizations for help with administrative tasks, funding, and program support. Therefore, incorporating standards for dealing with the school community at large is also a wise plan. When designing these standards, take time to consider your school community. Identify the core make-up of your school in terms of ethnic groups, business networking groups, and local employers. You will want to reach out to all these groups as resources for you media program. Consider all these groups when writing your standards for community interaction. A sample community interaction statement might be: *The media center will seek partnerships with local partners in education who serve and are served by our school.* Such partnerships could include mentoring programs for low-achieving students, donation of volunteer hours, or funding for a special program or need.

Ideal versus Real World: Meeting Your Standards

When writing your own standards, it is important to recognize they are ideals. You will not meet all the standards you establish. One year you might do a great job of recruiting community partners and the next year all your sources may dry up for reasons beyond your control. You may have excellent clerical support one year who meet all your operational standards and expectations, and then because of staff changes, you may go for a period marked by clerical inattention to detail. The important thing is to have your standards to communicate to your school community and to yourself (when you are tired and over-worked) what your vision and goals are for your school program.

Writing standards is not an exercise in futility or even busy work. It is an exercise in stating the positive, the goals, the vision, for everything your media center and program is and can be. Take time to create individual standards for your program. Share them with your principal, staff, clerks, and community. Get their feedback and revise them as needed; then continue to update them on an annual basis. You will be glad you've made this professional effort to define the program at your school. Clearly stating your vision through written standards defines your professional principles and allows everyone to work with you, and that cooperation will truly make your program thrive.

Bibliography

Alaska Association of School Librarians. *Library/Information Literacy Standards, Student Content Standards for School Libraries.* Available online at: http://www.akla.org/akasl/lib/studentstandards.html#document

American Association of School Librarians. *Information Power: Building Partnerships for Learning.* Chicago: American Library Association, 1998.

Florida State Department of Education. *Sunshine State Standards Language Arts Grades 3–5.* Available online at: http://www.firn.edu/doe/curric/prek12/pdf/langart3.pdf.

National Board for Professional Teaching Standards. *Standards: Library Media/Early Childhood through Young Adulthood.* Available online at: http://www.nbpts.org.

9

Developing and Promoting Your Media Program

Have you heard the old saying, "There's no bad PR"? This is definitely true for your library. School library media centers are often called the information center, and we should live up to that name. The program you create should attract your entire school community into the media center. Your students, teachers, administration, and parents should think of your media center whenever they think of your school. But how do you begin to develop a program that you want to promote?

Developing Your Program

Whether you are a seasoned library media specialist or this is your very first year in the media center, each year you will want to present a program that will engage students and increase achievement. First, take into account all of your knowledge of students. Think about the children at your school. What excites them? What would encourage them to visit your media center, to read more books and to be inquisitive, engaged learners? Next, consider what you enjoy. Do you love to give book talks and watch children enjoy the books you promoted? Does it delight you when students find the answer to that difficult research question? Do you like big programs that involve the entire school or would you rather concentrate on individual teachers and try to reach students through classroom activities? After considering the types of students at your school and your own passions, create a plan to reach all of your students. Start small, but each year you should build on the plan to elevate your program. Your plan begins by understanding your goals and deciding how to plan for them.

Every school has a mission statement—do you have one for your library media center? Do you have stated goals that you discussed with your principal when you presented your budget? Your mission and goals should determine your program. Your goals may be broad, such as increasing your school's reading scores, or more limited, such as increasing the quantity and quality of science materials discussing the heart and how it works. Your

A well-developed media program attracts students like Chad, who enjoys coming to the library daily.

I like to go to the media center because it is a great place to be with friends. The books also provide an escape from the stress of classes and the troubles of daily life. The media center is my home away from home, and there's no other place I'd rather be.

Chad Erickson
Sophomore
Timber Creek High School

goals may be long term, such as weeding and updating the video collection in the next five years, or short term, such as promoting cookbooks during a visit from a local chef. Whatever they are, these goals will help define your yearlong program and its promotion.

Using your goals, begin developing your program during the summer before school begins. Analyze your program as it stands right now. What is working and what is not working? Survey students and teachers to get information from your customers. Find out what they enjoy and benefit from when they spend time in the media center.

Ask fellow library media specialists what programs work best for them. Attend local meetings, state conferences, or national meetings such as the AASL Conference, which is held every two years. These gatherings allow you to network with other media specialists and gain insights into what is working for them in their media centers. Networking will spark program ideas you can adapt or adjust to benefit your students. Consider what the next year will bring. Is it an election year? Is your town or school celebrating a birthday? Have you just taken a vacation and become enthused about an area of the world that you want to share with your students? Your personal experiences might make a great addition to your library program.

Look at your school schedule and decide when your school will need you to infuse excitement into the curriculum. Look at national, state, and local library events that may fit into your program. Plan a tentative schedule and make adjustments as the year progresses. A typical program may look like this:

August:	Welcome Back to School Display New Teacher Orientation Student Orientation
September:	Banned Books Week Promotion and Display Library Card Sign-up Month Book Fair
October:	Hispanic Heritage Month Secondary: Teen Read Week (Promote Graphic Novels) Elementary: Literary Character Day and Parade
November:	Native American Indian Display Give Thanks for Good Books Display Children's Book Week
December:	Holidays around the World Display Donate Cans for Fines Program
January:	New Year New Attitude Display Paperback Book Exchange Meet the Author (invite an author to visit your students)

February:	Romance Novels Display
	Biography Promotion
	Black History Month
March:	Spring Collection Event (showing off new purchases)
	Read Across America (Dr. Seuss's birthday)
	Book Fair
April:	National Library Week
	National Poetry Month
	Women's History Month
May:	Super Summer Reading Display
	Paperback Book Exchange
	Free Summer Reading Book Giveaway to Every Student

Sidebar 9.01 Voice of Experience from Pat Franklin

Each June, I think about the goals I set at the beginning of the year. Did my program accomplish those goals? After reflection, I can focus on what goals I want to set for the upcoming school year. Outlining goals not only helps me stay on track during the school year, but also alerts my principal that I have aspirations that will help student achievement and that I will need funding to reach these goals.

Timber Creek High School (TCHS) Library Media Center Goals 2006–2007

Long-term Goals

1. To support the TCHS mission and curriculum by acquiring materials appropriate to the needs of students, teachers, and parents.
2. To create and promote a library media program which meets the needs of all stakeholders.
3. To maintain and increase the appeal of our physical space by being proactive concerning student and teacher interests.
4. To continually undertake professional development to update and increase knowledge and skills in the area of educational media and technology.

Short-term Goals

1. To increase collaboration with science teachers. Collaborating with science teachers will increase student standardized test scores as students become better purveyors of information. We will target ninth-grade integrated science classes.
2. To weed, update, and increase materials on Physical and Earth Sciences. This will support emphasis on the science curriculum as students prepare for state tests.
3. To investigate online databases which specialize in science materials.
4. To evaluate need and purchase new technology to support curriculum (LCD projectors, laptops, appropriate cables).
5. To evaluate and adjust subscriptions to leisure and professional magazines with an emphasis on science publications.

Pat Franklin

Sunrise Elementary School media specialist Agnes Shabat attended a Japanese exchange program in November of 2002. This experience ignited her passion for all things Japanese and continues to inspire her library program years later.

FROM THE LAND OF THE RISING SUN TO SUNRISE ELEMENTARY SCHOOL: INCORPORATING MY JAPAN EXPERIENCES INTO MY LIBRARY PROGRAM!

Japan is a gift that keeps on giving. It has been four years since I participated in the Japan Memorial Fund Teacher Program (JFMF), and I still carry the glow from Japan. The JFMF provides fully funded, three-week study tours of Japan to American educators from primary and secondary schools. In addition to learning about Japanese education and culture, participants meet with Japanese educators and government officials, visit schools, and experience a short home stay with a Japanese family.

My experiences in Japan translated into programs at my school and in the community. My Japanese programs at Sunrise Elementary School left a great impression on the children. Each of the 720 students in the school received a brand new *goen*, or five yen piece, which I put on a red ribbon and presented to the children during our Japanese New Year lesson to bring them good luck in the coming year. The students proudly wore their coins around their necks.

Other lessons on Japanese culture included Japanese vocabulary. Japanese video, music, and artifacts enhanced the presentations. The students enjoyed hands-on activities that immersed them in the culture. Students were challenged to demonstrate their expertise with chopsticks, and many of the children gained a new respect for the skills involved. A favorite lesson focused on Japanese clothing. Two children from each class dressed from head to toe in Japanese footwear, *yukata/hachimaki*, and kimono/*obi*/geisha wig with all the accessories.

We began a pen pal program, and the Japanese parents at our school helped translate letters from the students at our sister school in Urayasu. These same parents donated valuable family treasures to display at our Living Museum of Japanese Culture. Through their contacts, we were able to book a world-renowned taiko drumming group, Matsuriza, to perform for our students.

I also presented programs for the local public library system. I shared many of the same things that my Sunrise Elementary students experienced with these children. I featured Japanese vocabulary, music, and realia such as *goen*, daruma dolls, lucky cats, and a decoration called *kadomatsu*. The children experienced Japanese New Year by playing *hanetsuki* with *hagoita*. Each child received a daruma doll coloring sheet and a "Happy Japanese New Year" page to decorate using Japanese Happy New Year rubber stamps I bought in Japan.

I am grateful to the Fulbright Memorial Fund for giving me the gift of Japan and continue to share the things I learned there with my students, colleagues, and community. I am deeply honored to have been a part of the program and the experience will always remain a highlight of my life. For more information about this program, refer to the JFMF Web site at: http://www.fulbrightmemorialfund.jp.

Agnes E. Shabat

Promoting Your Program to the School and Community

Promoting your media program is not a job. It's fun! One of the first steps in marketing and promoting the library program is to make sure that anyone on staff at your library media center greets all stakeholders with a smile and a pleasant attitude. Everyone coming in contact with any aspect of your program on the phone, on the Internet, or in person should come away with a positive feeling about the program. In reality, the job of every employee in the library media center is service. Marketing your program is everyone's job and part of the excellent customer service that users should expect from your staff. Remember, our job is "all about them." We exist to help and serve patrons

Since the media center is the heart of your school and since recent research shows that an effective media center staffed with trained and certified personnel improves student achievement, one of your priorities is to get the attention of your customers so that they are aware of your program. Your customers include parents, administrators, teachers, and students. Reaching each of these groups is essential.

Parents support your efforts to encourage reading. They can also support your program with time and money. Parent volunteers help expand your program by giving you more time for planning. They lend an extra hand during special programs such as books fairs or paperback book exchanges. Parents are an integral part of your collection development plan—recruit them to donate a book on their child's birthday or to commemorate their graduation from your school. Purchase bookplates to put in the front of the book explaining who donated the book and why. Because parents are willing to support you, you must make

Sidebar 9.03 Voice of Experience from Rebecca Gross

WORKING WITH THE SCHOOL COMMUNITY TO IMPROVE YOUR PROGRAM

In an effort to promote reading among students, the school improvement plan at Discovery Middle School in Orlando, Florida, includes a free book giveaway to all students at the end of each school year. During my first year as Discovery's media specialist, I learned that it was my responsibility to purchase and disperse the books to the students. With almost 2,000 students and a budget of $2,000, this was quite a daunting task. In previous years, the books were ordered through Scholastic Book Club's annual 99 books for $100 promotion. Then they were dispersed through language arts classes. However, this method did not allow me to choose the titles or to see which books the students selected. A student survey showed a low level of satisfaction with the giveaway program, so I decided to try another approach. I requested a larger budget, making a persuasive case to the parents that the additional funding would improve the program and make it more successful. They approved the request, and I handpicked over 2,000 books at the Scholastic Book Fair Warehouse Sale, then I sorted the books by grade levels. I scheduled a week in the media center for the free book giveaway so I could ensure that each student had a good selection of books to choose from. This entire process was time consuming, but my efforts paid off. The students obviously loved picking their free book and a follow-up survey showed a much higher satisfaction rate with the free books received by the students.

Rebecca Gross

Sidebar 9.04 Promote Your Program!

Your school newsletter is a great way to promote your program and communicate with parents. This sample article appeared in the Timber Creek High School monthly newsletter during the 2006/2007 school year.

CHECK OUT THE MEDIA CENTER

TCHS is reading! Ask your child about the Florida Teens Read Books. This is a list of outstanding books chosen by the Florida Association for Media in Education for high school students in Florida. Students are reading so many of these books that there is a waiting list. (But don't worry. It goes really fast!) In April, students who have read three books are eligible to vote for their favorite book. For a complete list of these engaging books, look on the TCHS Web site at www.tchs.ocps. net. Many teachers are giving extra credit to students reading these books.

The media center is collecting cans for the needy during the holidays. If you have an overdue book or owe a fine, turn your book in and bring a can and we will delete your fine. It's a good deal for you and you are helping those less fortunate than you.

Looking for other good books to read? Check out Mrs. Franklin's blog at: http://teachers.ocps. net/weblog/franklp/. There are even podcasts!

them aware of your program. Consider getting involved by attending meetings of the PTA, the SAC, and any other steering committees that plan the vision for your school. These groups have a hotline to other parents who can help you put on your programs. Talk to them about what is going on in the media center. Fundraisers, such as book fairs, are very lucrative, especially in elementary and middle school. By understanding your program, parents groups may provide monetary resources for you to implement special programs such as an author's visit or a summer reading program.

Use your school's newsletter and Web site to show what you have done and advertise upcoming events. Local papers may be interested in events such as author's visits or Book Battles.

Your administration is your biggest ally. When you join the PTA or the SAC, your administration notices and appreciates your effort to promote your school to your parents. Make sure your monthly report to your principal stresses your activities and promotional ideas. Use the marquee in front of your school to advertise your programs. Put up signs around the school to advertise activities. Make sure you are visible and accessible to your principal. If your administration is looking for a volunteer, make every effort to find time to help. Your program will be in the forefront if you become a part of your school's leadership team. Show an interest in your school and your principal will show an interest in your media center. If you feel your principal has been especially supportive, nominate him for an award either locally or through the ALA. Any honor he receives is a reflection on your program.

Create a summer reading list for your students. In high schools, this is usually left to the English department, but you know what kids love to read, so make sure you actively participate on the committee that creates this list. In elementary and middle schools, create a list that pleases both parents and students, and your administration will also be pleased. Demonstrate that you are serious about reading, and your principal will understand how important student achievement is to you. Choose new books for this list that parents will enjoy talking to their children about and that students have not read.

Sidebar 9.04A *Voice of Experience: Gail Przeclawski*

Media Specialist, Grand Avenue Elementary School
Orlando, Florida

There are many benefits to publicly recognizing excellence, and that is true with a media programs as well. I am blessed with an outstanding administrator who completely understands not only the benefits of a quality media program, but also what a quality program looks like. More importantly, he also understands what is needed in order to produce a quality program and does all he can to provide those resources and support. Therefore, it made perfect sense to me to nominate him for our district media organization's Outstanding Administrator award, which he won. That win led to a nomination for our state's Advocate for Excellence in School Library Media Programs Award, which he also won. The repercussions of this award continue to bless my program. Through winning the state award, my principal received a $300 check and a beautiful plaque which is prominently displayed at our school. A few months later, I received five boxes of brand new books donated by the book vendor who sponsored the award. I applied for and received a library grant for $5,000. The grant application had a section asking me to describe the administrative support given the library program. I believe that the awards my principal won aided our grant process.

Gail Przeclawski

Consider books from state reading lists that are chosen in the spring. Even if your state does not produce a yearly reading list, other states have spent an enormous amount of time choosing quality books. You can take advantage of that effort by selecting from those lists. Historical fiction is a good choice because students learn background information that may help them in their social studies classes the next year. Interesting science fiction titles that tie into science and math programs are another good choice. Choose books with a variety of reading levels. Students benefit from reading slightly above their level because they learn vocabulary and practice using context clues. They also learn when they read below their reading level by practicing fluency. Their self-esteem is boosted as they read faster and finish more books.

Consider writing grants that benefit your school. Whether they are small local grants or large national grants, your administration will like the publicity and your teachers will love the extra dollars your grant generates. Grant writing is not hard once you discover the formula for specific grants. Look at the projects teachers are undertaking at your school right now. Are there any that could benefit from more technology? Would a field trip or more resources help the students better understand the concept being taught? Would the teacher like recognition for a project well done? Collaborate with a classroom teacher and write a grant. By doing this you will benefit all the stakeholders in your school.

Promoting Your Program to Teachers

To promote your program to teachers, send out content area booklists or ask them what they are teaching, then create special bibliographies or book carts specifically for them. Remember, they are just as busy as you are and don't have extra minutes to browse your catalog or discover what programs you are undertaking, so attending department or team meetings is a good way to start getting their attention. This may seem impossible because of time constraints, but it is worth the effort. Ask to be on the agenda; you can present information about new materials, learning strategies, or technology. Anything you think might help support their efforts in the classroom is a relevant topic. Don't present and run. Stay for the entire meeting, listen to the discussion, find out ways you can be a help to your teachers. Word will travel when you help one teacher with something new. Soon you will have others asking for assistance from you and the media center.

Present an overview of your program to new teachers during a meeting before school begins in the fall or during the beginning of the school year. Give them a brochure of all the services that you offer and show them your professional resources, which will help in their planning. But just telling teachers what is available doesn't heighten excitement or bring in customers. Bring your program to them by having a breakfast or luncheon for your teachers to promote the books you have purchased with your budget. Talk to your principal about funding.

Encourage teachers to collaborate on lessons and create a book display to coordinate with the lesson you are teaching together. Give fabulous prizes at faculty meetings to teachers who bring their students

---

Sidebar 9.05 Sample Grants Available to School Libraries

American Association of School Librarians. Available at: http://www.ala.org/ala/aasl/aaslawards/aaslawards.htm.

American Library Association. Available at: http://www.ala.org/ala/ppo/grantsandevents/ppograntsevents.htm.

Best Buy. Available at: www.bestbuy.com.

Funding and Grant Sources. Available at: http://www.libraryhq.com/funding.html.

Funding for Libraries and Museums. Available at: http://www.technologygrantnews.com/grant-funding-sitemap.html.

Grants for Nonprofits: Libraries. Available at: http://www.lib.msu.edu/harris23/grants/2lib.htm.

Grant Writing and Fundraising Information Resources for Libraries. Western New York Library Resources Council. Available at: http://www.wnylrc.org/Librtalk/Grants.htm#Programs.

Institute of Museum and Library Services. Available at: http://www.imls.gov/.

The Laura Bush Foundation for America's Libraries. Available at: http://www.laurabushfoundation.org/.

Lesko Loves Libraries. Available at: http://www.lesko.com/libraries/.

3M Company. Available at: http://charitychannel.com/publish/templates/?a=2671&z=0.

We the People. Available at: http://www.wethepeople.gov.

This is just a short list of grants available to school libraries. Additional sources may be found by doing a general Internet search. Note: your school district may have a grants office with specific rules for grant writing. Consult with them before submitting any grant and for additional grant resources.

into the media center. Prizes can range from inexpensive gift certificates to a local bookstore to promotional items with your school logo. Local businesses may agree to donate gift baskets, movie rentals, and so forth. to help support your school. Ask art teachers to display student work in the media center and ask other teachers to exhibit student projects, then develop a display around the student work. Ask teachers to schedule their parent nights in the media center. Target teachers who work with special needs students such as the gifted teacher, the English for Speakers of Other Languages (ESOL) teacher, and various Exceptional Student Education (ESE) teachers. Work with them to spotlight their students and to create programs that include invitations to parents. Use National Library Week to give each teacher a gift thanking them for their patronage and reminding them that your job is to serve them.

Promoting Your Program to Students

To alert students about activities you have planned, use your closed-circuit TV. Become a regular on the morning news, wearing a funny hat or using a signature sign-on. Give away bookmarks that promote activities and create book displays centered on student interests. Invite students or special interest clubs such as Students Against Drunk Driving (SADD) to help you create interest centers and prominently exhibit their work. Ask students to

Sidebar 9.06 Voice of Experience from Pat Franklin

Storing class sets in the media center increases access for all teachers.

I learned that the teachers were having trouble accessing class sets of novels and other books stored by the English department, so I spent some time brainstorming with our teachers and staff. Now, the media center houses these books so that they are in a central location. In this way, ESE and ESOL teachers, as well as other content area teachers, have access to the novels. This helps our English department because they do not have to store the novels, and the books are used more frequently because of their easy access.

Sidebar 9.07 Voice of Experience from Pat: Promoting Your Program to Teachers

Each year I organize an event in the media center to promote our program to the teachers. When I worked in middle school, we purchased donuts and coffee from our internal accounts fund and invited the teachers down for breakfast. Now at the high school, our principal has paid for a catered meal during the teachers' lunchtime. They eat lunch and then peruse books and other materials set out on tables by their Dewey decimal numbers.

Pat Franklin

create bulletin boards advertising your programs. Ask them for suggestions and invite them to create videos to advertise the latest activities on your closed-circuit TV. Utilize student assistants to get feedback on what is popular with their peers. Go into classrooms and give book talks on new titles. Plan an activity when a large shipment of books comes in to promote the new books. Invite students to peruse the new books and offer a piece of candy if they check one out.

As you look at your promotional calendar for the year, create or purchase items to lend a festive air to each event. The ALA, as well as supply companies such as Upstart and Demco, offer a vast array

Sidebar 9.08 Voice of Experience from Pat

Here is an idea we used to promote our school's media center. The teachers loved it! I think the important thing is to have fun and be creative in promoting your program. You never know when an idea you think is no big deal will be the one that touches that hard to reach student, teacher, administrator, or parent!

Create a small basket for each of your teachers. We use a die cut from a letter cutting machine. Include a few pieces of candy, a pen, a package of post-it notes, or other supplies. The things can be small, for example, a "library lovers" pencil. Use things you think teachers will like. Attach a special poem like this. Place it in their mailboxes to kick off National Library Week.

National Library Week

I know you're excited!
Keep it under control.
It's National Library Week;
Time to Rock and Roll!

Bring in your classes;
Do a project or two.
We have lots of databases
And good books for you!

Our professional room
Has lots of good resources.
Our audios and videos will support
All of your courses.

Our techies will fix
Computers with ease.
Just e-mail them your problems
For them it's a breeze.

So when you need resources,
Grab that party coat and hat
And think of your media staff:
Connie, Diane, Vickie and Pat.

Pat Franklin

of promotional products that can inspire you to create displays and programs. These products enhance events to attract patrons and create excitement. You should include promotional items in your budget each year. Keeping new, fresh, and current posters, signage, and other promotional items in your media center will help keep it interesting and inviting to students.

Promoting your library program may seem like an uphill battle, but it will benefit you and your students. Do not let limited funding deter you from promoting your program. Many promotions involve little or no money—just be creative. Promotion is all about attitude. Make your program highly visible and your customers will benefit.

Promoting Literature and Reading

Whether you were a library media specialist 30 years ago or just stepped into your position today, promoting reading has always been one of our primary jobs. In fact, many teachers choose to become "librarians" because they love to read. Reading quality new and classic literature is definitely one of our most important tasks. However, with collaborative teaching, library administration, and providing expertise about emerging technologies, we must often make time to read. Only by keeping abreast of new books can we share our joy of reading with our students. Another concern for all teachers in the twenty-first century, no matter what grade level or content area, is that we are asked to be reading teachers. Take a reading course if you are not familiar with current reading strategies. Read professional books on teaching reading. The knowledge you gain from this professional development will help when you are collaborating with teachers or working with students individually. Promoting reading to students can be accomplished one-on-one, through entire classes, or on a school and community-wide basis.

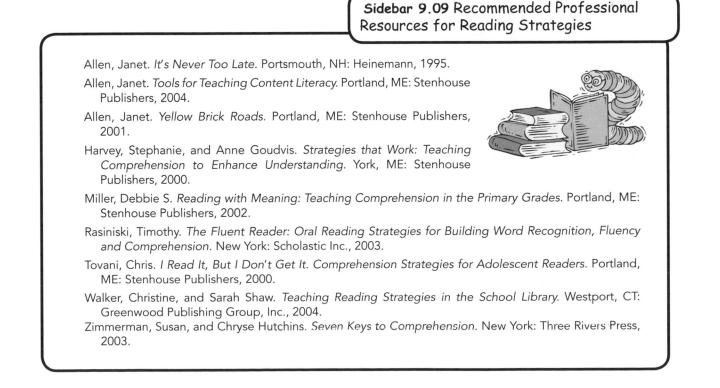

Sidebar 9.09 Recommended Professional Resources for Reading Strategies

Allen, Janet. *It's Never Too Late.* Portsmouth, NH: Heinemann, 1995.

Allen, Janet. *Tools for Teaching Content Literacy.* Portland, ME: Stenhouse Publishers, 2004.

Allen, Janet. *Yellow Brick Roads.* Portland, ME: Stenhouse Publishers, 2001.

Harvey, Stephanie, and Anne Goudvis. *Strategies that Work: Teaching Comprehension to Enhance Understanding.* York, ME: Stenhouse Publishers, 2000.

Miller, Debbie S. *Reading with Meaning: Teaching Comprehension in the Primary Grades.* Portland, ME: Stenhouse Publishers, 2002.

Rasiniski, Timothy. *The Fluent Reader: Oral Reading Strategies for Building Word Recognition, Fluency and Comprehension.* New York: Scholastic Inc., 2003.

Tovani, Chris. *I Read It, But I Don't Get It. Comprehension Strategies for Adolescent Readers.* Portland, ME: Stenhouse Publishers, 2000.

Walker, Christine, and Sarah Shaw. *Teaching Reading Strategies in the School Library.* Westport, CT: Greenwood Publishing Group, Inc., 2004.

Zimmerman, Susan, and Chryse Hutchins. *Seven Keys to Comprehension.* New York: Three Rivers Press, 2003.

One-on-One Reading Promotion

Each student is unique, and every time a student comes to the media center, they look for us to be a primary resource helping them to locate what they need. Yes, we want to teach students to use OPAC and to understand the Dewey Decimal System, but just as in any business, people want to talk to real people. By talking to individual students, you find out what type of reader they are, what their interests are, and what they are really looking for. You can direct them to the right book for their project or for pleasure reading. Talking to students about books has an added benefit—many times they will give you great ideas of titles or subjects of books to add to your next book order.

Hold contests for students throughout the year. Use the statistics available through your media management system to identify your avid readers. Give a prize to the student who has checked out the most books since starting school. Give the first five students who read 100 books this school year an award. Prizes can range from whatever might excite your students, such as local bookstore gift certificates to a special lunch with the media specialist.

Classrooms Visits

Going into classrooms is fun, promotes goodwill with teachers, and promotes reading at the same time. Often teachers ask for a cart of books specific to their current lesson. Buy colorful book carts and send them to classrooms full of exciting books. Include any books that might be applicable, even if it's a stretch, to show the teachers and the students the wide variety of materials available to them. Include fiction books with nonfiction books on topics for their content area. Give a five-minute book talk on these fiction books showing how they relate to the topic the class is studying.

Book talks in classrooms take your library beyond its walls and entice students to come to the media center. Create book talk themes based on current promotions such as Banned Books Week. You could also choose seasonal themes and spotlight books that are featured on a monthly display. Book talks on new books appeal to all students, including those who think they have read everything you have and those less than interested readers who may be enticed by the idea of taking home something new. Make a special point to go into classrooms where students are struggling readers. Talk about books that appeal

---

Sidebar 9.10 High Interest/Low Reading Level Publishers

This list identifies just a few publishers and jobbers of titles for reluctant readers. To find other high/low vendors, ask other media specialists and teachers about books students like. Attend professional conferences and browse the vendor hall looking for titles you think your students will enjoy. While there, network with the sales representatives to learn about their products and upcoming titles.

Orca Books. Available at: http://www.orcabook.com.

Townsend Press. Available at: http://www.townsendpress.com/.

Capstone Press. Available at: http://www.capstonepress.com/aspx/auVision.aspx.

Brodart. Available at: http://www.picks.brodart.com/highlow.htm.

Perfection Learning. Available at: http://www.perfectionlearning.com/ctcrp/ctc.whitepaper.pdf.

to those low-level readers. If you are new and not sure of what books to suggest, ask your peers for recommendations and check vendor catalogs. Many publishers specialize in developing high-interest, low-reading level lists specifically targeted for reluctant readers.

Know the curriculum and put together bibliography lists of fiction and nonfiction books on topics discussed in history or science classes. Find out what teachers are teaching and adapt your bibliographies to their subject matter. Ask teachers if you can talk about some of the books with their classes or leave a book cart in their room for students to browse. Have you been on a trip, have a special passion, just saw a good TV show on a topic? Look for books both fiction and nonfiction on the topic and market those books to teachers.

Schoolwide Programs

Schoolwide, you have the opportunity to influence instruction and be of service to all your teachers. Offer to house class sets of books for English teachers, then suggest companion novels to teachers and students. Purchase professional books on how to teach reading and offer in-service workshops on these books. Purchase small sets of books for teachers to use in literature circles. Invite teachers to use these books as their own private book club books. Invite teachers to hold lunchtime book clubs with their students in the media center.

Sidebar 9.11 Thematically Connected Literature

As you get used to your collection, develop bibliography lists related to different curriculum subjects. Share these lists with your teachers. Elementary teachers may discover good read-aloud titles for their classes and secondary teachers may discover a great picture book that supplements and expands on their student's studies. The two lists below identify titles on various reading levels that have subject matter.

Civil War–Related Books

• *Pink and Say* by Patricia Polacco	Grades K to 12
• *The Blue and the Gray* by Eve Bunting	Grades K to 8
• *Across Five Aprils* by Irene Hunt	Grades 4 to 8
• *Shades of Gray* by Carolyn Reeder	Grades 4 to 8
• *Soldier's Heart* by Gary Paulsen	Grades 7 to 12
• *The River Between Us* by Richard Peck	Grades 6 to 12

Weather-related Books

• *Snowflake Bentley* by Jacqueline Briggs Martin	Grades K-4
• *Snowy Day* by Ezra Jack Keats	Grades K-3
• *Night of the Twisters* by Ivy Ruckman	Grades 4–9
• *Out of the Dust* by Karen Hesse	Grades 4–9
• *Stormy Weather* by Carl Hiaasen	Grades 10–12
• *Wide Blue Yonder* by Jean Thompson	Grades 9–12

Sidebar 9.12 Resources for Literature Circles and Book Clubs

If you need information about organizing literature circles, and book club programs, try these books:

Daniels, Harvey. *Literature Circles: Voice and Choice in Book Clubs and Reading Groups.* Portland, ME: Stenhouse, 2001.

Daniels, Harvey, and Nancy Steineke. *Mini-Lessons for Literature Circles.* Portsmouth, NH: Heinemann, 2004.

Gilmore, Barry, and Harvey Daniels. *Speaking Volumes: How to Get Students Discussing Books And Much More.* Portsmouth, NH: Heinemann, 2006.

Sidebar 9.13 Helpful Hints for Choosing the Right Book for You

1. Study the front cover.
2. Read the back cover.
3. Ask a friend if they have read the book.
4. Ask your teacher or media specialist for a recommendation.
5. Try the five finger test. Begin reading the first page. When you come to a word you do not know, hold up one finger. When you get to another word you do not know, hold up another finger. If you hold up five fingers before you finish the first page, the book is too hard for you!

Hold a book fair once or twice a year. This is a great time to encourage parents to be a part of their child's school experience. Promote your book fair several weeks before the actual date with posters, TV announcements, and flyers posted around the school and given to individual students to take home. Set up your media center for maximum use other than the area you are using for the book fair. Schedule class visits to the book fair on a rotating basis. This is a good time to teach a lesson on how to calculate tax on an item and one on choosing the right book for you.

A reputable book fair company will deliver your book fair customized to your school population. Parents and other volunteers can help you set up and administer your book fair. Book fairs are fun and can be profitable. Monies earned at the book fair may be used for miscellaneous items for the library or prizes for students. Consider asking teachers for a wish list of books featured in the fair. Send that list to parents who will buy those books for their child's classroom. Teachers will love you! Also, consider making one book fair during the year a special promotion, such as a "buy one get one free" fair for students. This promotes good will and encourages students to choose more good books.

Hold a paperback book exchange once or twice a year, ideally about a month after your book fair. Then every student who has purchased a book from your fair is ready to exchange it for another. Use your profits from the book fair to purchase snack foods for the students, and invite them to spend time before school or after school in the media center exchanging books.

Create a book club program at your school. Choose books everyone will enjoy. By alternating your selections and the types of books, your book clubs will remain vibrant and interesting to students. Offer

refreshments and ask English teachers to give extra credit to students who read the book and attend the meeting. Ask students for their suggestions for each month and read what they like.

Hold your book club meetings when it is convenient for your students. If your students are mostly bus riders who cannot stay after school, have a Brown Bag Lunch Club. Discuss the book club selection while you and your members are eating lunch. Meet in the media center, in a conference room, or in a classroom. If your school runs an after school program, attach to that program and hold book club meetings after school.

Use your school newsletter, Web site, and TV announcements to promote your book club. Invite parents to read selected books with their children and then attend the meeting. Does your community have a One Book, One Community program? Choose that book for your book club selection one month. The community may bring the author of that book to your town for a book signing or lecture. If so, try to get that author to visit your school along with the bookstores and public or university libraries he or she will visit to promote the book. Many schools have adapted the One Book, One Community program to their school creating their own One Book, One School reading program. Talk with your administrations, teachers, and parents about developing a similar event at your school.

Collaborate with your teachers to create summer reading lists for students. Make them suggested lists, especially for elementary and middle schools, or required lists such as those used in high school. Include classic titles or the newest releases that make connections with the curriculum or provide a good read while reclining at the beach during summer vacation. Use a software program to create a brochure of these titles and take them to your feeder schools. Give one to each student and have them handy for your registrar when new students enroll in your school during the summer.

Have a Summer Reading Giveaway. Right before school is over, give each child a book to read over the summer. Many book fair companies have outstanding sales throughout the year such as 50 books for $50. Investigate these book sales online and talk to your local bookstores for discounts. This book giveaway can be funded by the PTSA or by fundraisers. Many schools have monies to specifically target reading. Tap into this fund. If you give a child a book to read over the summer, they will realize that you are serious about reading and that you will do whatever it takes to help them find the joy of reading. Hold a contest the first week of school in the fall. Have students fill out a short questionnaire on their book and drop it in the prize box. Randomly select a winner to encourage participation in the summer reading program.

One of the most popular and controversial ways to promote reading is by using a computerized reading management program such as Accelerated Reader or Reading Counts. To use these programs, you must label your books so students know their point value and purchase software so that when students read books they can take tests measuring their comprehension. Students receive grades or garner prizes depending on their point accumulation. The media specialist managing these programs encourages students to choose books on their reading level and manages the student accounts on the computers. These

Sidebar 9.15 A Word about Computerized Reading Incentive Programs

Reading programs such as Accelerated Reader and Reading Counts remain controversial. For more information about these programs and their impact on student learning, check out this Web site by noted educator and author Jim Trelease: http://www.trelease-on-reading.com/whatsnu_ar.html.

programs are controversial. Many library media specialists feel that students should choose books by interest not by point value. They feel that students should feel an intrinsic reward from reading, not be given a prize. Other media specialists rave about reading scores improving as students read books in higher quantities and of increasing difficulty. Usually the final decision on purchasing a program of this type is made by a committee. No matter what your personal feelings are, it is important that you assume a leadership role in the program. Starting and maintaining computer-based reading incentive programs frequently means an infusion of money for the media center to buy books and software. As the media specialist, you should be the head of this project, using your expertise to select books appropriate to your school and community. As the program gets up and running, you must make sure the books are circulated and the program is supported.

Create displays in your media center that draw students to books. Displays can be seasonal or about an upcoming activity at your school. Many promotional companies sell posters, bookmarks, and display items. Or create your own unique displays. They could revolve around a student display of artwork or projects from a particular classroom. Sponsor contests and display the results. Creatively cover large boxes and ask for student suggestions of titles needed for your collection. Invite classes to decorate your bulletin boards with their favorite books.

Create areas in your media center that invite quiet reading. Purchase a child-size table and chairs and place them beside a bookshelf full of picture books. Purchase leisure seating where children can sit together and curl up with a good book. Buy beanbag chairs and arrange them around a low table filled with magazines.

Beyond Your School

As a professional, you are tasked with encouraging reading not only within your library media center, but also within the community. If community members are reading, it will rub off on your students and encourage them to do the same. Look for activities or promotions that will not only involve your students, but also take them beyond the boundaries of your school in order to understand the importance of reading. In order to reach out into the community, some schools sponsor parent/child book clubs or seek to involve volunteer student mentors in reading programs.

Does your school or district have a Battle of the Books? If not, create one! Get buy in from schools on your level and write questions to popular books. Ask schools to bring teams of five students to answer questions about the books. Set up a competition schedule and have the two final teams battle it out by answering more questions! Reward winners with prizes of books (what else?!) and a huge trophy to place in their school's front office.

Does your state have a State Reading Program or Annual State Book Award? Use these books for your Battle of the Books or to promote reading in your school. Buy 10 paperback copies of each selected title and ask students to read three to be able to vote for their favorite book. Encourage teachers to read parts of the books to their classes to entice students to read more. Sometimes teachers read the entire book to the class, allowing students to count that book as one of their three books. Invite students who read a set

Attractive displays help draw students' attention to books.

Grant Funds Great Media Center Promotion at Timber Creek High School

Last year, my high school received a $25,000 grant to create a coffee shop in a conference room near the front of our media center. Collaborating with our business department, we enlisted the help of Barnie's Coffee and Tea Company. The Beans, Books, and Brains Cafe opened as an actual Barnie's franchise. We fill the room with well-stocked paperback book racks, magazines, and newspapers for students to enjoy with their coffee The cafe is very popular with students, especially before school and during lunch shifts. We ask students to exchange paperback books at their leisure, but if more books are missing than exchanged, who cares? The kids are reading.

Sidebar 9.17 Book Battles

Organizing a *Battle of the Books* contest is a great way to get students involved in reading. Use these Web sites to get more information about book battles.

The America's Battle of the Books Web site. Available at: http://www.battleofthebooks.org/index.html.

The New Mexico Battle of the Books Web site. Available at: http://www.nmbattleofthebooks.org/.

Battle of the Books, a Statewide Contest. Available at: http://viking.bwsd.k12.wi.us/battle/libstatebattle.html.

Novi Public Library: Battle of the Books. Available at: http://novi.lib.mi.us/youth/BattleoftheBooks.htm.

Sidebar 9.18 Does your State have a Reading List?

Check out this Web site sponsored by H. W. Wilson called *State Book Awards*. It contains links to reading lists from all over the country and even provides basic information about the list contents. http://www.standardcatalogs.com/lib_book_awards.htm.

number of books to the media center for an ice cream or popcorn party and to talk about the books. Give students who read all the books a special prize. Announce winners to excite and entice student participation. If your state doesn't have an annual state reading list, use a list from another state.

Bibliography

Accelerated Reader. *Renaissance Learning*. Available at: http://www.renlearn.com/ar/default.htm.

The American Library Association. *A Communications Handbook for Libraries*. Available at: http://www.ala.org/ala/pio/availablepiomat/online_comm_handbook.pdf (accessed May 7, 2006).

BookEnds Online Café. Available at: http://www.friendcalib.org/index.htm (accessed May 7, 2006).

California Library Association. *California Young Reader Medal Program*. Available at: http://www.cla-net.org/awards/cyrm.php.

Florida Association for Media in Education. Available at: http://www.floridamedia.org/.

Friends and Foundations of California Libraries. *Library Lover's Month at Your Library*. Available at: http://www.librarysupport.net/librarylovers/ (accessed May 7, 2006).

Geneva School's Library Themes. Available at: http://wwwgen.bham.wednet.edu/libtheme.htm (accessed May 7, 2006).

Hawaii State Public Library System. Available at: http://www.librarieshawaii.org/.

Library Avenue School Library Consortium. Available at: http://www.libraryavenue.com/id29.htm (accessed May 7, 2006).

LibrarySupportStaff.com. *Marketing Our Libraries On and Off the Internet*. Available at: http://www.librarysupportstaff.com/marketinglibs.html (accessed May 7, 2006).

Pizza Hut. *Book It*. Available at: http://www.bookitprogram.com/.

Reading A–Z.com. Available at: http://www.readinga-z.com/.

Scholastic Inc. *Scholastic Reading Counts*. Available at: http://teacher.scholastic.com/products/readingcounts/.

Study Dog Inc. *Study Dog*. Available at: http://www.studydog.com/.

Sylvan Learning Center. *Book Adventure*. Available at: http://www.bookadventure.com/.

University of Illinois at Urbana-Champaign Graduate School of Library and Information Science and Library and Information Science Library. *UI Current LIS Clips University of Illinois at Urbana-Campaign Graduate School of Library and Information Science*. Available at: http://clips.lis.uiuc.edu/2003_09.html#01 (accessed May 7, 2006).

10

Research and You

It doesn't matter whether we work in elementary, middle, or high school, teaching research skills is an integral part of our job. When a class comes to the media center to explore anything from the foods eaten in different countries to the chemical structure of an atom, we are there to teach students how to find the information they need. The library research skills we teach vary depending on the grade level, project focus, time constraints, and the teacher's purpose. Suppose a teacher wants students to research food. If it is a third grade teacher who wants students to get basic information about what types of food people eat in Japan, we might teach how to use an encyclopedia or the index of a book. If a seventh grade class is studying the culture of Japan and wants students to find and make recipes from that country, we might teach using our OPAC to find books and Web sites featuring Japanese recipes. If a ninth grade health teacher is discussing heart disease and wants students to investigate Japanese foods to understand why heart disease rates are lower in that country, we might teach media literacy skills such as Web site evaluation and the difference between search engines and online databases that are available for student use.

Since the advent of flexible scheduling, the emphasis has been on teaching research skills in connection with the curriculum, because teaching them in isolation does not work. Therefore, the perceptive media specialist is always looking for opportunities. You must find a teacher who is willing to collaborate with you. While they teach a portion of their content, you are presenting information skill lessons. Since your lessons directly relate to the class's subject matter and assignment, students will not stare at you wondering, "Why is she telling me this?" The information skills you teach will support and extend the classroom teacher's lessons; you will have immediate student buy-in. Your lessons make their task easier. Your lessons must convince them that by using your advice and research strategies, they will do less work and receive a higher grade. A curriculum connection is critical to teaching research skills.

Once you team up with a teacher, begin your collaboration by helping the teacher design a lesson that incorporates research. No matter the age or ability of the student or the length of the lesson, a few research steps can be taught. Be sure to consult your state and local standards and benchmarks and to address them specifically in your lesson plans. The media specialist and the classroom teacher both share in the teaching of the skills, but students must feel an urgency to research correctly for lessons to be successful. Sometimes a teacher only wants students to begin the research process by leaning how to brainstorm to narrow a topic. Sometimes they want students to focus on search strategies. Possibly, they are practicing note taking or citing sources, and writing the entire paper is not the goal of the lesson. Teachers may want you to be a part of the process from assigning the topic to evaluating the presentation, whether a paper or a multimedia presentation, or they may want you to step in to speed up the search process. Sometimes the media specialist must take the leadership role and let teachers know how they can collaborate to help students learn. You may want to consider doing an in-service to help teachers understand your role and the services you provide. However you work it out, determine what capacity the teacher wants you to have and fulfill their needs to the best of your ability.

Typical Lessons

Lessons usually begin in the classroom with the teacher introducing the unit that will involve the research. For example, it may be a unit on the Civil War, but perhaps the teacher hopes to complete it soon in order to make it to the twentieth century. Why not have each student take an aspect of the war, research it, and contribute to the class when it is discussing uniforms, arms, prisons, supplies, generals, the home front, and so forth? Sometimes a class completes a unit and the teacher wants students to delve deeper into the content by investigating a specific aspect of the subject. The study of bugs is a great example for this situation. When finished with their class study of insects, why not have each student choose a bug and find our more about it? In each scenario, the teacher makes the assignment giving deadlines and expectations. The teacher then schedules the media center for as many days as she and the media specialist believe is necessary. The media specialist may want to help students write a rubric before they begin researching so that they know exactly what is expected of them and how it will be graded. Research may include print and nonprint sources so all research tools should be available to the teacher and students. The classroom teacher may teach lessons during the research on note taking. On days not spent in the media center, the teacher may provide background material in the area students are studying. The media specialist may teach lessons on library skills, such as using a table of contents or an index. She might also teach lessons in technology, such as using the OPAC, evaluating Web sites, ethics in citing sources, presentation software such as PowerPoint, and more. Your collaboration with the classroom teacher and the experience level of your students will determine your teaching duties. As the research continues, you and the classroom teacher may find that you must adjust your lesson plans to include more instruction in one area and less in another. For example, if all of your students are familiar with PowerPoint, you do not need to teach them how to use this software. If you notice students choosing Web sites without thought or consideration, a lesson on media literacy and Web site evaluation is needed.

Using Research Models

No matter what the assignment, when students do research, they need a plan to follow. Promoting a consistent research model for all teachers and students to use at your school does not make more work for students, but actually makes their job easier by providing a structured series of steps to guide their work. Likewise, it helps teachers by giving them a framework for evaluating student projects. Your first step is to choose a model that aligns with the curriculum at your school. No matter what model you choose, if students continually use it, they will become familiar with the steps and they will soon use them without even thinking about it. Your district may recommend or require all schools use a specific model. If your district has no specific model, investigate national models and choose one that is right for your students. Students from kindergarten

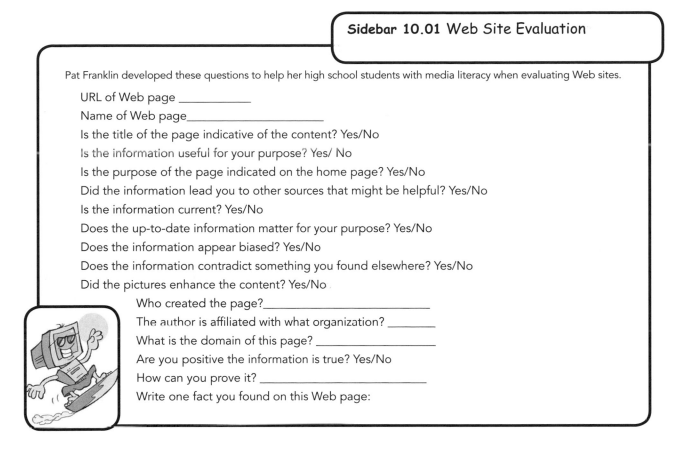

Sidebar 10.01 Web Site Evaluation

Pat Franklin developed these questions to help her high school students with media literacy when evaluating Web sites.

URL of Web page _____
Name of Web page_____
Is the title of the page indicative of the content? Yes/No
Is the information useful for your purpose? Yes/ No
Is the purpose of the page indicated on the home page? Yes/No
Did the information lead you to other sources that might be helpful? Yes/No
Is the information current? Yes/No
Does the up-to-date information matter for your purpose? Yes/No
Does the information appear biased? Yes/No
Does the information contradict something you found elsewhere? Yes/No
Did the pictures enhance the content? Yes/No

Who created the page?_____
The author is affiliated with what organization? _____
What is the domain of this page? _____
Are you positive the information is true? Yes/No
How can you prove it? _____
Write one fact you found on this Web page:

to high school seniors can and should be researching. Although the depth of the projects will vary, all students need to learn the steps of the research process, not just for future use as they continue their formal education, but because we want to build lifelong learners. In today's world, we are able to find the answer to almost any question through basic research. We want to produce students who can do that with ease.

Try these resources if you are looking for a research model:

- The Big6™ (http://www.big6.com)—The Big6™ is a research problem solving model created by Mike Eisenberg and Bob Berkowitz. The model takes students through the research process in an orderly manner. The six steps include task definition, information seeking strategies, location and access, use of information, synthesis, and evaluation. For K to 2 students, Eisenberg and Berkowitz created the Super3, a scaled down version of the Big6™. The Super3 steps are plan, do, and review.
- IIM (http://www.iimresearch.com)—The Independent Investigation Method was created by Virginia Morse and Cindy Nottage. IIM also creates a logical, easy to follow process for students and teachers to use when researching. IIM's seven steps are topic, goal setting, research, organizing, goal evaluation, product, and presentation.
- Many states promote their own models so that there is consistency across school districts. For example, the Florida Department of Education Library Media Services Office developed

a model called FINDS (http://www.sunlink.ucf.edu/finds/). Its five steps include focus, investigate, note, develop, and score. Check with your district support staff, local professional group, or state department of education to find out if your state has a preferred research model.

TABLE 10.01: Comparison of information skills process models.

Eisenberg/ Berkowitz Information Problem-Solving (The Big6 Skills)	Kuhlthau Information Seeking	Irving Information Skills	Pitts/Stripling Research Process	New South Wales Information Process
1. Task Definition	1. Initiation	1. Formulation/ analysis of information need	1. Choose a broad topic	
1.1 Define the problem	2. Selection		2. Get an over view of the topic	Defining
1.2 Identify info requirements	3. Exploration (investig info on the general topic)		3. Narrow the topic	
			4. Develop thesis/ purpose statement	
2. Information Seeking Strategies	4. Formulation (of focus)	2. Identification / appraisal of likely sources	5. Formulate questions to guide research	
2.1 Determine range sources	5. Collection (gather info on the focused topic)		6. Plan for research & production	Locating
2.2 Prioritize sources	6. Presentation			
3. Location & Access	7. Assesment (of outcome/ process)	3. Tracing/locating indiv. resources	7. Find, analyze, evaluate resources	
3.1 Locate sources		4. Examining, selecting, & rejecting indiv. resources		Selecting
3.2 Find info				
4. Information Use		5. Interrogating/ using individual resources		
4.1 Locate sources				Organising
4.2 Extract info		6. Recording/ storing info	8. Evaluate evidence take notes/compile bib	

(continued)

TABLE 10.01: Comparison of information skills process models. (*continued*)

Eisenberg/ Berkowitz Information Problem-Solving (The Big6 Skills)	Kuhlthau Information Seeking	Irving Information Skills	Pitts/Stripling Research Process	New South Wales Information Process
5. Synthesis 5.1 Organize 5.2 Present		7 Interpretation, analysis, synth., and eval. of info	9. Establish conclusions/ Organize info in outline	Presenting
		8. Shape, presentation, and communication of info	10. Create and present final product	
6. Evaluation 6.1 Judge the product 6.2 Judge the process		9. Evaluation of the assignment	(Reflection point—is the paper/project satisfactory)	Assessing

This chart compares five nationally used research process models.
Source: Big6.com. Available at: http://www.big6.com/showarticle.php?id=87. Used with permission.

Bibliography

Active Learning Systems LLC. *Independent Investigation Method.* Available at: http://www.iimresearch.com/iim/demo.php (accessed May 15, 2006).

Big6 Associates LLC. *The Big6: Information Literacy for the Information Age.* Available at: http://www.big6.com/ (accessed May 15, 2006).

Copeland, Brenda S., and Patricia Messner. *Collaborative Library Lessons for the Primary Grades: Linking Research Skills to Curriculum Standards.* Westport, CT: Libraries Unlimited, 2005.

Department of Education Victoria, Australia. *Wrapping up Research.* Available at: http://www.highlands.vic.edu.au/research/index.html (accessed May 15, 2006).

Duncan, Donna. *I-search, You Search, We All Learn to Research: A How to Do It Manual for Teaching Elementary Students to Solve Information Problems.* New York: Neal Schuman Publishers, 2000.

Florida Department of Education. *Library Media Services Research Process Model—FINDS.* Available at: http://www.firn.edu/doe/instmat/pdf/22lessoncorrelation.pdf (accessed May 15, 2006).

Info Zone Pembina Trails School Division. *Are you about to do Research?* Available at: http://www.pembinatrails.ca/infozone/ (accessed May 15, 2006).

LibraryHQ.com. *Teaching Library Research Skills.* Available at: http://www.libraryhq.com/libresearch.html (accessed May 15, 2006).

The Library of Congress. *The Learning Page.* Available at: http://lcweb2.loc.gov/ammem/ndlpedu/ (accessed May 15, 2006).

Miller, Pat. *Stretchy Library Lesson: Research Skills.* Fort Atkinson, WI: Upstart Books, 2003.

Resources for School Librarians. *Information Skills Instruction.* Available at: http://www.sldirectory.com/libsf/resf/libplans.html (accessed May 15, 2006).

Stebbins, Leslie F. *Student Guide to Research in the Digital Age: How to Locate and Evaluate Information Sources.* Westport, CT: Libraries Unlimited, 2005.

Thomas, Nancy Pickering. *Information Literacy and Information Skills Instruction: Applying Research to Practice in the School Library Media Center.* Westport, CT: Libraries Unlimited, 2004.

11

Television Production and You!

Depending on your point of view, one of the best or worst parts of any media specialist's day is the time spent producing a daily school news show. This time can be an engaging, fun-filled hour overflowing with creativity and hands-on learning activities for your students, or you can view it as a lost hour, a frustrating time when you could be doing other more important things to make your media center run smoothly. Many times, those of us who see it as an intrusion feel that way because we really don't know enough about television production to feel as confident producing our school news show as we do when we present a book talk or some other more traditional library activity. For those who are new to the profession and who may have had very little training in video production, the school news show can be a scary time. Trying to teach students how to use all the technology involved in the production process while you yourself are just learning how it works is intimidating to say the least. It can also be embarrassing because your learning curve involves a daily public performance viewed by the whole school. No one else on your campus is held up for such scrutiny.

The good news is—your television production problem is not unique to you or your school setting. Over the past 30 years, video production has become a standard part of school curricula across the nation. New schools are built with state of the art production facilities, while old schools seek to retrofit spaces to accommodate cameras, lighting, and the other equipment needed for production. Some schools simply mount a camera on a tripod and point it at an improvised news desk, while others create slick shows with fancy graphics, special effects, and student produced news reports. The success of most television production programs rests squarely on the instructor. It is their vision, their willingness to learn the equipment and spend experimental time creating projects and then teaching them to students that makes a good program work. While some schools make different arrangements, in many schools that instructor is you, the media specialist.

Don't allow teaching television to become the low point of your day. Instead, look at it as an exciting new learning opportunity. Embrace its creative potential and allow

News set at NorthLake Park Community School, Orlando, Florida. Photos courtesy of Amy Alday, Media Specialist.

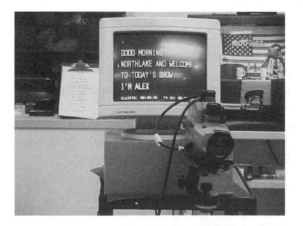

News set at NorthLake Park Community School, Orlando, Florida. Photos courtesy of Amy Alday, Media Specialist.

News set at NorthLake Park Community School, Orlando, Florida. Photos courtesy of Amy Alday, Media Specialist.

Sidebar 11.01 Voice of Experience from Claire

If you read the introduction to this book, you know I became a media specialist *accidentally*; I wanted to teach in a TV program at the school where I worked. So, I took media specialist courses to gain the required certification. Unfortunately, my media classes only lightly touched on TV production, and my newly built high school boasted better facilities than what the university had to offer at that time.

I was lucky, however; the teachers of the television program where I worked were Keith Kyker and Chris Curchy. These two gifted educators generously spent hours of their time working after school with students and a few teachers like me who were interested in learning the art and craft of TV. I learned by doing. I spent time experimenting with the equipment, shooting tape, practicing camera angles, and so forth. I learned how to handle microphones and soundboards, and eventually advanced to editing equipment. I still remember how excited I felt when I finished my first project. It was short, only a few minutes long, but it felt like I had accomplished something big.

As a media specialist, I used these TV production skills for nine years at Walker Middle School in Orlando. I do not consider myself an expert at television production, and my new job assignment does not require me to teach it anymore, but I still routinely use the skills I learned while working with Keith and Chris. Frequently, I must videotape teachers, students, or school events. For teachers in our alternative certification program or those seeking National Board certification, I must correctly mic their rooms for sound. We regularly help students and teachers dub video onto tapes and now DVDs for various reasons. I also feel confident that if need be, in the future, I could walk back into a television production classroom and hold my own.

For those of you who are new to this profession and to the art and craft of television, I must strongly recommend the books written by my peers and teachers, Keith Kyker and Chris Curchy. After teaching TV for several years, they realized there was a need in the education community for simple introductory texts for both teachers and students. Their classroom experience translated into a series of books published by Libraries Unlimited. The titles are listed below.

Television Production: A Classroom Approach, 2nd ed. Westport, CT: Libraries Unlimited, 2004.

Educator's Survival Guide to Television Production and Activities, 2nd ed. Westport, CT: Libraries Unlimited, 2003. (Note: A worthwhile DVD accompanies this title for an additional cost.)

Television Production for Elementary and Middle Schools. Westport, CT: Libraries Unlimited, 1994.

Video Projects for Elementary and Middle Schools. Westport, CT: Libraries Unlimited, 1995.

Keith and Chris's Web site, SchoolTV.com, is another great resource. On this site, you will find links to resources, articles they've published in professional journals, and a very helpful frequently asked questions section. Check it out at http://www.schooltv.com.

yourself time to learn how things work. There are many good books available on television production in the classroom setting. Locate a few of these and read up on equipment. Several feature easy projects for students that teach camera operations and functions. Do these projects yourself, and then lead your students through them. You'll be surprised at how quickly you adapt to working with the equipment and become a knowledgeable person in the area of video production.

So take a deep breath and relax—you can teach TV production! You may be learning on the job, but you can do it. You need to become familiar with three TV production areas: equipment, facilities, and teaching curricula. Don't expect to know all three instantly. Take your time, work at it, and most importantly, relax and have fun. Teaching and doing TV production is great. You get to know your students in a wonderfully different way and will watch them grow academically, creatively, and personally as they work with each other to produce their projects.

Video Equipment

The most basic equipment needed for TV production at your school includes camcorders, a tripod, a video monitor, and industrial or professional grade VCRs. With these basics, you could do an elemental school news show. Additionally, you will want to acquire a video mixer, character generator, microphones, an audio mixer, a computer, and a document camera. These pieces of equipment will allow you to add a few bells and whistles to your news show and wow the audience. As you become more knowledgeable, you may want to invest in computerized editing equipment and software products that make it easy for images to be digitally manipulated into final projects. Detailing all this equipment requires more space than is available in this text, but you will find a brief explanation of each of these items to help you understand what they are and some things you might consider when planning an equipment purchase.

Camcorders

The backbone of your TV operation, camcorders work by converting light energy into an electronic or digital signal that is recorded on some form of storage media such as a VHS or MiniDV tape. Like many electronics, in the past years, camcorders have become progressively smaller. Today most models record on MiniDV tapes almost exclusively, and models using mini recordable DVD discs are now appearing on store shelves. As a media specialist, you may inherit a mixture of camcorders at your school, and many of the old VHS models will continue to work well for years to come, but, eventually, you will need to upgrade your camcorder collection.

You may want to purchase one or two professional grade cameras for your studio and smaller models for teachers and students to check out, but you need to understand the difference and establish criteria for your purchases. Check with your district office; some school boards employ video production professionals who do video production on the district level. These professionals can be a valuable resource and may have recommendations to assist your purchasing process.

Spend some time learning about camcorders before purchasing them. Familiarize yourself with the language and features related to video cameras. You can do this by reading one of the books recommended in this chapter. Before you buy new camcorders for your studio or school, it is important that you understand terms like CCD chip, video formats, lines of resolutions, electronic image stabilization, and so forth. Even if you do not thoroughly understand the vocabulary of camcorders, a working knowledge of related terminology will help you ask vendors appropriate questions. Listen as they respond and ask them to demonstrate the camera features. As they show off their camcorders, pay attention and take notes; you will be surprised at how quickly your superficial knowledge of camcorders turns into in-depth understanding.

If possible, try to use the camera before you buy it. Ask the sales person to allow you to examine the camera closely, record some footage, and play it back to get a feel for using the unit and check the picture quality. Everyone at your school will be using your purchase for several years. You will be called upon to demonstrate how it works. Take the time to be sure it is a camcorder you can live with!

Although rapidly becoming obsolete, VHS camcorders are still an important part of many school television studios.

A larger digital video camera will be a good addition to your studio; however, because this equipment costs more, you may not want to check it out for classroom use.

Tripods

The tripod holds the camera in place, providing a steady position for recording. They have three adjustable legs that can be set at varying heights to provide for the best shot, and are essential for school-based TV production programs since it is frequently difficult for students to hold a steady shot. Because your students will take your tripods out into the field for recording projects, they must be well made. Spending the money to purchase a sturdier tripod with a quick-release mounting plate will be worth it in the end.

When buying a tripod, try to imagine your students using it. Will they be able to set it up and take it down with ease? If you teach elementary students, is the tripod adjustable to their height? Will young people be able to mount the camera on the tripod securely and safely? Will they understand how to use the pan and tilt mechanisms to move the camera? If the tripod has a dolly, is it secure or could students knock the tripod off the dolly base and damage your camera? Will students be able to move the dolly with the tripod mounted on it in a smooth manner?

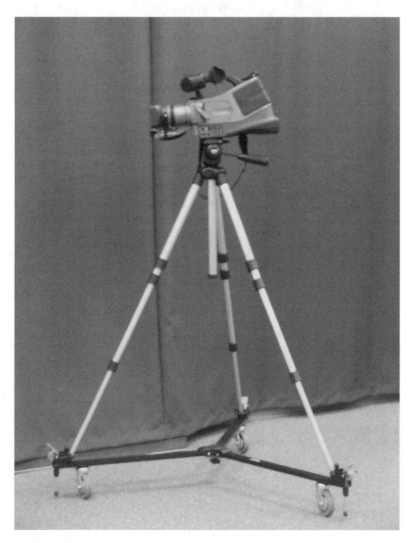

This sturdy tripod has an added dolly base to allow movement in the TV studio.

Tripods are not difficult to use, but it is still important to take a few minutes and read the instruction manual. Practice setting the equipment up and taking it down. Mount the camera on the tripod head so you understand how to securely lock it in place before you demonstrate this to your students. If you are a tripod novice, ask for input from someone you know. They don't have to be a professional videographer to help you learn how to use a tripod correctly. Amateurs and still photographers use tripods too and can probably answer many of your questions.

VCRs

The professional television production world is moving away from videotape and going digital. Schools will eventually follow the same path; however, most school budgets will not support a quick change into digital television production. Your school will probably still be using videotape in either a VHS or MiniDV format for several years to come. If you are in the position of working in a new school, you will probably not need many VCRs in your television studio space. If you are in an older school, you will have to carefully weigh your equipment purchases to decide if you should continue to replace VCRs. Consult with your district video personnel about VCR purchases and the direction your program is moving. Their suggestions will help you align your program to local standards and expectations.

This special dual function VCR allows users to copy tapes from the newer mini digital video format to traditional VHS and vice versa. A machine like this is worth the cost if your school and students still use VHS players in the classrooms and at home.

As with any television equipment, check the manual; be sure it is clearly written and illustrated. You will probably be alone setting up this equipment and integrating it into your TV production equipment, so be sure you can read and understand this important book. Ask vendors if they provide set-up and training on the machines you are considering. It may cost a little more, but it will be worth the price if it means you are able to get the equipment installed and can begin using it faster.

As with camcorders, familiarize yourself with the language of VCRs. Some terms will be similar, like format, inputs, and outputs. Others are unique to the VCR, such as jog/shuttle control, four-head system, and adjustable sound recording levels. Depending on your program, you may not need all these features, but they can make a difference in the appearance and sound of your final projects so it is important to understand them before you buy equipment.

Finally, be sure to ask yourself what your program really needs, what your budget will allow, and what you think the future will bring. If you are only teaching one small class of students in your TV program each day and doing very basic production, then a consumer grade VCR may be fine for your needs and will cost much less. Many of the machines designed for home use are now coming equipped with features such as jog/shuttles and multiple input/output jacks thanks to the advent of computer video editing software for the home. If your budget will not support a professional level machine, check the high-end consumer models available through some of the dealers in your area. You may sacrifice some features but still get a good machine that more than adequately services your needs. Another important consideration is planning for your TV program's future growth. Do you plan to convert your school to digital technology in the near future? While a VCR may still be needed in this scenario, it is not going to be used in the same way. If your plans include going digital within the next year or two, you may decide going with a less expensive model VCR is a better solution for the present.

Video Mixers

These units allow the user to select and combine video images, which are then sent to a VCR for recording or broadcast. For example, a student using a video mixer might select an input coming from a studio camcorder showing an anchor on your news show. The student then mixes it with another image coming from your character generator displaying the anchor's name. This combined image, anchor and name, would then be sent to the VCR for recording or input into the school closed-circuit system for broadcast. Other common features on video mixers allow for transitions such as fading in and out, incorporating digital special effects, and superimposing one image over another (chroma keying). Users are also able to change background colors and more. A true video mixer allows for the seamless editing of the final output. There should be no jump cuts or glitches between one source and the next in the final product. You can expect the price of the machine to increase with the number of features it offers.

Since video mixers are expensive, consult your district video production staff. Ask them to help you identify criteria for purchasing your new equipment. Be prepared to share with them any existing equipment the video mixer must work with in case there are any compatibility questions. Check the number and type of inputs available on the unit you are considering. Check the cable inputs, be sure they will accommodate existing equipment that you still need to use, and allow for expansion to newer technologies such as FireWire cables for digital editing down the road.

As with the selection of all video equipment, analyze your needs before buying a video mixer. Each year, schools spend thousands of dollars buying these units and many overbuy for their actual needs. Be sure that you plan to use most of the features available on the models you are considering for purchase. Again, it also pays to ask your vendor about installation and training for a mixer you are considering for purchase. Your students are another consideration. Will they be able to operate the equipment you might buy? Don't let showy features distract you from functionality and ease of use.

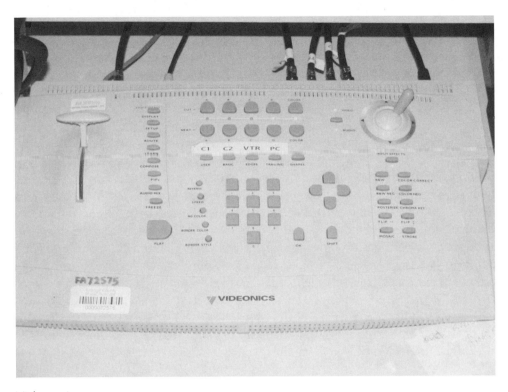

Video mixer.

Character Generators

Imagine watching TV news without the graphics. You would not know the reporter's name or location if you missed the verbal toss from anchor to reporter. You might not learn additional information that the graphics can add to a story, such as time, place, or cost of an event. Graphics are an integral part of TV production and your students will want, even expect, to be able to add them to their projects. The character generator allows them to do this. As with the video mixer, you need to shop carefully for a character generator. They can be expensive and offer you many features beyond your true needs. It is important to get your hands on these units. If possible, have both you and your students try any unit you are considering. Is it easy to use? Does it come with some sort of training?

You may want to consider using a computer as a character generator. A machine with a video output jack and the right software can interface with your video mixer with ease. Keep in mind the cost of the computer will be more than most character generators, but you may have an older model machine around your school that could easily be upgraded to work with your video system for around the same cost. If you are considering using a computer in this way, consult with your school and district technology staff to get their recommendations for compatible hardware and district video production personnel for software recommendations.

Preview Monitors

Monitors allow students to see the video they are working on. This is important because students must be able to cue up videotapes, graphics, and other sources in order to assemble their final project or news show. A preview monitor can be black and white, although color is necessary when working with graphics and video mixers that supply color backgrounds and special effects so that students can accurately see what they are setting up. It is also important to note that a video preview monitor is not the same as a television set, the difference coming from the type of signals they process. Generally speaking, monitors cost more, but provide a superior picture. While you can spend additional money to buy an RF modulator that will convert a lesser costing television set to a monitor, the resulting picture will probably not be of good quality. Combination TV/monitor units are available that work well for most school applications. They have a slightly diminished picture quality, but are also more economically feasible. These units have inputs on the back for video and audio signals in addition to the regular television inputs.

After you decide which type of preview monitors you want to use, be sure you also look at the number of inputs on units you are considering. Many sets have a second set of inputs on the front panel, which allows two sources to share the same monitor. You can generally access the second source by tuning the monitor to an auxiliary channel below channel two on the set. Finally, notice the type of input jacks on the monitor you are considering. Common input jacks will receive either BNC connectors or, more often, an RCA jack. RCA jacks are less secure than BNC connectors, which feature a twist-lock design, but RCA connectors are more readily available and less costly. For most school purposes, RCA connectors will be fine.

As you become more adapt at TV production, you may want to shoot some video on location outside of your studio. A portable preview monitor is important for this situation. In most cases, a small portable television set will suffice. If electricity is not available, you may wish to purchase a battery-operated model.

Preview monitors allow students to see their work before broadcasting or recording.

Audio Equipment

Microphones

There are several different types of microphones, and selecting the right one can make or break your production. While you do not have to be a serious audiophile to make good quality audio for your TV production class, it helps to be armed with some basic information about how microphones work.

Just as the camcorder gathers light and converts it into a digital signal, microphones do the same thing with sounds. Microphones differ in three ways. They capture and convert sounds differently and the directionality of the sound pickup differs depending on the microphone. Another variation comes in their resistance to signal flow, which is called impedance. Eight possible microphone combinations result from mixing these differences in individual microphones. It will not take long to read up on microphones and understand their basic workings. Consult any of the texts suggested in this chapter for more information.

Another consideration is the format or type of microphone. Do you need a handheld model? Is it for your news anchor? Then you may need a lavaliere microphone. Are you trying to gather a specific sound but cannot get close to it? You may need a shotgun microphone. These are just three of the microphone types you may have to choose from when buying new equipment. To help you select the

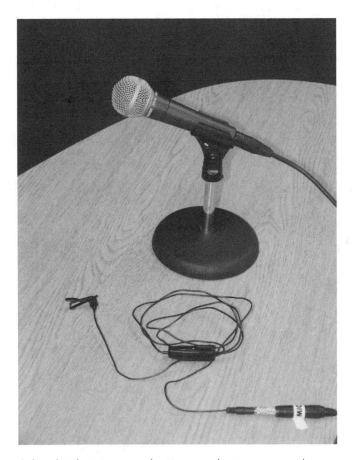

School television production students commonly use both small lavaliere microphones and larger table stand setups.

right microphone format, consider what you need the equipment to do. Do you need to mic the school chorus or band? Are you just trying to mic your news anchor in a studio setting? Do you need a microphone students can take outside to interview the track coach? Be clear and specific with your needs and then contact someone more experienced with sound reproduction to assist you in making good microphone selections. Your district office video production personnel should be of assistance. Don't overlook your music teachers, who may have some experience setting up sound systems for concerts. They may also be able to offer suggestions for that type of sound gathering. You may find some of the students at your school have parents who are employed in this field and are willing to help you learn the ropes of microphone selection. Many hotels, businesses, and churches now employ audiovisual staff to help with the many new technologies being used in their buildings. They may be willing to become an education partner with your school and assist you in purchasing and setting up a workable sound system that meets your needs. Ask questions, seek referrals, and start slowly building up a collection of microphones that work for the needs at your school.

Audio Mixers

Students use an audio mixer to choose combinations of audio signals for recording or broadcast purposes. Mixers take in a variety of inputs, such as microphones and videotape audio, then the sound technician controls the volume of each sound, making it possible to blend background music with a voice or to fade one sound out while raising another. Professional audio mixers can cost thousands of dollars and will probably be more than you need for your school TV production studio. Good planning is important when selecting an audio mixer. Be sure you take into account your present needs and growth since it is likely that you will want to add different audio sources as time goes by.

A simple audio mixer like this one will be sufficient for most school productions.

Audio mixers have microphone inputs and line inputs. Consider how many of each you will need. Typically, you will need three or four microphone channels for most school productions, although advanced students may require more. Line inputs cover any additional audio sources you may wish to connect to your system. These might include a compact disc (CD) or MP3 player, the sound coming out of a VCR or an old-fashioned cassette player. A simple mixer that allows for blending between 7 to 10 different audio inputs should be more than adequate for most school programs. Be sure you have calculated the number of inputs you need before purchasing your mixer. You don't want to find out you are short inputs after spending all your money.

Other common features on an audio mixer include a line out jack to allow you to send the mixed sound signal out for recording or broadcast. VU (volume unit) meters that indicate signal strength are a desirable feature, along with a headphone jack that allows the sound technician to monitor the mixer's output. A crossfader allows for the simultaneous lowering of one audio source while another source's volume is raised. A cue function is very helpful if you plan to use the audio mixer during broadcasts. It allows the technician to listen to and cue up one audio source while another is being broadcast through the main line out.

Additional Audio Sources

You will also wish to acquire additional audio sources for your TV production setup. Equipment such as a CD player, audiocassette player/recorder, and an MP3 player will be used by students to play

---

Sidebar 11.02 Audio Tips

These tips will help you as you learn about dealing with sound.

Students tend to hold microphones directly in front of their mouth, blocking their face. To help them, videotape a few network news segments and watch them with your students. Discuss how the reporters handle the microphones so students understand how to present themselves with the equipment.

In general, keep microphones as close to your anchor as possible, unless you are recording a group. To record a group, move the microphone so it is near the group, but not close to anyone individual. This insures that no one person's voice dominates the sound recording.

Learn about audio cables. The main types are XLR and RCA. XLR cables provide superior signal transmission but cost more.

Invest in a good set of headphones for your audio system. Headphones will help you hear any background noises that you need to eliminate before recording.

Always do a sound check before beginning any recording. Test each person's microphone by having him or her speak, read their script, or count. It is also a good idea to record a few minutes of tape and play it back to be sure all the audio levels are appropriate.

Clip-on microphones can get caught on jewelry and pick up the sounds of necklaces clicking against  each other. Train your announcers to place necklaces under high-necked shirts or to remove them temporarily if clothing design does not allow them to be hidden.

You never know what you will be required to connect to your system. Begin a collection of adaptors that will allow you to convert audio signal between various types and sizes of connections. Examples of such adapters include XLR to RCA, 1/8 inch to 1/4 inch and the reverse of each. Purchase a small multi drawer storage container or tackle box to sort and store your adaptors.

background music for their projects. Higher end consumer grade units will probably be sufficient for your school TV production program, but be sure each supplies line out jacks so that they can be connected to your sound mixer. Many consumer grade products are now packaged without these necessary outputs. Other amenities such as headphone jacks and time/counter functions are great assets and worth a few extra dollars since they will make it easier for students to use the equipment. If you are just starting a program, begin with a CD player since it is currently the most common audio source, but be aware of the increasing use of MP3 players by students. You may need to add one of these units in the near future. Even though it is old technology, an old-fashioned audio cassette player/recorder may still be useful for some purposes. Check around your school. Do the chorus and band teachers still use cassette tapes? If so, you will probably need the cassette player to input recordings of your school's performance groups.

TV Production Facilities

If you are a new media specialist at an existing school, chances are you will inherit a TV studio space. Depending on your school, this space could be large and spacious, filled with state of the art equipment, or it could be a small, cramped area, barely big enough to house the camera and one news announcer. Because the idea of TV production was not considered when many older schools were built, school staff have adapted, often quite creatively, to the spaces available to them. If your school is newer, you may have a dedicated space complete with high ceilings, a light grid, and built-in audio connections. Those of you who inherit newer facilities should count yourselves lucky. Many school TV programs are literally crammed into storage closets at some facilities. Whether you are in a new or old facility, as you begin to work in your existing TV production space, take stock of the following issues:

- Look at the overall TV production space. Typically, there are two areas, a production area and a performance or studio area. If your production and studio spaces are in one room, the two work areas should be clearly evident. Hopefully you have enough space to allow your crews to spread out so they are not tripping over each other as they try to work. If you are in a newer school, you may have a separate control room for the production space. Typically, the control room has a glass window overlooking the performance space so the teacher can supervise all the students in the program. If you are a new media specialist, just take this opportunity to become familiar with the surroundings. Locate electrical, cable, and audio outlets. Look at the studio lighting situation. Is there storage space? Where are the light switches? These may seem trivial, but you need to build your knowledge base before you take on the entire studio.
- Inventory the equipment, what do you have? If possible, make a list identifying the equipment make and model, serial number, condition, and if you have an instruction book for that particular unit. This information will be helpful as you begin to learn how to work the equipment. Instruction books are often available on the Internet, so a detailed list will be helpful.
- Check for safety issues. TV equipment requires many cables connecting the various pieces of equipment. In newer spaces that are correctly designed, these cables are hidden inside specially constructed furniture and under removable floor panels. In older facilities, the cables can become a hazard, causing people to trip over them or accidentally pull them out of equipment by walking into them. These accidents can injure people and damage equipment. They can also ruin your news broadcast or a student's project work. Address any safety concerns immediately. You may need to purchase longer cables to allow sufficient slack for them to lie on the ground. You may need to bundle and tie cables together, pulling them up, out of the way using zip or twist ties. You might be able to purchase some specially designed floor molding to encase floor cables and protect

them and your students. Note that you will not be able to solve all the safety issues. Unfortunately, in many converted older facilities, the cables are a necessary part of life—something has to run from the camcorder to the line in on the back of the video mixer. So that 12-foot long RCA cable may just need to be there whether you like it or not. At least you will be aware of this hazard in your new space and will be able to discuss it as a safety concern with your students, staff, and administration.

- Check out your equipment arrangement. Often things are the way they are for a reason and you may decide to leave them alone for the first month or so until you learn the reasons for the organization. However, in general, you should find your audio equipment grouped together and the video editing equipment grouped together. Equipment should be close enough to allow students to communicate during production, but not so close as to crowd your crew. Typically, these are lined up together either facing your anchor desk area if all in the same room or on the same wall if housed in a separate control room area.

Sidebar 11.03 Creating Studio Space

Author's note: Sam Morris worked in professional television for many years before becoming an educator. The judges in local, state, and national contests consistently recognize his award winning WFCN news team at Walker Middle School in Orlando, Florida.

When setting up a new TV studio, particularly in an area not designed for such use, you will need to consider a few points before actually bringing in equipment.

- What kind of show are you doing? Is it live, full newscast, or is it just some quick announcements? The bigger the show, the more room you will need.

- How many people will be involved in each production? A full studio crew is 8 to 12 people, not including your talent (news announcers). There must be adequate room to move around and stay safe from cables, lights, and so forth.

- How much equipment do you have? Some schools have everything they need for morning announcements on one utility cart, while some have separate rooms for full studio production. Make sure you have adequate power outlets for everything. You don't want your floor to be a nest of extension cords as this presents fire and tripping dangers.

- Where is the room located? Not only do you need to be wired to your school's cable system (the head end), but you don't want your productions to be filled with noise from a busy hallway. How accessible is the room you are considering for studio space? Administrators generally don't like to go on a long hike to reach the room just to turn around and head back across campus to return to their duties.

- Is the room secure? Check for locks, windows, and find out who may have access to the room when you're not around.

After considering these things, plan your studio out and then plan your show.

Sam Morris
Television Production Teacher
Walker Middle School
Orlando, Florida

- Locate your video head end unit. This equipment controls what is going out on the school's closed-circuit system channels; it is usually housed in a sturdy metal rack. Hopefully it will be located in or near your studio space. Most schools have several VCRs attached to this unit, and by pushing switches, it is possible to control what is playing on the closed-circuit channels. Ask if there is an instruction manual for this unit. If not, is there someone at the school or in the district who understands how it works and can provide you with training? You will need to understand how the head end works, not only for your TV news broadcast, but also for assisting teachers who need videos played in their classrooms.

Remember the old adage, "Rome wasn't built in a day"? Well, your TV studio won't be done in a day either! Look at your TV production facility as a work in progress. Even if you are blessed with a new school featuring state of the art equipment, the technology time clock is ticking, and what is new and novel now will be old and used in just a few years. Approach your TV studio like you do your book collection. Write a five-year plan identifying equipment maintenance and updates you would like to do. Share the plan with your principal and other interested parties at your school such as the PTA or school advisory council. Include the costs in your annual budget submission to your principal. By doing this, you will know that you plan to replace camcorders one year and audio equipment the next. You will also know that you need to budget for annual purchase of cables or lighting supplies to keep your system up and running. This also places you in the position of not having to learn everything all at once because of a dramatic change in your production equipment. Of course, your plan can be altered as needed in the event of the sudden demise of a necessary part of your system, but having the plan in place will help to raise your principal's confidence in your program and budget requests. It will also give you a sense of direction that will lessen your stress. If you are new to the position of media specialist, you may not be able to create this plan right away, but by the end of your first year, you'll be surprised at how much you have learned about television production and your studio facility. You should be able to put some thoughts on paper at that time outlining a plan for your studio space.

Teaching TV

Once you have become familiar with television production equipment and your studio facility, the question becomes, what should I teach the students? This can be very scary if you have no background in video production, but you can do the projects you ask your students to do before assigning them. This will help you gain experience, skill, and knowledge sufficient to lead your students through the same assignment. Couple this with the understanding you gained from experimenting with your equipment and reading the instruction manuals, and you'll be surprised how much you already know.

Often media specialists find themselves involved in the teaching of TV production with little or no guidance. If this is the case in your school, begin to ask questions of your curriculum resource teachers, other media specialists, and district personnel. You may be surprised to find out that there are course descriptions, objectives, and state standards that will guide you in establishing your curriculum. In general, at the end of a first year television production course, students should have some rudimentary knowledge of the following things: basic video camera operation, basic production skills such as adding graphics and audio to a project, basic editing, and simple storyboarding and scriptwriting skills.

Obviously, the degree of skill will vary with the age and ability of the student. For example, elementary students might learn simple camera operations such as turning the camera on and off, doing simple macro focus projects, and adding a simple voice-over narration to a project. Their graphics may be simple handwritten or computer generated signs that the camera focuses on at the beginning and end of

Be aware of safety issues when adapting television studio space in older schools. A larger space is better so that students have room to maneuver around freestanding lighting and cables on the floor.

their project. Middle school students may do the above plus learn about using tripods, beginning microphone techniques for field interviews, and how to use video and character generators to do more complex graphics and editing. High school students will be able to understand more complex techniques of television and film such as pans; tilts; long, medium, and close-up shots, and so forth. They should be able to develop detailed storyboards and scripts, then turn them into completed short projects. Many students on all levels are also now using computers and specially designed softwares to produce video projects and record them on DVD. This technology is already making videotape obsolete; hopefully, our schools will all be using digital editing technology in the very near future.

Robert F. Kenny, PhD, in his book, *Teaching TV Production in a Digital World* (Libraries Unlimited 2004), lays out a comprehensive course outline for upper-level students. His course of study includes learning equipment and lessons on media literacy, current trends in the broadcast industry, and extensive production vocabulary. There are teacher and student editions of this text available. Even if you teach a younger age group, you may want to use the teacher edition of this book as a resource and adapt the lessons to your student's abilities.

If you have no state guidelines or course descriptions to follow, ask around. What are your fellow media specialists doing in their schools? You will find a wide variety of activities taking place. Some schools use scanners and computer software to convert pictures to digital video format, which is then recorded onto tape or DVD. Ask your peers for copies of lesson plans and assignment sheets. Ask to view finished student projects to see what their classes are doing. Imagine what your students could do

A video head end unit controls the broadcast signal going out over a school's closed-circuit channels.

that is similar or different. Try to reproduce the projects yourself. Can you do them with the equipment available at your school? Are your students ready to master the skills required by the project? How difficult is the project? Do you need to make any adaptations for your students? How will you score the completed projects? Spend a good deal of time developing video projects for your students and you will be surprised at the results you get back in return. Students of all ages enjoy working with the medium of television and will rise to the challenge of producing quality projects. All you have to do is point them in the right direction.

There are many excellent books on television production available for the new media specialist. These books provide much more detailed information than is possible in these pages. Invest some of your budget money in purchasing these books and reading them. Look for books that are simple and easy for novices to understand. You will want books that are clearly illustrated with recent equipment, not machines

Sidebar 11.04 Voice of Experience from Claire: Control Your Studio Space!

Unfortunately, sooner or later you will have to take your TV studio apart. The custodians may want to clean the room or the principal may decide to relocate the space (hopefully to a larger facility). As scary as this may sound, you can take control of the situation and handle it with ease. Here are some tips.

1. Take pictures of the studio before breaking it down so you have a record of how everything is set up.

2. Create a diagram showing each piece of equipment and how things are interconnected.

3. Identify your cables. Tape a label at each end of each cable describing what piece of equipment it is connected to and which input jack it goes into.

4. Purchase cable ties from a local hardware or computer store. Carefully wrap and tie each cable so it does not come unwound and become knotted. Use large ziplock bags to group cables together by equipment. Label the bags so you can identify the cables if things become separated.

5. If you no longer have the original packaging for your equipment, purchase plastic tubs and bubble wrap to cushion things as you pack them for storage or moving.

6. Before packing things up, think about how you need to reassemble the equipment. Organize your packing so that equipment you need to access first is on top. Be sure to include the cables that match the equipment in each container so things are kept together.

7. Get some soft rags and cleaning solution. You'll want to dust equipment and wipe off cables. Studio equipment gets dusty, and cables that often lay on the floor become filthy. Wear old clothes on the day you plan to pack everything up. Be prepared to clean up as you break down your studio.

that are obviously 20 years old. Simple, easy to follow directions for projects on your students' level are mandatory, especially when you are new to the field. In a few years, you will be dreaming up and creating your own projects, but when you are just learning TV production skills yourself, take advantage of some of these instructional books developed by experts in the field. You'll be glad you did.

All This, and I Have to Produce the News, Too!

In addition to teaching media production skills, many media specialists find themselves in the position of producing a daily news show for the entire school. This can be frustrating when you yourself are just learning the equipment, but relax. Take a deep breath. It can be done.

First, find out how the news program has been done in the past. Perhaps your school has some archived tapes you can watch. Get a feel for the format of the show. The format is the order things are presented during the program. For example, at an elementary school, students might hear an announcer ask them

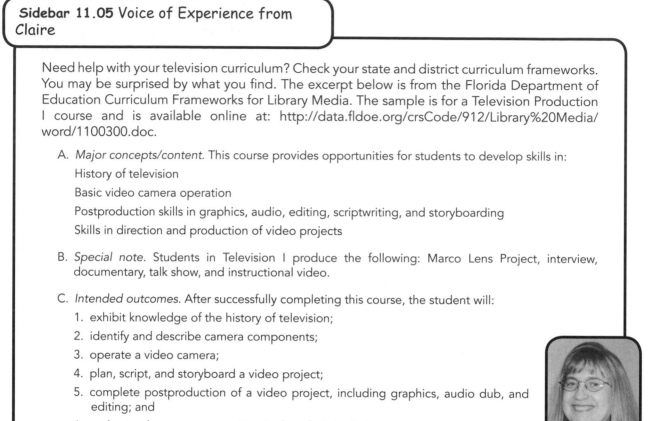

Sidebar 11.05 Voice of Experience from Claire

Need help with your television curriculum? Check your state and district curriculum frameworks. You may be surprised by what you find. The excerpt below is from the Florida Department of Education Curriculum Frameworks for Library Media. The sample is for a Television Production I course and is available online at: http://data.fldoe.org/crsCode/912/Library%20Media/word/1100300.doc.

A. *Major concepts/content.* This course provides opportunities for students to develop skills in:

History of television

Basic video camera operation

Postproduction skills in graphics, audio, editing, scriptwriting, and storyboarding

Skills in direction and production of video projects

B. *Special note.* Students in Television I produce the following: Marco Lens Project, interview, documentary, talk show, and instructional video.

C. *Intended outcomes.* After successfully completing this course, the student will:

1. exhibit knowledge of the history of television;
2. identify and describe camera components;
3. operate a video camera;
4. plan, script, and storyboard a video project;
5. complete postproduction of a video project, including graphics, audio dub, and editing; and
6. understand career opportunities in the television industry.

to rise for the national anthem and pledge to the flag. This may be followed by the word of the day, then a few students read announcements and a principal's message. Older students will have more complex news shows including student-produced segments on everything from last weekend's football game to the upcoming homecoming dance. Depending on the equipment level at the school, these news shows can be surprisingly sophisticated and begin to resemble network news programming. Once you've identified the format students and teachers at your school are used to, resolve to continue it for a little while. Once you master your equipment and have your students trained, you can begin to rearrange things.

After you've identified the format, ask about student news crew staff. Some school news crews rotate from among the student body. Others schools require students to apply for news crew positions. If their application is approved, these students may be in the class for a quarter, semester, or the entire year. Again, begin by working with the status quo at your school. Once you are used to the system, you can decide to leave it as is or propose changes you believe will improve the program. If you know who your news crew is, begin to get to know them. If the school year has not yet begun, make some phone calls. Perhaps you can arrange for them to come in before school starts for some initial training and placement into crew positions. Depending on the amount of equipment and the layout of your video production studio, you will probably need between 5 to 10 students on your crew. Positions include announcer (one or two), camera operator (one or two), graphics, video switcher, audio, and computer/teleprompter. Newer

Television production teacher Sam Morris uses digital editing software to produce a sample project for his students at Walker Middle School in Orlando, Florida.

schools with up-to-date equipment may need a crew member to control the lighting. Older students in high school programs also frequently have student floor directors and news show producers. Find out if any of your student crew have any prior experience and build on their prior knowledge. Ask students what positions they would feel comfortable doing. If possible, rehearse a few shows with them and see how they work in different positions, then assign them to a job they seem adept at doing. This will get you started. Make sure they understand that they may not do that particular job all the time; their position may change so that they can learn about all the jobs associated with the news program.

If you are new to television production and you do not have a lot of lead time to learn your equipment before beginning your job as media specialist, don't panic. Take a deep breath and resolve to keep the news show format as simple as possible while you learn the ropes. Even if you have to do a one-camera show for the first part of the school year with little or no bells and whistles—it's okay! Don't be deterred by the advice givers or the people who compare you to the previous media specialist who did all sorts of wonderful things. Remember who you are, and that you are learning. That previous media specialist who did all the wonderful things was once in your shoes and had to start at the beginning just as you are doing. The important thing is to build your program, not to replicate someone else's. So relax, breathe deeply, and open the door to your television studio. Build your skills one step, one day at a time, and most importantly, enjoy this wonderfully creative class with your students. You'll be surprised at how quickly it becomes your most favorite part of the day.

Author's note: We asked Libraries Unlimited author Keith Kyker, an expert on teaching television production in the classroom setting, to provide some advice for our readers. For more information about Keith and his coauthor, Chris Curchy, visit their Web site: http://www.SchoolTV.com.

Claire and Pat have asked me to provide some advice for media specialists who create TV news programs for their schools. Here are some of my ideas.

1. LEARN YOUR EQUIPMENT

You probably have several items of TV production equipment already at your school. As a media specialist, you need to learn how to use this equipment. The best way to learn is to experiment. Take the camcorder home for the weekend. Videotape a few scenes around the house or in a park. Learn how to play the tape on your television. Learn how to get the date and time off the screen so your program won't have "JAN 01, 2000" in the lower-left corner!

Spend a few minutes each afternoon experimenting with a new item of production equipment in your studio. Get the manual and work through a few sections. Learn how your equipment is connected so you'll know how to reconnect all of the video sources when the janitor accidentally disconnects your video mixer during spring cleaning.

Equipment challenges can appear at the most inopportune times. Maybe a menu screen appears on the television, or no sound comes from the announcer's microphone. A media specialist who understands how her studio equipment works can quickly troubleshoot simple problems, allowing production to continue.

Unfortunately, some educators take a different approach—they show their students the one button that they are allowed to push, and threaten dire consequences for attempting to use any of the equipment's advanced features. They continuously worry and fret about technical problems that might appear. My advice: don't put yourself in this situation. Learn about your equipment, and earn the security of knowing that you can solve problems as they arrive.

2. TEACH YOUR STUDENTS

This advice might seem unnecessary in a school setting. However, media specialists often discount the importance of actually teaching the skills of television production. Teach students about camera operation, shot composition, microphones, and graphics creation. If you need to learn this yourself, then grab one of our recent books (Kyker and Curchy, Libraries Unlimited). You can use the lessons that we created or make your own. Either way, plan several 15-minute sessions for teaching your news crew the basic skills of audio and video production.

3. INSIST ON QUALITY

Decide right now that you will produce a high-quality news program, and don't deviate from those plans. Am I saying that you have to have the latest and greatest production equipment? No. I'm saying that when you do something, do it with excellence.

For example, make sure that your announcers create a professional atmosphere for your program. Require them to sit up straight. Make sure that their hair is combed and their faces are washed. Make sure that they are dressed appropriately.

For years, I have enforced a "No T-shirt, No Logo" dress code with my student announcers. Young men wear a shirt with a collar, and young ladies wear an attractive blouse. I purchased

(*continued*)

several inexpensive polo shirts of various sizes and colors. Some students wear their own clothes, but others enjoy our simple wardrobe department. Also, we do not "advertise" for any clothing company that emblazons their name on every shirt they sell. Our dress code creates a crisp, smart-casual look, drawing attention to the program content, not our clothing.

Here's another example of quality; will your student be interviewing people around campus? If so, insist that they memorize their questions and practice the interview with you before recording with a guest. If they're not ready, they need more practice before going into the field.

You probably understand the point now. Insist on excellence. I have to smile when I watch the news shows my students made 12 years ago. I had just been hired as a media specialist at a middle school that had a camcorder, a microphone, and a VCR—that's it! We made some great news shows. We didn't have graphics and we couldn't edit, but the students were always well groomed, smiling, and prepared.

4. FOLLOW A FORMAT AND WRITE A SCRIPT

Make a list of the elements that will appear in your news show each day, and arrange them in an order that makes the most sense. This is your format. Your local network-affiliated news program follows a format every day—opening, welcome, news, weather, sports, human-interest story, and so forth.

Here's what a high school program's format might look like:

Opening

School announcements

Interview segment

Club news

Sports news, results, and schedule

Today in history

Ending credits

Of course, the content of each news show will change, but your audience and your news crew will appreciate the consistent format.

Format also applies to interviews, reports, and segments as well. For example, each interview ends with, "For Cougar News, I'm (*reporter's name*)." This format tag provides a graceful and professional way to end each segment, and allows your technical director or editor to know when the interview has concluded.

Your on-camera announcers (anchors) also deserve this professionalism and security. Give them a script to read. Assign the task of scriptwriting to an advanced student, or write the script yourself. On our Web site, SchoolTV.com you can learn about Easy Prompter, an inexpensive software program that transforms a PC into a teleprompting system. You can save scripts on the computer and simply make the necessary changes each day. Without a script, your anchors are simply reading stacks of announcements, most of which begin with the word, "ATTENTION!" Your anchors will sound like army drill sergeants: Attention, attention, ATTENTION! Provide a script instead.

5. IMPROVE SOME ASPECT OF YOUR SHOW EACH YEAR

As you continue your news show journey, try to improve one aspect of your program each year. Notice, I didn't say improve *every* aspect of your show each year. You can feel good about

(*continued*)

focusing on just one aspect each year. For example, you might decide to improve the graphics of your program. You could buy a character generator, or learn how to integrate computer graphics into your program. Here's another example: you could decide to replace your anchors' shared desk microphone with individual lavaliere (tie-pin) microphones. You can probably think of more examples.

Most media specialists have similar plans for their book collections. "This year, my first priority is to expand our reference collection," or, "This year, I plan to add a collection of historical fiction to support our social studies curriculum." Media specialists would love to improve the selection on every shelf each year, but we have to work within our budgets. You can apply the same principle to improving your news show production.

Hope that helps! For more information and advice, check out the Kyker/Curchy Web site at http://www.SchoolTV.com.

Keith Kyker

Sidebar 11.07 Sample News Show Format

Date_____

Taping for _____Day #_____

Switcher bus	Format—Description	Audio
Titlemaker	Graphic	CD
VCR	Opening (Friday—school song)	VCR
Camera 1	Desk—Anchors	Mics 1 & 2
VCR	Patriotic song/pledge	VCR
Camera 1 Title maker	Desk—Anchors Lunch menu	Mics 1 & 2
Camera 1	Announcements	Mics 1 & 2
Title maker	Anchors—Birthdays	Mics 1 & 2
Camera 1	Anchors Introduce special guest	Mics 1 & 2
Camera 2	Special guest	Mic 3
Camera 1	Desk—Anchors Closing	Mics 1 & 2
Title maker	Ending credits	CD

Provided by Amy Alday, media specialist at NorthLake Park Community School, Orlando, Florida.

Bibliography

Florida Department of Education. *Curriculum Framework—Grades 9–12, Adult Television Production I.* Available at: http://data.fldoe.org/crsCode/912/Library%20Media/pdf/1100300.pdf (accessed May 20, 2006).

Kenny, Robert F. *Teaching TV Production in a Digital World*, 2nd ed. Westport, CT: Libraries Unlimited, 2004.

Kyker, Keith, and Chris Curchy. *Educator's Survival Guide for Television Production and Activities.* Westport, CT: Libraries Unlimited, 2003.

Kyker, Keith, and Chris Curchy. *Television Production: A Classroom Approach.* Westport, CT: Libraries Unlimited, 2004.

Utz, Peter. "The 10 Most Important Things to Know about Buying Cameras/Camcorders. How to Buy a TV Monitor for Desktop Video. Field Mikes: Great Audio on Location. VCR, TV, and Camcorder Connections: Taming the Wire Jungle." *How-to Info and Books for Videographers: Learn Video Equipment Set-up, Operation and Production.* Available at: http://videoexpert.home.att.net/index.htm.

Whittaker, Ron. *Television Production A Free, Interactive Course in Studio and Field Production.* Available at: http://www.internetcampus.com/tvp_ind.htm.

Part III

Long-term Vision— Managing Your Collection

12

Collection Development

What exactly is included in your collection? Your collection consists of everything a patron checks out or uses in the library media center. In the past, that may have included just the physical items on the shelves. Today, that includes any information your patrons can find, not only on your shelves, but also beyond your walls using the online resources you select for your school. Your collection is the reason the library exists and, therefore, helping it grow is one of your most important jobs.

With so much information bombarding us, how do we ever decide what to buy? A collection development policy is a good starting point for purchasing decisions. This policy is a written plan developed to prioritize, support, and explain your purchasing strategy for the library collection. Creating a collection development policy results in a well-rounded and up-to-date collection of books, magazines, newspapers, online databases, equipment, and audiovisual materials, and is worth the time it takes to write or update each year. The written plan states goals for your collection that should integrate with your school goals. It explains the purpose for purchasing items and who is responsible for buying, processing, and caring for items purchased. Update your policy annually to reflect changes in your school curriculum and community.

For many overworked media specialists, taking the time to write out a collection development policy seems like extra work. However, it is important to have a written collection development plan in order to articulate your short- and long-term goals to your principal and community. Even if you are the only media specialist in a school, you are not working in isolation. Establishing a plan to acquire materials that meet all the needs of your school is an important responsibility. A written collection development plan communicates your rationale for purchases and will help you in the event that some of your purchases are questioned. By following professional guidelines, you will ensure that you make informed decisions benefiting all your stakeholders as you build your collection.

Most school systems have a comprehensive collection development policy for the entire district. Use this policy as a starting point and customize it to create a collection development plan that is unique to your school. The procedures you create for your school will increase the effectiveness of your staff as your collection grows and changes. As you begin the process of writing your collection development plan take time to consider these things.

Know Your Collection

Before you can begin purchasing things for the media center, you have to know what you already own. Take time to explore the media center shelves; get to know your collection. Notice what areas lack materials requested by teachers and students. Assessment should be frequent and ongoing. As you get to know your collection, you will notice holes in areas and find out which books are not meeting the needs of your students. Your media management program allows you to print data that will help you analyze your collection. Find out how many books you have in each area of the library and find out the average age of that Dewey category. Many book vendors also provide free collection analysis. Use your management software reports and the vendor provided analysis to identify the strengths and weaknesses of your collection.

Non-Fiction Collection Information		
■ 30 years or older	1783	33.39%
☐ 20 to 30 years	554	10.37%
■ 10 to 20 years	1193	22.34%
☐ 10 years or newer	1809	33.88%
18.24% of Non-Fiction items in this collection were published in the past 5 years.		

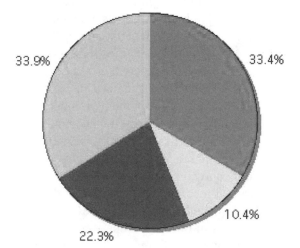

How old is your collection? This table and pie graph from SUNLINK, Florida's K12 union catalog, represents the age of one school's *nonfiction* collection. Tools like this are available from many management softwares and vendors. Using them can help you determine where to best allocate your budget money.

Weed this book! Even though the rest of the book may still be useable, the damaged binding will lead to its rapid deterioration and makes it unappealing for checkout.

Statistics alone will not paint an entire picture of your collection, however. Analyze the condition of your collection by physically examining every section of the library. How do the books, videos, and DVDs look? Are some old and unappealing? Analyze the content of your collection. Are you missing balanced viewpoints? Critically consider your findings and compare them to your curriculum needs. Write your collection goals based on these findings.

Know Your Students

Knowing your students also drives your purchasing. What level are your readers? What interests your students? What do they do for entertainment? What is their ethnic makeup? What is their socioeconomic makeup? What languages are spoken in the homes of your students? Do you have students with special needs? You can gather this information through everyday interaction with your students. You might also create a student survey in order to have statistics to back up your findings. Tell students you will publish the results and they will anxiously await your analysis. Use the survey to decide what is working and what is not working in the library media center. Also, use it to determine what areas need bolstering depending on the interests and needs of the students.

Know Your Curriculum

Be familiar with your state standards. Know what benchmarks teachers must meet so that your collection can enhance their teaching. Know your teachers' passions. If your science teacher spends extra weeks on hurricanes because he finds them fascinating, look for nonfiction and fiction materials that will appeal to him and his students. Gather information about your curriculum by using your state standards and by surveying teachers for their needs. Surveys not only provide information for you, but also give information to teachers about your program that they may not already know.

Sidebar 12.01 Media Center Student Survey

It is the goal of the media staff at Timber Creek High School to offer all the resources and services that will help you be successful in your studies and enrich your reading enjoyment. Please help us by completing this survey. Circle the one answer that best answers the questions below. Feel free to make additional comments in the margins or on the back of this survey. Your input is important to us!

Grade Level: Freshman   Sophomore   Junior   Senior

How often do you visit the media center *per week* outside of class time?

Never   1 to 3 times   4 to 7 times   7 to 10 times   Almost every day

When do you most often visit the media center outside of class time?

Before school   During lunch   After school   I don't

What are the most common purposes for your visits to the media center? (circle all that apply)

Work on class assignments   Research   Check out books for class

Use the computers for class work or research   Check out books for pleasure reading

Use the computers for games and unrelated school work   Just to hang out with friends

I only visit when a teacher brings the class   To read   Do homework

Other _____

How often do you visit the Orange County Public Library *per month*?

Never   1 to 3 times   4 to 7 times   7 to 10 times   On a weekly bases.

Please list two or three of your favorite fiction authors or titles:

_____   _____
_____   _____

What do you most prefer to check out?

Paperback books   Hardcover books   Doesn't matter

Please list your favorite magazines you would like the media center to subscribe to:

_____   _____
_____   _____

Think about the research you did this year. From your experience in the TCHS media center, what types of nonfiction topics do we need to help you with research for your classes?

Examples: books on drugs, prehistoric life, political leaders, and so forth.

_____   _____
_____   _____

Write any additional comments or suggestions on the back of this paper. Thanks for your help!!

Know Your School Community

Survey your parents. Evaluate what is important to them and what their expectations are of your school and your library media center. If you are part of parent organizations at your school, such as the PTA or the SAC, get to know the committee members. Invite them to be a part of your School Library Media Advisory Committee, which is put in place to advise you on matters important to your stakeholders. This committee is also valuable in the event of a book challenge.

Consider materials that may be challenged. Knowing your school community will help you be prepared for complaints. Be familiar with the ALA's Freedom to Read Act. It supports the tenets of intellectual freedom. Our position as library media specialists compels us to make purchasing decisions for all of our readers. We must not shy away from controversial material; however, we want to choose wisely using our collection development policy as our guide. We must consider grade level, social and ethnic makeup, and community values and mores when we purchase. Are you willing to support your purchase if there is an objection? Know your school district's policies to confirm that you are choosing wisely.

Sidebar 12.02 Voice of Experience from Pat

Several years ago when I opened a new high school, I was told all freshmen would take biology so there was no need to purchase materials on earth science. Two years later, the curriculum changed and we are now teaching earth science courses. To meet this need, we are focusing on purchasing books in that content area. As curriculum needs change, so does our collection.

Content area purchases are similar for every school, but your collection must provide materials that will enhance the learning of *your* students. People are basically interested in other people like themselves, so your shelves should reflect that. Local celebrations and history should be taken into account. All students should be encouraged to excel beyond even their own expectations, but consider professions of parents in your community. Support them by including information about their careers and lives.

The Collection Development Plan

After analysis of your collection and your stakeholders, you are ready to create a written plan. This plan includes long- and short-term goals so that when money is available, you are ready to create a budget and implement your plan. Your written plan must include the long-term goals for your collection. Here you set forth your philosophy on developing a collection that meets the needs of your school. You explain how you are going to carry out this plan. Your district collection policy probably includes a selection policy, a format for creating a budget, and the process for ordering materials. It also includes procedures for handling materials when they arrive and how to maintain and continually evaluate your collection. Using this policy, you create a plan that includes a yearly budget based on your analysis of your current collection. Here you include short-term goals that need to be funded in order to reach your long-term goals.

Collection Goals

Articulate your collection goals to your principal. After explaining your goals and objectives and making sure he understands that you have a plan to accomplish these goals, your principal will understand why you need money, staffing, and other resources to build a quality collection. Your principal may ask you to articulate your goals for the next year when you submit your budget each year. He or she may ask you to prioritize your plan in case all the funding you need is not available at this time. Even if your principal does not ask for a copy of your future plans, submit your goals to him or her anyway. He or

Sidebar 12.03 Timber Creek High School Faculty Survey

Please help us to help you. Fill out this short survey to let us know how we are doing and how we can serve you better. Please return this completed form to your media specialist.

1. Do you use the media center for...? (check all that apply)
   ___ Entire class checking out books.
   ___ Individual passes.
   ___ Research using books.
   ___ Research using computers.
   ___ Meetings.
   ___ I have never sent students or brought students to the media center.

2. A media specialist has assisted my class by . . . ? (check all that apply)
   ___ Collaborating and helping teach a research unit.
   ___ Giving book talks to encourage reading.
   ___ Helping facilitate a contest to encourage literary skills.
   ___ Locating materials and sending them to my classroom.
   ___ Conducting professional training.
   ___ Other _____

3. My students use the online databases purchased by the media center . . .
   ___Often   ___Sometimes   ___Never

4. Do you have the technology you need in the classroom to facilitate learning?
   ___ Yes, I have all I need
   ___ No, I need the following items for my classroom _____

5. When I check out AV equipment from the media center . . .
   ___ It is always available and works well.
   ___ We need more equipment because what I want is always checked out.
   ___ What I want is not available. It is_____.
   ___ I never check out equipment from the media center.

6. Does our print collection (books, magazines, newspapers) meet your needs?
   ___ Yes, I find lots of materials on all topics.
   ___ No, we need more information on _____.
   ___ I never read books or assign them to my students.

7. I take advantage of these media services . . . (check all that apply)
   ___ Laminating   ___Bulletin board paper
   ___ Material requests (books, magazines, and videos)
   ___ Die cuts (shapes/letters)   ___Scantron
   ___ Locate materials via SUNLINK   ___Reserving materials for classes

8. Does our nonprint collection (videos, DVDs, Books on Tape) meet your needs?
   ___ Yes, I find lots of materials on all topics.
   ___ No, we need more information on _____.

(continued)

___ I never watch videos in my class.

___ I never use Books on Tape.

9. I peruse the media center's professional materials . . .

___Often   ___Sometimes   __Never

10. Do you use the class sets of novels available in the media center?

___Often   ___Sometimes   __Never

Please comment on our . . .

Strengths_____

Weaknesses_____

Sidebar 12.04 Collection Development Goals

These goals were developed by Pat Franklin for her school. Writing goals help you formalize your thoughts and define your vision for your media center. List four goals you have for your media center and describe how you plan to meet them during the school year.

TIMBER CREEK HIGH SCHOOL

Library Media Center

Goals 2006 to 2007

1. To increase collaboration with science teachers. Collaborating with science teachers will increase student standardized test scores as students become better purveyors of information. We will target ninth grade integrated science classes.
2. To weed, update, and increase materials on physical and earth sciences. This will support emphasis on the science curriculum as students prepare for state tests.
3. To investigate online databases which specialize in science materials.
4. To evaluate need and purchase new technology to support curriculum (LCD projectors, laptops, appropriate cables).
5. To evaluate and adjust subscriptions to leisure and professional magazines with an emphasis on science publications.

she will know you have researched and contemplated your program and have a plan to make your media center better each year.

Articulate your goals to your school community. Talk to your teachers about collaborations that will encourage their classes to use the media center to its maximum. Attend PTA and SAC meetings so that you can communicate with parents about your media program. Many times these stakeholders will find funding for collection development if they know your library media program is an energetic, effective one.

Create a Selection Policy

Set standards as to how you will select materials for your school. The standards should address the quality of the information as well as the format of the material. What tools will you use to select the appropriate materials? What criteria will you apply to taking books out of your collection?

Selection tools provide an authoritative source to help you become familiar with the many new materials on the market. This helps library media specialists avoid their own prejudices and widens their knowledge of materials. Recognized selection tools include:

- Reputable, professional selection guides such as H. W. Wilson's *Senior High School Catalog*, *Middle and Junior High School Catalog*, or *Children's Library Catalog*. Many selection guides are in book form, but many are also found through Internet sources.
- Book reviews in professional magazines and journals such as *School Library Media Activities Monthly*, *School Library Journal*, *BookList*, *Book Links*, or *Library Media Connections*.
- Salespeople often offer new materials at a discount with the advantage of being able to touch and look at the material before purchase. Vendors may come to your school or be available at state and national conferences. Make sure you purchase from vendors that are approved by your school district.
- Listen to suggestions. Ask students, teachers, administrators, and parents for their input, but their suggestions must meet your selection criteria before actually purchasing the material.
- Donated materials that meet the standards of your collection development policy are useful. Evaluate donated materials carefully; sometimes groups with particular agendas donate items to school libraries that may be inappropriate or even controversial in nature. Make sure these materials meet your standards by evaluating for content, condition, and age.

Selection Considerations

After analysis of your collection, you will become aware of what you need. By using reputable selection tools, you are aware of what is available. However, there are still other factors to consider before deciding what to purchase.

- Does the material have literary merit and add value to your collection?
- Is the material accurately written by authoritative sources and published by a reputable company?
- Will the book fit on the shelves without falling behind the shelf? Is the binding of a quality that will withstand many readings?
- Is the video or audio format one that you have equipment to support?
- Is the reading level or appropriateness of the materials right for your students? Does it treat the subject in a fair and just manner? Is the scope of the materials too limited or too advanced for your students? Does it appeal to diverse groups? Does it foster all viewpoints, even if you don't agree with them personally?
- Is this the only material available on the topic you need?
- Is the look or arrangement of material detrimental or helpful to your students?

- If you are buying equipment, is it easy to use with simple, yet complete instructions?
- If the material is for limited use (such as magazines), is it necessary? Can you find it in other formats?
- If it is an electronic format, how will you get the information to your students about the availability of the information?
- Have you considered cost? Is this the best price you can find?

Professional Materials

Don't forget your teachers—they need a professional library. In a teacher workroom or an area of the media center, create a collection for teachers, staff, and interns. In this area, put books and audiovisual materials on best practices in teaching. Include materials on the philosophy of education, outstanding lesson plans, and emerging educational trends. Also, purchase practical items such as helpful guides for taking your state teacher's exams or tips on completing the National Board certification process. Ask teachers working on advanced degrees to recommend materials they have used or learned about in their classes. Use the same selection policies that you do for any part of the library media center.

Communicate with Your Stakeholders

Communicate with students, teachers, administrators, parents, and community about your plan to update and modernize your library media center. Explain what areas you will concentrate on first and why. Parents and other community members may have an interest in specific areas and may want to help with time or monetary contributions. Have a party when your new books are in! For example, invite the math and science teachers to a small breakfast after you have updated your Dewey Decimal 500 section. Leave the books on display all day so students can browse through them. Put them on a new bookrack for a week or two before they are shelved to draw attention to your new items.

Weeding

At the same time you are considering materials for purchase, you must consider items already on your shelves. After evaluating your collection, you will find materials that are inappropriate for a variety of reasons. We call the process of discarding materials from our collections weeding. If done consistently, your media center remains a vibrant, exciting garden of knowledge. Have you ever noticed your garden after you weed it? The process of removing the weeds makes the plants more visible. All of the flowers and shrubs seem to pop out and ask you to take notice. This also happens in your library media center when you have removed the old, worn books. Your teachers and staff will be able to find what they need quickly and with more ease.

Many library media specialists make excuses for not discarding materials. They have a problem with throwing things away. They fear limited resources because of dwindling dollars. They fear retribution by teachers who want unlimited amounts of materials in their content areas. They say it takes too much time away from other tasks. Although all media specialists share some of these feelings, it is ultimately necessary to discard items. Although it is time consuming, weeding must be ongoing and systematic. One way to make sure you are assessing your entire collection is to choose a different area of your media center to weed each month.

Your weeding criteria must be a part of your written collection development plan. There are many sources to help you determine how long it is appropriate to keep materials in different Dewey Decimal categories and how to know if an item needs to be weeded.

Weeding old, out-of-date books helps students locate the current resources they need for projects and assignments.

Reasons to Weed Materials

- It is old! Books become torn, yellowed, or damaged. Videos become outdated. Take away the old, dusty raggedy materials, and your students will think you have purchased all new books and videos.
- It is not current. Books and videos that use about career titles such as a "mailman" are undoubtedly out-of-date with old, unreliable information about letter carriers. Covers that show styles of 20 years ago alert readers and viewers that the material is dated.
- Information is inaccurate or biased. State books may show populations that are 10 years old and industries that have long left the state. Find a newer book that contains information you need without being misleading or wrong.
- The shelves are too crowded. Crowded shelves give the impression you do not need funding for new materials.
- Student needs, interests, and checkout patterns have changed. In the 1980s, "chic lit" included *Sweet Valley High* books and in the 1990s it was *The Baby-sitters Club*. Today, girls like *Gossip Girls* and *A-List* books. Tomorrow it will be another series.

Check to see if your district has policies for discarding books. If possible, have a book sale for old fiction books. Charge a small donation and you will win friends and not have to worry about how to

Sidebar 12.05 Try Target Weeding Using Guides like the SUNLINK Weed of the Month

© The Weed of the Month is a project of SUNLINK, administered by the University of Central Florida, College of Education, under a grant from the Florida Department of Education, Office of School Library Media Services
This example from October, 2005.

WHY WEED WORLD WAR II?

The year 2005 marks the 60th anniversary of the end of World War II and the first anniversary of the WWII Memorial in Washington D.C. Recognizing that under five million U.S. veterans now survive of the more than 16 million who served in those war years, a flurry of commemorative events, educational activities, and publishing is currently taking place. There are wonderful new and interesting titles available to supplement or replace aging titles in school library collections.

SUGGESTED DEWEY NUMBERS TO CHECK:

Check 940.53 (World War II, 1939-1945) and 940.54 (Military History of World War II). It's especially important to review your AV and reference collections due to the number of new AV titles and reference resources recently released. There may be some titles in the biography section that should be updated.

SPECIFIC CRITERIA FOR WEEDING:

As with any historical event, save any primary source materials that are still appropriate for the collection but reconsider titles that deal with interpretation and controversies that might have changed over the years. Don't keep "post war" accounts of WWII countries that are misleading to the current state of those countries. Be wary of keeping encyclopedias that are old, especially if located in the reference collection. Older AV titles may have the same archival photographs as newer titles, but new replacement AV titles will likely include enhanced photographs as well as reenactments and may include contrasting current views of those past locations in order to make the events more interesting to students today. Replace any "borderline" print or AV titles with some of the attractive new titles on the market now due to the renewed interest in this time period.

Consider Weeding Titles Like These:

- The case against Adolf Eichmann, 1960.
- Causes of World War II [filmstrip], 1970.
    - Illustrated World War II encyclopedia : an unbiased account of the most devastating war known to mankind, 1978.

Consider Adding Titles Like These:

- Always remember me : how one family survived World War II, 2005. Grades 2-4. ISBN 0689869207
- B-17 flying legend [videorecording], 2004. Grades 7-up. ISBN 1568391382

Sidebar 12.06 Weeding Guidelines

The guidelines in this chart are used by one of the authors at her school. You may want to set up a schedule so that you weed your collection routinely, concentrating on certain Dewey areas each year. In this way, you can be sure you routinely weed the entire collection every three to five years, depending on the schedule you establish.

Dewey Decimal Number	Area	Guidelines
000–099	General	Usually 5 years, but review technology-related items after 3 years.
100–199	Philosophy	Usually 5–10 years. Check use and interest.
200–299	Religion	Usually 5–10 years. Check use and balance.
300–399	Social Sciences	Usually 5–10 years. Careers 3–5 years. Check currency and appeal.
400–499	Language	Usually 5–10 years. Historical perspectives may be older.
500–599	Science and Math	Usually 5 years. Currency is very important in this area.
600–699	Applied Sciences (Tech nology)	Usually 5 years. Review content and format.
700–799	Arts	Usually 5–10 years. Check sports figures, art, and music for currency and wear.
800–899	Literature	Usually 5–10 years, except for classics, but update for format and appearance.
900–999	History	Usually 5 years. Check for accuracy and bias. Check travel books and maps for accuracy.
Bio	Biography	Usually 10 years. Check for appeal of pop culture biographies.
Fic	Fiction	Weed by appearance, bias, and appeal.
Ref	Reference	Same criteria as nonfiction. Important to keep up to date. Encyclopedias 3–5 years.
	Periodicals	Usually 1–2 years.
	Professional Material	Usually 5–8 years.
	Audiovisual	Usually 5–10 years. Check need and appearance for currency.

dispose of your weeded books. Don't let teachers intimidate you into keeping old materials because they are afraid you won't have enough books for their next project. Stick to your weeding guidelines. It is better to have fewer books with accurate information than lots of books with inaccurate information. Another caution—teachers will often ask for the weeded books to keep in their classrooms. Before giving the books to them, consider what types of books they are. If they are weeded nonfiction books,

Examine books as you weed. Be sure each copy meets your criteria for removal from the collection.

allowing students to use them in the classroom may promote learning inaccurate and outdated information. If they no longer belong in your media center, perhaps they should not be in a classroom, either. Sometimes it is best to remove old, weeded materials from the school property. Teachers will only be upset until that new book order comes in and they see all your beautiful new books. If your school has been neglected for a number of years, consider having a weeding party. Invite your library media specialist friends to your school to weed sections of your collection; serve pizza, snacks, and soda. Refreshments are a small price to pay for their expertise and the opportunity to network with your peers. At the end of your weeding party, you'll be amazed at the amount of work that has been accomplished and thrilled with the many new ideas and insights you've picked up along the way.

Gifts

Gifts of new books that fit your selection policy are welcomed! Gifts of old worn out books are not acceptable. Why process a book you would normally weed because of its old copyright date, its poor condition, or its inaccurate information? But we never want to alienate friends of the media center by not accepting generous gifts. Accept all gifts, but find a place for everything. One of your teachers may want all those old *National Geographics* for her students to cut up for a poster project. An ongoing paperback exchange rack or "Free Stuff" table in the media center will make those older donations disappear.

Setting up a give-away table for unneeded items allows teachers and students to pick up things they can use or read.

Ordering and Purchasing

Now that you have defined your collection development policy, weeded your collection, and set your goals for the new school year, it is time to develop a purchasing plan. Develop a five-year plan that tells your administration the order in which you plan to update your media center and why you chose this particular plan of action. Include this plan with your budget. A thorough knowledge of the curriculum and your resources will help administrators understand why you need specific money to meet your collection development goals. This depends on the size of your school and the state of your collection. If your school has been consistently weeded and updated, your plan will be minimal. If your school has been neglected, choose the areas most used by your clientele to update first. Your next budget should include a section to provide money to purchase replacement materials for at least one area of your media center.

Dewey Decimal Number	Area	Cycle Guidelines for a 5-year Purchasing Plan
		Note—Concentrate on the Area(s) Shown Each Year, But Do Not Ignore Other Areas If there is a Legitimate Reason to Purchase for that Section.
000–099	General	Year 1—But review technology section every third year.
100–199	Philosophy	Year 1—Depending on your school curriculum, this may not be a very large area in your collection.
200–299	Religion	Year 1—On an annual basis, review your student population and update selected religions if your school population requires it.
300–399	Social Sciences	Year 2—Review careers and testing every third year. Update section on law each year if needed, depending on current events.
400–499	Language	Year 2—On an annual basis, review your student population and update selected languages if your school population requires it.
500–599	Science & Math	Year 2—Currency is very important in this area. Be aware of scientific breakthroughs and discoveries. Update as needed.
600–699	Applied Sciences (Technology)	Year 3—In this area, be aware of updating current technologies and medical information annually if needed.
700–799	Arts and Sports	Year 3—You may want to add a few updated sports and music titles each year for currency.
800–899	Literature	Year 3—Depending on your school curriculum, this may not be a very large area in your collection.
900–999	History	Year 4—This is a large area. Concentrate on it exclusively for the year, updating country and state books, history, and so forth.
Bio	Biography	Year 5—Update annually for a few popular figures of interest to your students and important people such as a new president or prominent world figure.
Fic	Fiction	Annually include new award winners, popular series, and entertainment books.
Ref	Reference	Follow the same pattern as nonfiction, updating the reference areas at the same time you do that area of general nonfiction. Purchase one or two new encyclopedia sets each year to replace outdated volumes. Year 5—Purchase new large display atlases.
	Periodicals	Review annually and alter your order as needed
	Professional Materials	Year 5—Update any important new trends or educational policy concerns annually as needed.
	Audiovisual	Follow the same pattern as nonfiction, updating audiovisuals at the same time you do that area of general nonfiction.

Use your selection tools to maintain an ongoing list of books and materials you wish to purchase. After books are selected, double-check your list against your collection to avoid unwanted duplicate titles. It is impossible for any of us to memorize our entire collection. This double-checking helps to eliminate extraneous purchases. Many book vendors now offer free online ordering which can match up potential titles with your collection, checking for duplicates by using the book's International Standard Book Number (ISBN). These services also allow you to keep ongoing order lists on their Web sites and make it possible to know the total cost of an order, including processing and shipping, as you develop you list. Since they are online, it is also possible to access your order list from home during nonworking hours, which can be useful for busy media specialists.

Many schools have standing order materials. These are usually for updates on reference materials or series that are updated or include supplemental texts. These materials are automatically shipped and invoiced to your school. Make sure your district collection policy does not restrict or prohibit standing orders and be sure your annual budget contains sufficient funds to cover any standing order you make. Most orders, however, are new and must be initiated by generating a purchase order. Request price quotes form various sources before you make a final decision. When money is available, write purchase orders that reflect the goals of your library media center program. Your purchase orders should reflect your commitment to quality, well-selected materials. Keep a running list of materials you have found in selection resources or that have been suggested by parents, teachers, or students. Use this to prioritize your purchases.

Order as many items as you can that are fully processed. This means that books and audiovisual items have bar codes and spine labels that are compatible with your media management system. For more information about handling your books and other materials once they are received, refer to chapter 15, "Cataloging and Processing."

Maintaining Your Collection

As the school year progresses, you must constantly maintain your collection. You will see books that are damaged, and you must decide if the damage is easily repaired (a new book cover) or if the book should be discarded. Equipment will break or need cleaning. Routinely performing preventative maintenance will help you maintain your collection. Repair damaged books before they are beyond repair. When changing lamps on overheads and multimedia projectors, clean the equipment to prevent dust buildup. Clean VCR heads and test DVD players to make sure they are working. Make sure patrons are aware of how to use each piece of equipment before it is checked out.

Evaluating Your Collection

Routinely evaluate your collection. You can informally evaluate materials as you check them in and out to your patrons. When you order new materials, check them against materials you already have in that content area or by that author. Formal evaluations are done each year as you prepare your plan and budget for each new school year.

Perform a complete inventory of your entire collection each year. Even if your district office or your principal does not ask you for a copy of this inventory, it is an important part of your collection development process. Inventory is an integral part of keeping track of how your library media center is growing. Is one area constantly neglected? Inventory numbers will tell you. Have you lost an unexpectedly large number of items in your collection? Maybe security is a problem.

The best part of taking an inventory is that while you are physically touching each item in your collection, you can make a quick assessment if the item is cataloged in an area unsuitable for optimum use or simply placed in the wrong area on the shelves. Many missing materials are found in this way. By physically examining each item, a determination can be made as to the need of discarding particular items.

Taking an inventory also alerts you to problems in your database of materials. As you work through the inventory process, you will notice if things are not correctly entered in the management system. Correct any problems you find immediately.

Inventory may be taken at any time of the year. The most effective way to perform an inventory is to continue to circulate while the inventory is ongoing. In this way, the number of materials physically inventoried by the staff is minimal since most of your items are circulating. You need not close any areas while taking inventory. The media center is closed often enough because of meetings, testing, and other community or school functions. Closing it for a simple inventory procedure limits your patrons even more. The media center must be perceived as an accessible area where students and teachers can get help at any time.

Bibliography

Baltimore County Public School Selection Criteria for School Library Media Center Collections. Available at: http://www.milbank.k12.sd.us/jschwab/Default.htm.

Baumbach, Donna J., and Linda L. Miller. *Less is More: A Practical Guide to Weeding School Library Collections.* Chicago, IL: American Library Association, 2006. Burgett, James, John M. Harr, and Linda L. Phillips. Collaborative Collection Development: *A Practical Guide for Your Library.* Chicago: American Library Association, 2004.

California Department of Education. *Weeding the School Library.* Available at: http://www.cde.ca.gov/ci/cr/lb/documents/schoollibweedng.pdf.

Harbour, Denise. "Collection Mapping." *The Book Report* (March–April 2002): 6–10.

Kerby, Ramona. "Weeding Your Collection." *School Library Media Activities Monthly* 18, no. 6 (2004): 22–24.

Kramer, Pamela K. *Weeding As A Part of Collection Development.* Available at: http://www.islma.org/pdf/weeding.pdf.

Lowe, Karen. "Providing Curriculum Support in the School Library Media Center: Resource Alignment." *Knowledge Quest* 32, no. 1 (2003): 46.

Lukenbill, W. Bernard. *Collection Development for a New Century in the School Library Media Center.* Westport, CT: Libraries Unlimited, 2002.

Van Orden, Phyllis J., and Bishop Kay. *The Collection Program in Schools: Concepts, Practices and Information Sources.* Englewood, CO: Libraries Unlimited. 2001.

13

Resources for the Journey

Media specialists strive constantly to reach out to students in unique ways. It doesn't matter if we are trying to cultivate a new lesson designed to teach critical thinking skills or simply connecting students with interesting books that may trigger a lifelong love of reading. One of the things new media specialists learn quickly about the job is that cultivating resources to help with the work is essential. We cannot do the job alone; it is bigger than all of us combined, much less the individual media specialist usually working at each school. In order to last on the job, we must develop resources that will provide us with the means to survive and thrive. We need to know where we can turn for assistance when we need it, whether the help we need is financial, professional, or personal. The successful media specialist cultivates resources for the road.

Financial Resources

Money is a constant issue for a media specialist. Your budgets are strained and balancing your spending to get through the year is a difficult task. The constant search for funding can consume all your time, taking you away from valuable student contact, so it is important to develop an awareness of the financial resources available to you. In previous chapters, the importance of writing a budget was stressed. Your budget identifies your planned expenditures for the school year and the estimated costs. Include budget lines for all the areas of your media program, such as supplies, online databases, equipment purchases, and maintenance costs, audiovisuals, books, magazines, student programs, and so forth. Make sure your budget is realistic; don't inflate costs, but be sure they accurately reflect your needs. Present your budget to your principal and discuss the plans it represents. You may not get all the funding you ask for, but not presenting a budget insures an uncertain financial future for your program. Once your principal has established how much money can be allotted to the media center, revise your budget to reflect the actual amount and discuss it with him again. Communicating with your administration about plans is important. Many times administrators receive additional monies once the school year gets going. Let your administration know what you had to trim from your budget and they will keep your worthy projects in mind when they come into extra funds.

Besides the school budget, there are additional resources available to most school programs. Start networking with your school staff and ask about additional funding sources. Your principal may know about a local business group that would like to do something for the school. Perhaps you could approach them about donating money for new library books or covering the cost of a new piece of video equipment. Your school parent teacher organization raises funds for the school; they are a potential source of money. If your school has a school advisory council, find out if they receive funding from the state or district. You can approach them for funding to purchase something specific for your program or collection. Many school districts offer grant programs for teachers—find out if your district does this and learn how to apply for funding.

Fund-raising is another way to get money for your program. Before you begin a fund-raiser, check with your administration about the rules governing these events. Schools often have specific guidelines for holding fund-raisers; you don't want to risk your professional reputation by mishandling a fund-raiser. Common fund-raisers for media centers include book fairs, book donation programs, and selling school supplies. Many creative media specialists take advantage of their video production capabilities to make and sell special videos. They may make a video yearbook, for example, or a sports highlights video profiling the school's teams and games. Whatever fund-raiser you decide on, be sure to organize carefully. Advertise your fund-raiser to the students and community. Let them know how the monies raised will benefit your program to encourage participation.

Many school libraries charge fines for overdue books. Charging fines is controversial and in some states is against the law, but can raise money to support a variety of programs. If overdue fines are customary in your school, find out what rules apply to spending this money. Often fine money must be spent directly for students. In that case, these funds might be useful for purchasing books or prizes and incentives for students.

Grant writing is another way to increase funding for your program. Many major corporations and foundations sponsor grant competitions throughout the year. Selecting and writing a grant requires careful attention to detail. Determine the project you need to fund, then research available grants to determine which opportunities match up with your project. Do your research and write the grant carefully to increase your chances of winning the funding you need. To locate information about grants and grant writing, check with your district office. Most school districts have professional grant writers on-staff. These people can assist you in locating appropriate grants for your project and creating the paperwork needed for your application. Consulting with your district office on grant writing is also a good idea in case there are any rules for submitting grants. Be sure you ask about procedures for submitting grants for your school before you spend hours of time writing a grant you may not be able to submit because of district policy.

Professional Resources

Most schools usually have only one media specialist, and it is easy for that one media specialist to begin to feel isolated. Because of this, it is important for new media specialists to develop professional resources to help them adjust to their new positions. Within your school, seek out experienced staff such as department chairs, team leaders, or grade-level chairpersons. Begin to cultivate professional relationships with them. You will need the collective experience and memory these people can share with you. They can explain how or why things are the way they are at your school and in the media center. This information will be of great value.

Get to know the other resource teachers at your school. These positions go by many names, such as, classroom resource teacher, instructional coach, testing coordinator, reading resource teacher, and so forth. Each of these faculty members are in a similar position to the media specialist because there is usually only one per school. Find out about their jobs and begin to discuss how you can collaborate with them to assist teachers and students. As you begin to work with the resource teachers at your school, they will help you to learn the ropes in your building and district.

Outside of your school site, look for professional support on the district level. Does your district have a supervising media specialist? Get to know this person and take advantage of his or her expertise. What other schools are near to your own? Call or email their media specialists, ask if you can drop by for a brief meeting and to see their media centers. These professional contacts will be invaluable; sometimes you need the knowledge only a fellow media specialist possesses. If your district does not have a mentor program for new media specialists, contacting your peers at nearby schools may be the key to developing a mentoring relationship with an experienced school library professional.

Join your local and state professional organization. Attend meetings and conferences so that you can network with other media specialists. Join a Listserv or a Web site such as LM_Net (http://www.eduref. org/lm_net/) which allows you to communicate with your fellow media specialists. Take time to read professional journals. Besides much needed product and book reviews, these magazines are idea treasure chests. They contain great articles about best practices in school library programs, hints for how to manage your media center, and the latest research supporting student learning and school libraries.

Your professional support network is important. It will help you through the first several years of being a media specialist. On days when things are not going smoothly, you need someone you can call to find out how to work your media management program, what the required purchasing procedure is, or how you can teach media literacy. Don't feel that you are imposing. Your colleagues will delight in helping you become a terrific media specialist, and in a few years, you can return the favor by helping the next generation of new media specialists.

Personal Support

Teaching is a time-consuming profession. It is easy for your job to take over your life when you work in the media center. You usually do not have a planning period like most teachers, so you come early and stay late. In addition to regular teaching duties, you must develop and maintain collections of books, videos, and audiovisual equipment. Staying current requires time spent studying trends in new technologies, publishing, and educational best practices. Many new media specialists are surprised to find they are working harder and longer than they did in the classroom. Some even return to the classroom after a year or two because the workload and expectations are overwhelming. For most of us, however, it is a job we relish and would not give up for the world. But, at the same time, media specialists who last in the profession recognize the importance of personal support networks to maintain a healthy balance between work and life. Without this balance, teachers in all subject areas are prone to burn out from stress. Many teaching professionals come into the field with a sense of idealism; they want to make a difference in the lives of their students. That sense of idealism drives and pushes them to give more, more, more. Quickly, they find they are in over their heads because they have more on their plates than they can handle. Striking a balance between your personal and professional life is key to surviving in the education field.

How do you ensure that you have a personal support network? Start by looking at your life realistically. Identify the friends and family members who matter to you, the people you go to for emotional support or just to have fun. Be sure you schedule and keep regular appointments with them. Go out to lunch or dinner, and don't cancel because you have book orders to finish or need to spend time at your computer researching Internet sites for a new Web quest. Listen to these people if they tell you that you have neglected your friendship with them and take time to nurture the relationship. By cultivating the friendship, you will also be nurturing yourself.

Establish boundaries for how much time you will work outside of your established duty day. It is easy for media specialists to put in several hours of overtime each day. The principal wants the media center open before and after school. Teachers bring you things on their way out the door that need to be fixed for tomorrow's classes or come up with last minute resource requests and wonder if you could pull together a book cart for them. Your day was spent teaching classes about note taking so you did not have time to check your e-mail, finish up the order list that needs to be submitted, and finalize the lesson plans for the next day's class. Before you know it, you've put in a couple of extra hours after the end of the school day. You are tired, frustrated, and not in a good frame of mind. This scenario repeats itself often for most media specialists and leads to burnout very quickly. This is why it is important to set boundaries and prioritize your professional activities. Determine how much time you are able to commit before and after school, then stick to your plan. The work will always be there and there will always be more, so recognize it and leave. Go home, take time to relax and enjoy your family. Work at a favorite hobby, read a book by your favorite author, maintain yourself! You are your best resource when it comes to being a first-class media specialist. Remember, if you burn out, you will not be serving your students, faculty, staff, or administration well. Keep this in mind and recognize that sometimes it is better to say, "No, it will have to wait until tomorrow." By taking time for yourself, you'll arrive at school the next day refreshed and invigorated to face the challenges of a new day in your media center.

14

Budgeting and Purchasing

Did you become a library media specialist because you love to read? Maybe you became a media specialist because you love to research and help others. Or, perhaps you not only wanted to be a teacher, but also wanted to be able to reach all the students at your school. These are all great reasons, but in order to run an effective library media program, you must also have good business sense. Besides being a place of learning, your media center also functions as a major supplier of equipment, books, technology, and more. As the media specialist, you are the chief executive officer of your media center. If you run your company well, your entire school will benefit. Foremost in your administration is preparing a budget. Whether your principal asks for a budget or not, it is a good idea to have a budget on paper to help focus your spending during the year. This is not only an ethical issue, but also a practical one. As professionals, we need to have goals, and proper funding is necessary to reach those goals. If you believe in your program, you will also believe that you need money to run your program. On the practical side, if you do not request a fully funded budget, your principal will not understand why you need any funding at all. Unless you make your needs known, he will allocate money to programs that do specify why they need those precious dollars available to your school.

Usually budgets are determined the spring before the new school year. As with any action taken in the media center, planning is most important. Before you begin planning for the new school year, look back at last year with a critical eye. Examine your funding and the programs you implemented. Assess their effectiveness and try to remember any programs you considered but were not able to get off the ground. Why was that?

Do you have a budget from last year that you can evaluate to decide what worked and what needs to be updated? If so, ask these questions. Did you have enough money to:

- maintain your collection?
- purchase as many new print and audiovisual materials as needed?
- maintain and utilize online databases and programs?

Sidebar 14.01 Why Write a Budget?

Consider the following:

- *Defines your vision for the media center*—A written budget helps you identify your goals for the media center and media program.
- *Helps balance expenditures*—A written budget forces you to look at how you plan to spend the funds you have and points out inconsistencies.
- *Helps communicate your thoughts*—The budget is a means of sharing your plans with your principal, staff, and school community.
- *Helps prioritize spending*—Once written and discussed with your principal, you will be able to use the budget to establish priorities with the funds available to you.
- *Provides justification for your requests*—Purchase requests throughout the year will not be seen as random expenditures; your principal will know you are working within the budget plan you discussed with him or her.
- *Helps you keep track of spending*—Writing and maintaining the budget throughout the year helps you track expenditures and stay focused on your plans.

- begin new programs to ensure your media center is the heart and hub of the school?
- maintain your AV equipment and purchase new items as needed?

Decide how to modify your previous budget to reflect your actual needs for the new school year. Make adjustments that you feel will benefit your teachers and students.

If this is your first year in the media center, and the previous budget is not available to you (or non-existent), contact media specialists in your area to discuss the categories that make up their budgets and how much they typically spend in a year. Work with your bookkeeper who may be able to give you an estimate of how the media center was funded last year. She will explain to you how money is categorized and if there are restrictions on how and when to spend certain funds. Due to constantly increasing costs, it is a good idea to increase your budget by 5 to 10 percent each year.

The first step in creating a budget is to assess your needs. After careful analysis and with a concrete plan for the new school year, you can create a budget that makes sense. Your budget can be general or detailed, but if you are thorough, your principal will have a better understanding of your needs.

Needs Assessment

First, evaluate the needs of the media center and base your budget on those needs. Involve all stake-holders in this process, including your school administration, faculty, students, clerical staff, and parents, then consider your own analysis of your program and your collection.

Work with your administration on their needs. You are the expert on purchasing, so if they need help in finding information on where to purchase items for areas of the school besides the media center, be ready and willing to help. Cultivating a relationship with your principal will be beneficial when you ask if there are additional funds that can be allocated to your program.

Create a teacher evaluation form to find out if your program has been successful in its service and collaboration with teachers. By carefully wording your teacher form, you can not only ask for input from your faculty, giving them a voice in your program, but you can also use it as a tool to inform teachers

Sidebar 14.02 Average Book Price Increasing

Source: St. Lifer, Evan. "2005 Book Prices." *School Library Journal*, (March 2005), http://www.schoollibraryjournal.com/article/CA507329.html.

According to *School Library Journal*, the cost of school library books has been steadily increasing for the past 25 years. In fact, in 2005, the average price of a hardcover children's and young adult book topped the $20 mark for the first time.

about your programs and services. Make sure you create an area on the form where teachers can add comments anonymously. These constructive comments may spark ideas that will help you when asking for funding. New resources or programs requested by teachers are sure to be used and therefore should be fully funded.

On a separate form for students, ask questions that give you an insight into how effective your program is with its most important customers—your students. Again ask questions that inform students about aspects of the library media center that are underutilized. Ask students about online databases that your school has purchased to determine if students are using these resources or if you should adjust the type or quantity of online subscriptions purchased. Students need to understand that your main job is to serve their needs. They need to know you are receptive to their needs and will honor their requests.

Your budget is also based on needs identified by your clerical staff. At any time your staff should be able to give you a needs list of items such as office or processing supplies.

Do your staff members have any ideas of ways to make the media center more efficient? Many times their suggestions will streamline mundane tasks, leaving more time for teaching classes and implementing programs that truly impact student achievement.

Parents are also stakeholders in the quality of your school. If you have formed a School Library Media Advisory Committee, hold a meeting or send out an email to ask for their views. Attend an SAC or PTA meeting and poll members. Ask them their opinions of the resources and programs offered by your library media center. Make sure you take note of any suggestions they may have to improve your program, making it more user-friendly to them and their children.

Finally, analyze what you know about your library media program. Have you really accomplished all that you set out to do during the school year? Do you know that areas of the media center are lacking in materials? Have you noted throughout the year that you have not been able to meet the needs of specific content areas? Consider this analysis of your collection and program. Using this information, create plans for the future. Do you plan to weed the career section this year? You will need funds to replace outdated material. Do you plan any new promotions such as an author visit during Children's Book Week in November? That program will definitely need funds. Are you planning a parent night for low-level students where parents are encouraged to check out books along with the book on tape and a small tape recorder for their child? That new program will require dollars. All of these programs will take lots of funding, be sure to account for them in your budget.

Creating the Budget

After carefully analyzing assessments from all stakeholders, create your budget. Address all areas of your program, even if you feel you do not need funding for them at this time. The following are a listing of budget categories that you should consider:

Print Needs

It is impossible to run a quality program without the print materials students and teachers need to implement their curriculum and to increase student achievement. This includes not only content specific books for student research, but also fiction books. The more students read each day, the higher their test scores.

Print needs include:

- Books (fiction, nonfiction, reference)
- Periodicals (magazines, newspapers)
- Professional materials (books, magazines)

Nonprint Needs

Because we know that we must appeal to all students no matter what their learning style, we also must build and maintain a collection that speaks to diverse styles of learning. The visual learner may learn more from a movie clip than a lecture. An auditory learner will retain information longer if they hear it at the same time they are reading it. Because we seek to reach all learners, we need to purchase materials for these students. In doing so, we will also help the traditional learner by appealing to more than one of their learning styles. Nonprint needs include:

- Visual needs (DVDs, videos)
- Audio books (recorded books, textbooks on CD)

Online Subscriptions and Support Fees

Each year, our students and their families become more dependent on computer technology for information. We need to be a part of this technological revolution by providing information in the format users are used to accessing. By teaching how to effectively use the Internet and providing accurate, current, authoritative sites for students to use, we are meeting students where their needs are. These are not purchases which your bookkeeper or principal will physically see on your shelves, but you must make stakeholders realize they are an integral part of your program. These expenses commonly include:

- subscription databases;
- online skill practice programs;
- professional materials (such as databases that access ERIC);
- updated software programs such as tests for reading programs like Accelerated Reader or Reading Counts;
- online services that detect plagiarism in student work; and
- renewal of support agreements (such as technical support for your media management system, your reading program, your security system, your ID machine).

Equipment

When we evolved from librarians to library media specialists, we took charge of equipment and its maintenance. As equipment becomes more sophisticated, we need to be on the forefront, using and

Source: Anderson, R., P. Wilson, and L. Fielding. "Growth in Reading and How Children Spend Their Time Outside of School." *Reading Research Quarterly* 3, (1988): 285–303.

Sidebar 14.04 Independent Reading Impacts Learning Gains!

This chart correlates the amount of time students spend reading each day with increased performance on standardized tests and vocabulary acquisition.

VARIATION IN AMOUNT OF INDEPENDENT READING

Percentile Rank	Minutes/Day	Words/Year
(Books, Magazines, Newspapers)		
98th	67.3	4,733,000
90th	33.4	2,357,000
70th	16.9	1,168,000
50th	9.2	601,000
30th	4.3	251,000
10th	1.0	51,000
2nd	0.0	0

providing the latest technologies to teachers. Your budget should include funds to repair, purchase, and maintain your audiovisual equipment, including:

- library equipment (to be used in the library media center, such as a presentation system, a podium, audio enhancement, stereo speakers, etc.)
- classroom equipment (to be checked out to teachers, such as overhead projectors, LCD projectors, laptops, digital cameras, video cameras, tape recorders, DVD players, CD players, screens, headphones, calculators, visual presenters, etc.)

Supplies

Your media center will not function without proper supplies. This can be a large category because in addition to office supplies, you must include all the supplies needed to run your entire program. Don't overlook the following:

- simple office supplies (tape, paperclips, or notepads)
- substantial supplies (tape dispensers, staplers, scissors, or book carts)
- processing supplies (book pockets, spine labels, laminates, or bar codes)
- promotional items (bookmarks, prizes, posters, or items for displays)
- media supplies (videotapes and other storage media such as CD-ROMs)
- equipment supplies (projector, video and audio cables need to be in stock, along with replacement lamps and other things needed to maintain your AV equipment)

Furnishings

You may not make large furniture purchases each year, but it is wise to include this line in your budget. Perhaps you need to buy new metal shelves for your storage room or replace an old computer table; you should plan these expenditures and include them in your budget request. Sample furniture might include:

- storage shelving
- replacing old unsafe student chairs or tables
- proper computer tables

Funding Your Budget

We always hear about tight budgets, but education has lots of money; you just need to find it. Typical financial resources might include:

- federal funding such as Title I funds
- state money earmarked for your media program
- district funds given directly to your school
- fund-raising efforts (for example, book fairs, fines for overdue books, charges for printing documents from computers, copy machine charges, charges for making replacement ID cards, etc.)

You may discover you need more money than allotted by your school budget. Now is also the time to brainstorm a list of alternative funding sources. Be creative and ambitious.

- Ask your PTA for a grant to fund a special project that will benefit their children.
- Talk to your school steering committee or SAC and ask them for funding.
- Be creative in asking parents for help. Ask them to donate a book on their child's birthday or to commemorate graduation from your school (no matter what level).
- Look for grants that are local or on a district, state, or national level. The ALA has a plethora of grants waiting for you.
- Approach local civic groups and organizations that might be willing to provide funding to support your media center.

Most districts have a policy and procedures manual, which will help you understand how the budget process works in your district. Many times there are restrictions in spending or money is categorized and you must be careful to obligate funds from the correct category. Your best friend when you are implementing your budget is your bookkeeper. He or she is an expert on the rules and regulations of your district and can guide you in writing your purchase orders. Get to know him or her!

Submit Your Budget

After you have created your budget, make an appointment with your principal and give him or her a copy. Keep this meeting brief, but be prepared to discuss the budget and highlight any important requests you've included in it. Don't expect a financial commitment from your principal at this meeting, and be sure you let your principal know you don't expect an answer on your funding request at that moment. Stress that you are bringing the budget to share with him or her as a means of communicating about your plans for the media center. A typical budget is essentially the same each year, but includes updates so that your principal understands that the library media center is a vibrant, exciting place that needs feeding in order to grow.

Category	Requested Amount	
Print Needs		
Including library books, reference materials, professional books, and so forth.	State funds	$22,000
	Additional funds	$10,000
Periodicals		$3,000
Online Subscriptions		$14,000
Nonprint Needs		$5,000
Including audiovisual materials, computer software, reading program software, letter cutting machine and dies, and so forth.		
Supplies	Clerical supplies	$1,000
Including consumables such as clerical supplies, items for book repair and processing, projection lamps for overheads and LCD projectors, cables, batteries, promotional materials, and so forth.	Book repair and processing	$2,000
	Projection lamps/overheads	$1,000
	Projection lamps/LCD	$2,000
	AV supplies	$2,000
Equipment	DVD players	$2,000
Including equipment used in the media center and equipment for classroom checkout.	LCD Projectors	$5,000
	Overhead projectors	$1,500
	TVs	$10,000
	TV and overhead carts	$5,000
Maintenance Agreements		
Including media management system, ID machine, security system.	Media management	$2,000
	ID machines	$1,800
	Security system	$1,000
Maintenance Fees		
Repairs fees for equipment, furniture, and so forth.	Equipment repairs	$1,000
Furniture	Chair repair	$1,000
Including maintenance and new furniture.		
Internal Accounts Funding	Anticipated	$5,000
From book fairs, fines, ID card charges, and so forth. Used for promotional items, reading incentives, and so forth.		
Grant Funding	Anticipated	$3,000
From local and national grants and SAC funds. Used for collaboration materials, new ideas, and projects.		

Bibliography

Baltimore Public Schools. Available at: http://www.bcps.org/office/lis.

IUPUI School of Library and Information Science. Available at: http://eduscapes.com/sms/index.html.

Johnson, Doug. *Budgeting for Mean, Lean Times.* Available at: http://www.doug-johnson.com.

Minkel, Walter. "Painless Budget Planning." *School Library Journal*, 49, no. 4 (2003): 34.

Morris, Betty. *Administering the School Library Media Center.* Westport, CT: Libraries Unlimited, 2004.

St. Lifer, Evan. "2005 Book Prices." *School Library Journal* (March 2005), http://www.schoollibraryjournal.com/article/CA507329.html.

15

Cataloging and Processing: Getting It on the Shelf so It Can Go out the Door!

If you like to spend money, being a media specialist is a great job because each year you will get to shop, shop, shop! Even with tight budgets, you will still spend a great deal of money on everything from online resources to audiovisual equipment. New books for your media center will be one of your primary purchases each year. And, of course, after buying all these wonderful books, you will want them to be checked out by your students and faculty. When a new book order arrives, getting the books out of the box and onto the shelf is always a top priority, but as with everything else, it is never as easy as it seems. Vendors will tell you that their books come shelf-ready, meaning you can take them right out of the box and place them on the shelf for checkout. However, this is seldom the case. Before you receive your first book order, there are decisions to make and procedures to establish for your media center. The steps you put in place for cataloging and processing your book orders will dramatically affect how easy it is for your students to access the materials you purchased.

Cataloging

The cataloging you purchase or create yourself provides the bibliographic information that guides library patrons to materials. Most media centers now use computer management systems that include electronic or online catalogs. This catalog uses MARC records to allow users to sort through the information about the items in your collection and locate materials. Most vendors ask you to provide information about your cataloging requirements when you place an order so they can tailor MARC records to your needs (see page 35 in chapter 4). Vendors usually charge a small fee to provide a downloadable data disk containing your cataloging information. For most media specialists, this is worth the cost. Even if buying MARC records eats some of your book budget, purchasing the records will save you something else—valuable time.

Sidebar 15.01 Sample MARC Record

Source: Furrie, Betty. *Understanding MARC: Bibliographic Machine Readable Cataloging.* Washington, DC: Library of Congress in conjunction with the Follett Software Company, 2003. Used by permission.

If a librarian uploaded this record into a library automation system, the data entry screen might look like this. The descriptors in the left-hand column are not stored in a MARC record. They are part of the software program's screen display. Most systems are designed so that records can be edited to add additional fields containing local information.

Leader	01041cam		2200265	a	4500

Control No.	001		###89048230	
Control No. ID	003		DLC	
DTLT	005		19911106082810.9	
Fixed Data	008		891101s1990 maua j 001 0 eng	
LCCN	010	##	$a	###89048230
ISBN	020	##	$a	0316107514 :
			$c	$12.95
ISBN	020	##	$a	0316107506 (pbk.) :
			$c	$5.95 ($6.95 Can.)
Cat. Source	040	##	$a	DLC
			$c	DLC
			$d	DLC
LC Call No.	050	00	$a	GV943.25
			$b	.B74 1990
Dewey No.	082	00	$a	796.334/2
			$2	20
ME:Pers Name	100	1#	$a	Brenner, Richard J.,
			$d	1941–
Title	245	10	$a	Make the team.
			$p	Soccer :
			$b	a heads up guide to super soccer! /
			$c	Richard J. Brenner.
Variant Title	246	30	$a	Heads up guide to super soccer
Edition	250	##	$a	1st ed.
Publication	260	##	$a	Boston :
			$b	Little, Brown,
			$c	c1990.
Phys Desc	300	##	$a	127 p. :
			$b	ill.;
			$c	19 cm.
Note: General	500	##	$a	"A Sports illustrated for kids book."

(*continued*)

Sidebar 15.01 Sample MARC Record (*continued*)

Note: Summary	520	##	$a	Instructions for improving soccer skills. Discusses dribbling, heading, playmaking, defense, conditioning, mental attitude, how to handle problems with coaches, parents, and other players, and the history of soccer.
Subj: Topical	650	#0	$a	Soccer
			$v	Juvenile literature.
Subj: Topical	650	#1	$a	Soccer.

Before you fill in a cataloging information sheet for a vendor, take time to analyze the current state of your cataloging. Unless you are opening a brand new facility, you very likely inherited a mixture of call number styles and prefixes. For example, you may have some fiction marked with "F" and other books marked "FIC." Nonfiction may be a mixture of Dewey numbers stopping at the decimal point or extending beyond it. Cleaning these inconsistencies up is time consuming. You will simply have to tackle this as an ongoing project. However, when choosing cataloging specifications for a vendor, you want to opt for making things as consistent as possible in your media center. Scan the shelves or, better yet, check the reports section of your management system. It probably has one report that will print out call number prefixes. This report identifies all the variations in your classifications and allows you to identify potential problems. Examine the report looking for the most common type of cataloging. You will probably want to stick with that approach for your future orders.

The ability to buy MARC records makes cataloging seem easy; however, the art of cataloging is more than filling in a specification sheet. There will always be books that require you to create original cataloging. Perhaps you recently held a book fair and received free books or had a book drive that brought many donated books to your media center. Each of these items requires cataloging before students can check them out. You will probably be able to deal with some of the new books by adding them as copies to existing records, but you will not be able to do this with everything. What happens when you need to create an original catalog record?

Original Cataloging

Cataloging books is both an art and a science. If you went through any type of library coursework to become a media specialist, you undoubtedly took at least one class in cataloging. This course should have left you with a strong respect for the rules and procedures involved in creating good bibliographic records. Trained school media specialists usually begin their careers with this strict cataloging approach, but soften over time as they learn the ins and outs of helping students locate information. For example, using strict guidelines, the subject headings for many car-related topics use the term "automobile." For example, the *Sears List of Subject Headings* (17th ed.) lists the following as preferred subject headings: "automobile industry" instead of "car industry" and "automobile racing" instead of "car racing." Very few students would think to look under this word for books about cars; hence, the art of cataloging comes into play. School media specialists must understand the rules and regulations for proper bibliographic cataloging. They must also develop a sense of their students and community so they know when to bend the rules in order to help students access information.

Sidebar 15.02 Formatted MARC Display

Source: Furrie, Betty. *Understanding MARC: Bibliographic Machine Readable Cataloging.* Washington, DC: Library of Congress in conjunction with the Follett Software Company, 2003. Used by permission.

Formatted displays: The type of screens OPAC patrons use are formatted since MARC tags would be meaningless to the general public. Within each particular OPAC program is a routine that formats each record in the way the designers thought would best serve the public using the online catalog. A similar transformation takes place if catalog cards are printed from a MARC record, as illustrated in the third example.

Sample of a brief record display as seen by a patron

TITLE :	Make the team. Soccer : a heads up guide to super soccer! / Richard J. Brenner.
AUTHOR :	Brenner, Richard J.
PUBLISHED :	Little, Brown, c1990.
MATERIAL :	127 p.
Copies Available :	GV943.25 .B74 1990

Sample of a full record display as seen by a patron

TITLE :	Make the team. Soccer : a heads up guide to super soccer! / Richard J. Brenner.
ADDED TITLE :	Heads up guide to super soccer
AUTHOR :	Brenner, Richard J., 1941–
PUBLISHED :	1st ed. Boston : Little, Brown, c1990.
MATERIAL :	127 p. : ill. ; 19 cm.
NOTE :	"A Sports illustrated for kids book."
NOTE :	Instructions for improving soccer skills. Discusses dribbling, heading, playmaking, defense, conditioning, mental attitude,how to handle problems with coaches, parents, and other players, and the history of soccer.
SUBJECT :	Soccer—Juvenile literature.
	Soccer.
Copies Available :	GV943.25 .B74 1990

(*continued*)

Sidebar 15.02 Formatted MARC Display (*continued*)

Sample of a catalog card

GV943	Brenner, Richard J., 1941-
.25	Make the team. Soccer : a heads up guide to super
.B74	soccer! / Richard J. Brenner. -- 1st ed. -- Boston :
1990	Little, Brown, c1990.

127 p. : ill. ; 19 cm.

"A Sports illustrated for kids book."

Summary: Instructions for improving soccer skills. Discusses dribbling, heading, playmaking, defense, conditioning, mental attitude, how to handle problems with coaches, parents, and other players, and the history of soccer.

ISBN 0316107514 : $12.95

1. Soccer — Juvenile literature. 2. Soccer. II. Title: Heads up guide to super soccer. II. Title.

Dewey Class no.: 796.334/2 — dc 20

89-48230
MARC

When media specialists discuss cataloging, they are referring to three basic steps:

- Classification—This is determining the correct call number for the item in question. The assignment of the correct Dewey Decimal number will determine where the item is placed on the library shelves.
- Cataloging—Here the media specialist actually prepares the record for each item. The record will include information such as the title, author, physical description, subject headings, reading program, and so forth.
- Processing—This includes any steps needed to make the book shelf ready. With the advent of vendor supplied processing, this can be a quick check of the order or a more complicated procedure, depending on your school's policies and procedures.

Tools for Original Cataloging

Even with vendor cataloging, you will still need to create original cataloging from time to time. It is a good idea to have the following resources at your school to help you make appropriate decisions about classifying books and other materials.

- *Sears List of Subject Headings*, published by the H. W. Wilson Company, or *Subject Headings for School and Public Libraries: An LCSH/Sears Companion*, by Joanna F. Fountain and published by Libraries Unlimited.
- *Dewey Decimal Classification and Relative Index*—Abridged version adequate for schools—published by OCLC Online Computer Library Center, Inc.

If you inherited a program, the chances are you have an old copy of these books somewhere in your workroom or office. Don't throw these copies out. Instead, flip through them. You are likely to find notes written in the margins by your predecessors. These notes will help you identify choices that were made in cataloging materials for the media center. This valuable information will help you as you begin the process of making the media center your own. Check these books for copyright information. If they are over 10 years old, consider buying newer editions. Transfer any notes you feel are important to the newer editions, then weed the old books.

Classifying Materials

The Dewey Decimal System was explained in chapter 2. Before you begin the process of classifying anything for your media center, it is important to understand the classification categories. A good way to do this is to select several items from your collection that have similar subject matter, but different Dewey numbers. Examine each item carefully, comparing the content to its assigned Dewey category. What conclusions can you draw about the assigned classification? Remember the content of the material determines the assignment of the Dewey number, not the cover or immediately obvious subject. As media specialists become more familiar with the nuances of Dewey, they also become adept at asking students questions to help them locate the right materials. For example, asking, "Are you looking for information about the history of the civil rights movement or about how the civil rights movement impacted society?" will help you lead a student to the right place for the information they need.

When classifying materials, take a few minutes to look them over and determine their content. Scan the contents page and the index of books. Examine chapter headings, pictures, charts, and diagrams. If necessary, read a few chapters. It is usually fairly easy to determine the main focus of children and teen books by a simple scan. Check the cataloging in publication, usually referred to as the CIP. Most publishers provide this information on the back of the title page of a book. The CIP includes the classification information for the book and other cataloging information. Usually this information is accurate, but don't follow it blindly. The CIP is usually done before the final draft of a work is complete, so it could be inaccurate. You might also decide that for your school community, a book would be more accessible in another location. If you are unsure of the Dewey number assigned to the book in the CIP, check the Dewey and Sears reference books to verify the choice. Once you determine the Dewey number for a particular item, decide if any additional prefix (such as Ref, Prof, or AV) is needed. Use sticky notes with the classification written on them and attach to the book to help keep track of the information as the book moves onto cataloging and processing.

Cataloging Materials

Modern media management systems make cataloging much easier than it used to be by providing ways to create MARC records using templates built into the software. It is also possible to download the records from vendor provided data disks and online sources such as the Library of Congress. Patrons access these records through the OPAC.

If your media center is not yet automated, you and your patrons are probably using the old-fashioned card catalog to locate books in your collection. Creating catalog cards is more time consuming, and keeping the card catalog up to date is labor intensive for a busy school library media specialist. However, if you are still using this system, it is important to maintain this resource. Not creating and filing cards makes it impossible for patrons to know what is contained in the media center, and not removing all the cards for a weeded item will cause wild goose chases as patrons search for things that no longer exist in the collection. There are computer software programs available to help create the cards you will

Carbon 14 dating
    USE Radiocarbon dating
Carbon dioxide greenhouse effect
    USE Greenhouse effect
Carburetors 621.43
    BT Internal combustion engines
Carcinoma
    USE Cancer
Card catalogs 025.3
    UF ~~Catalogs, Card~~   *Use 'OPAC' & Online*
    BT Library catalogs   *Public Access Catalogs*
Card games 795.4
    SA types of card games [to be add-
        ed as needed]
    BT Games
    NT Bridge (Game)
        Canasta (Game)
        Card tricks
        Solitaire (Game)
        Tarot
    RT Playing cards
Card tricks 795.4
    BT Card games
        Magic tricks
        Tricks
Cardiac diseases
    USE Heart diseases
Cardiac resuscitation 616.02; 616.1
    UF Heart resuscitation
        Resuscitation, Heart   *Also use*
    BT First aid   *"CPR"*
Cardinals 262
    BT Catholic Church—Clergy
Cardiovascular system 612.1
    UF Circulatory system
        Vascular system
    BT Anatomy
        Physiology
    NT Heart
    RT Blood—Circulation
Cards, Debit
    USE Debit cards
Cards, Greeting
    USE Greeting cards
Cards, Playing
    USE Playing cards
Cards, Sports
    USE Sports cards

Also use specific sport ex. "Baseball Cards"

Care
    USE parts of the body, classes of
        persons, and types of animals
        with the subdivision *Care*,
        e.g. Foot—Care; Infants—
        Care; Dogs—Care; etc.;
        classes of persons with the
        subdivisions *Medical care*, *In-
        stitutional care*, and *Home
        care*, e.g. Elderly—Medical
        care; Elderly—Institutional
        care; Elderly—Home care;
        etc.; ethnic groups and classes
        of persons with the subdivi-
        sion *Health and hygiene*, e.g.
        Infants—Health and hy-
        giene; and inanimate things
        with the subdivision *Mainte-
        nance and repair*, e.g. Auto-
        mobiles—Maintenance and
        repair [to be added as need-
        ed]
Care givers
    USE Caregivers
Care of children
    USE Child care   *Also, "Babysitting"*
Care of the dying
    USE Terminal care   *Also, "Hospice Care"*
Career changes 650.14; 658.4
    UF Changing careers
        Mid-career changes
    SA fields of knowledge, professions,
        industries, and trades with the
        subdivision *Vocational guid-
        ance* [to be added as needed]
    BT Age and employment
        Vocational guidance
Career counseling
    USE Vocational guidance
Career development
    USE Personnel management
        Vocational guidance
Career education
    USE Vocational education
Career guidance
    USE Vocational guidance
Careers
    USE Occupations
        Professions
        Vocational guidance

Use "Careers" instead of Vocational

110

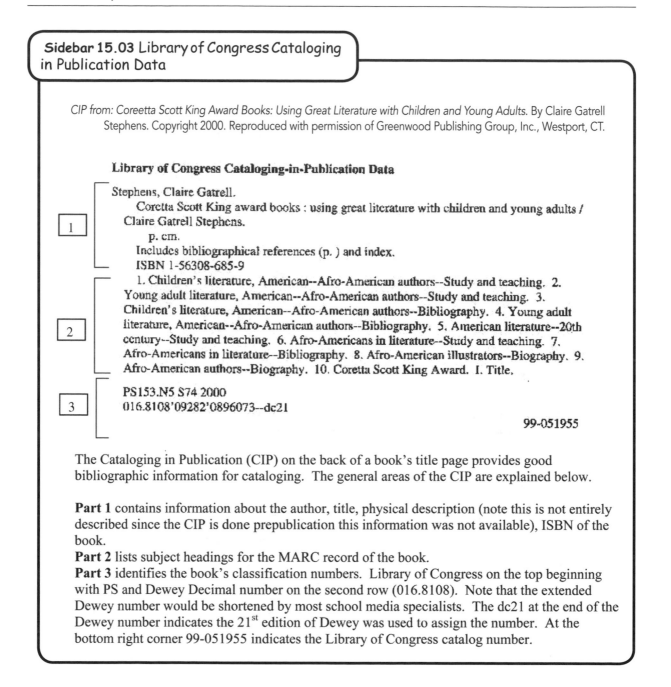

Sidebar 15.03 Library of Congress Cataloging in Publication Data

CIP from: Coreetta Scott King Award Books: Using Great Literature with Children and Young Adults. By Claire Gatrell Stephens. Copyright 2000. Reproduced with permission of Greenwood Publishing Group, Inc., Westport, CT.

Library of Congress Cataloging-in-Publication Data

1. Stephens, Claire Gatrell.
    Coretta Scott King award books : using great literature with children and young adults / Claire Gatrell Stephens.
    p. cm.
    Includes bibliographical references (p.) and index.
    ISBN 1-56308-685-9

2. 1. Children's literature, American--Afro-American authors--Study and teaching. 2. Young adult literature, American--Afro-American authors--Study and teaching. 3. Children's literature, American--Afro-American authors--Bibliography. 4. Young adult literature, American--Afro-American authors--Bibliography. 5. American literature--20th century--Study and teaching. 6. Afro-Americans in literature--Study and teaching. 7. Afro-Americans in literature--Bibliography. 8. Afro-American illustrators--Biography. 9. Afro-American authors--Biography. 10. Coretta Scott King Award. I. Title.

3. PS153.N5 S74 2000
    016.8108'09282'0896073--dc21

    99-051955

The Cataloging in Publication (CIP) on the back of a book's title page provides good bibliographic information for cataloging. The general areas of the CIP are explained below.

Part 1 contains information about the author, title, physical description (note this is not entirely described since the CIP is done prepublication this information was not available), ISBN of the book.
Part 2 lists subject headings for the MARC record of the book.
Part 3 identifies the book's classification numbers. Library of Congress on the top beginning with PS and Dewey Decimal number on the second row (016.8108). Note that the extended Dewey number would be shortened by most school media specialists. The dc21 at the end of the Dewey number indicates the 21st edition of Dewey was used to assign the number. At the bottom right corner 99-051955 indicates the Library of Congress catalog number.

need for a card catalog system, or you can create the cards yourself. Creating cards by hand requires strict adherence to specified formats for each type of card (author, title, and subject). If you do not know how to correctly type these cards, refer to your district policies and procedures manual or other library resources for directions. Most major book vendors can provide card sets for a small fee, and some will sell you cards for books that you did not purchase from them. These vendors will work from a list of ISBN numbers you provide to generate the cards for titles you may have acquired from your book fair or local bookstore. If time and money is not an issue, purchasing these preprinted vendor cards will allow you to spend more time working directly with your students.

Whether you are using MARC records or creating card catalog cards for your library materials, there are certain things you need to know in order to create a correct catalog record. These include:

- The complete title of the work.
- The name of the author(s).
- The publication information and copyright.
- The physical description. Commonly, this includes the number of pages, whether or not the book is illustrated, and the books height at the spine measured in centimeters.
- The classification number from the Dewey Decimal System.
- The work's ISBN.
- Any subject headings you plan to use. (Check the CIP and your Sears reference book.)
- Reading program information for Accelerated Reader or Reading Counts can be inserted into MARC records, but is not commonly placed on card catalog cards.

Many media specialists enjoy classifying and cataloging materials. It feels like detective work and they like the intellectual challenge it provides. Others feel creating original cataloging is a stressor since it robs them of valuable student contact time. These media specialists purchase cataloging from vendors and train clerical staff to download MARC records from reliable databases or create catalog records using the CIP inside the book. The media specialist then oversees the work and double checks the process in between classes. This may not be an ideal situation, but busy school library personnel recognize the benefits of a well-trained library assistant and know that a good clerk can become an expert cataloger.

Whatever choice is made, it is important to strive for consistency in the creation of records. To be sure of uniformity in your catalog records, examine the existing catalog looking for trends in capitalization, classification use, subject headings, and so forth. If you spot problems such as mixed styles in formatting records or inconsistent use of call number prefixes, decide on the standards for cataloging you want for your library and put it in writing. Be sure to share the information with your staff and any volunteers who assist you with the cataloging process. As time allows, you can go back and correct the existing records to accurately reflect your standards.

Processing

Even if you order books shelf ready, you will probably need to do some processing of new orders before placing them on the shelf. Vendor processing typically includes things such as spine labels, theft detection, book pockets, book covers, and bar codes placed according to your specifications. Having vendors do these things is a big help, but each media center has unique needs for materials processing that vendors simply cannot accommodate. Perhaps you like to stamp your books with a name and address stamp on a hidden page inside the book, or maybe you like to affix stickers on the spine to identify award winners, reading program information, or genre. Because of these individual school-based needs, most shelf ready vendor processing usually requires some additional handling when it arrives at the school. There will also always be donated books or titles you purchased at a local bookstore that require processing, so thinking about your processing requirements and steps is a good idea.

Since a clerk or volunteer usually handles processing, you may want to make a checklist to be sure all the steps you require are done. It is also important to order these steps so that helpers don't put book covers on books before attaching the bar code, spine label, and other identifying stickers you may require. The amount of processing required before materials can go on the shelf varies from school to

Sidebar 15.04 Processing an Order

Below are some things to consider when processing an order of new books for your collection.

1. Check books against shipping and order lists to verify the order contents.
2. Examine books for condition or special problems. Set aside and contact the vendor about any issues you find.
3. Stamp books with school address stamp on inside front and back covers. Many schools also stamp the top and bottom of the book.
4. Many schools also like to stamp a page somewhere in the book as a hidden identifier. If you do this, ask other media specialists in your district what page they use and stamp the same one at your school.
5. If you did not order the books with shelf-ready processing from your vendor:
   a. Apply bar code and protector
   b. Insert security tag for your system
   c. Apply pocket if needed
   d. Determine cataloging information for each book, call number, subject headings, and so forth.
   e. Create and attach spine label and cover with protector if needed
6. Identify any books that need special identification stickers:
   a. Newbery
   b. Caldecott
   c. Coretta Scott King
   d. Pura Belpre
   e. Reference
   f. Spanish Language
   g. Colleges and Careers
   h. Other, according to your school's needs
7. Verify books that are part of school reading incentive programs such as Accelerated Reader or Reading Counts.
   a. Are books marked so students will be able to identify them on the shelves?
   b. Do you have quizzes for the books?
8. Place clear plastic book covers on hardcover books or laminate to paperbacks if desired.
9. If you purchased MARC records, download the disk. Verify the download when complete and address any problems.
   a. Do you want to change any call numbers for your students?
   b. Do you need to add or change any prefixes such as Prof or AV on certain titles?
   c. Do you need to insert any subject headings for your students and curriculum?
   d. Is the school reading incentive program information in the MARC record?
   e. Does the purchasing information (vendor, cost, date of purchase, etc.) show for the book copy?
   f. Do you want to place the book in a bibliographic category you have set up so patrons can easily locate certain materials?
10. For orders without a MARC record download, create original cataloging according to your management software specifications.
11. Review order for one last time; consider any other issues that may need to be addressed.

Now for the fun part—display and promote the newest additions to your collection!

school. Check your district policies and procedures manual for recommendations. Ask other media specialists in your district for common practices in your area. Examine existing materials in the collection to see how they are marked. Decide what processing requirements are needed by your school and develop your checklist accordingly. Then train your staff to be sure they handle all orders according to your specifications.

The Results of Good Cataloging and Processing

As the media specialist of even a small school, you will be responsible for keeping track of thousands of books, DVDs and videos, audio books, equipment, and so forth. It is a daunting task that requires high standards, strong will, clear vision, attention to detail, and excellent organizational skills. When a media specialist takes time to carefully catalog and process materials, he or she is ensuring that students and staff will be able to identify, locate, and use resources. Good cataloging and processing is not a futile exercise in minutia; it cuts to the core of what libraries are about—accessing and sharing resources. Whether you are a new or experienced media specialist, time spent learning about cataloging is professionally valuable. Likewise, periodic evaluation and updating of your school processing standards benefits everyone in your community. Many library schools now offer online courses to help working professionals stay current in new trends of library science. If you've never taken a cataloging course or if it has been a long time since you last studied this subject, do some research and find a class to take. Review your processing procedures with staff at the start of each school year and make changes if necessary. All of the effort you put into developing good cataloging and processing procedures for your school will come back to you tenfold when you see the smiling face of a student who just found the book they were looking for.

Bibliography

Eberhart, George M., ed. *The Whole Library Handbook 3.* Chicago: American Library Association, 2000.

Furrie, Betty. *Understanding MARC: Bibliographic Machine Readable Cataloging.* Washington, DC: Library of Congress in conjunction with the Follett Software Company, 2003.

Miller, Joseph, ed. *Sears List of Subject Headings*, 17th ed. New York: H. W. Wilson and Company, 2000.

Wasman, Ann M. *New Steps to Service: Common-Sense Advice for the School Library Media Specialist.* Chicago: American Library Association, 1998.

Part IV

Equipping Your Library
Media Center

16

Equipped to Run!

When it comes to equipment, most media specialists are, as the old saying goes, a jack-of-all-trades and a master of none. The influx of technology into the modern classroom has brought more than computers. It is normal to find teachers and students using a variety of technologies, including:

- Multimedia projectors to interface between computers and interactive white boards, show videos and DVDs, or project documents from a visual presenter.
- Visual presenters that allow teachers and students to project from the printed page onto a screen for easy viewing by all.
- Scanning devices that allow users to create digital copies of a variety of texts, pictures, and photographs for incorporation into projects and reports. A newer version of the scanner blows up the contents of a sheet of paper to a variety of poster sizes.
- Digital cameras and camcorders that are used by teachers and students to document and illustrate lessons and projects.

The list is endless, and new technologies are born each day.

Gone are the days when the most complex thing a media specialist needed to know was how to thread the filmstrip and 16mm movie projectors. Instead, our clients expect us to know how to operate a wide range of equipment made by a variety of manufacturers. In addition, we must understand how to network these technologies to allow integration of the products and softwares that accompany them. We must possess more than basic computer skills. As we move through the day, we assist teachers and students with everything from simple word processing and PowerPoint presentations to complex Internet searches and Web page design.

The diverse range of technical skill required of the modern media specialist is dizzying to say the least. Many experienced media specialists have thrown up their hands and declared their unwillingness to learn these new tricks of the trade. This is unfortunate because students constantly experiment with new technologies and since our goal is always to positively influence student learning, we must embrace emerging technologies to assist our students in meeting their academic goals. The following is an overview of technologies commonly found in school media centers and classrooms across the country.

Computers

At this point, we may be tempted to look at computers as *old* technology. After all, they have been around schools for more than 20 years and have gone from being an extra add-on to being a mandatory requirement in each classroom. Indeed, many classrooms across the nation contain multiple computer workstations—one for the teacher and several others for student use. Today's students do not remember a time when there were no computers in the classroom. These machines are a centerpiece that allow for efficient record keeping, interactive lessons, quick creation of a variety of products demonstrating student mastery of ideas and concepts, and access to a wide variety of information resources via the Internet. Indeed, it is difficult to imagine a classroom or media center without them.

It is essential for the modern media specialist to be a technology leader at the school site. This does not mean the media specialist must be an all-knowing computer whiz. It does require that the school library professional have a working knowledge of computers in three essential areas: hardware, software applications, and online resources. On any given day, the average media specialist will find himself or herself using skills in each of these areas. He or she might connect a peripheral device such as a multimedia projector to a computer for a teacher's lesson, assist a student who wishes to use a reading enhancement program to take

Many people now expect computer labs to be part of school media centers. This lab is in McCoy Elementary School, Orange County Public Schools, Orlando, Florida.

a computerized test, and help locate information on the Internet for a student or teacher. In each of these situations, the media specialist demonstrates leadership skills by incorporating computers in the education process.

While it is unrealistic for a new school or library media specialist to know instantly all there is to know about technology in the classroom, the entering professional must take stock of her abilities and immediately begin to increase technological skills. Start by assessing your expertise in each of the above areas individually. Seek out and attend staff development classes related to computers and the software programs commonly used at your school site. Attend technology conferences and network with other media specialists to share information about hardware and software. Go online and explore resource databases available through your school, district, or local public library. Become familiar with the types of online products available and learn how to use them. Join professional groups that support computer technology in the classroom and become a regular visitor to their Web sites to keep current on trends and best practices. Your efforts will pay off quickly, and you will realize that your faculty, staff, and students turn to you for answers to their technology questions.

Computer Hardware

You will face many computer hardware related questions and issues as you assume the role of a media specialist. Here are a few:

- Do you know the basic vocabulary of computer hardware? It is important to understand the language and to be able to identify computer parts so that you can effectively communicate with faculty, students, and technology staff.
- What computers do you have in your media center? Most schools have a variety of machines purchased over time. Become familiar enough with your machines that you are able to discuss with tech staff the general brand(s), age, and condition of the machines in your library.
- What operating systems are running on your computers?
- What software packages are loaded on each machine?
- Are your computers connected to the Internet?
- Do you have peripherals that connect to computers in your media center? This might include scanners, calculators, multimedia projectors, portable keyboards, wireless laptops, MP3 players, and more. Identify each of these devices and commit to learning how they work, what they do,

Sidebar 16.01 Check Out This Technology Organization!

Logo reprinted with permission from the International Society for Technology in Education. E-mail: iste@iste.org. Web site: http://www.iste.org. All rights reserved.

A great organization to consider joining for more information about technology in education is the International Society for Technology in Education (ISTE; http://www.iste.org). This nonprofit organization dedicates itself to helping improve teaching and learning by implementing effective use of technology in K-12 education.

One important program of ISTE is the National Educational Technology Standards (NETS). Designed for students, teachers, and administrators, the NETS guidelines are being adopted by school districts across the country. For more information, go to: http://cnets.iste.org/index.shtml.

iste International Society for Technology in Education

and how to connect them. Try to learn one new device each month. It is not necessary to become a master of each device, but you should know each piece of equipment well enough to set it up, perform basic operations, and take it apart for storage.

- Does your school district have purchasing guidelines for computers? Some districts allow purchases of any computer make and model. In many other districts, however, it is necessary to follow guidelines so computer purchases are compatible with networks and easier for repair staff to work with.

Sidebar 16.02 Computer Tips from Pat and Claire

In preparing this section of *Library 101*, we became curious. Exactly how many computer software programs did we use on a regular basis? The list surprised us. We counted 10 software products that we routinely use in our jobs as media specialists. They include Microsoft Word, Excel, Outlook, Internet Explorer, Filemaker Pro, PowerPoint, Publisher, CICS (a common district level database in our schools), Smart Tools, and our media management software, Follett, which is actually made up of six different softwares that interact with each other. This list does not include online database resources that our schools subscribe to and are accessed through the Internet. If you add these in, the number jumps to more than 15 programs. Reflecting on this, we wondered how many career fields require their professionals to know and use so many different computer applications. The list is probably short—very short!

It is important for new media specialists to recognize that we did not learn these programs overnight. It took years of experience to master them, and even then, we understand that we are not expert users of each one. In fact, our knowledge of these softwares is frequently limited to what is required for our jobs. The important thing is to be open to learning new programs, Over time, you will find that there are common skill sets used in operating different softwares and you are able to transfer knowledge from an older program to learning a newer one. As media specialists, we are technology leaders in our schools, and computer skills are not only an important measure of how well we are able to do our jobs as managers, but also reflect our ability to assist our students, teachers, and staff as they navigate their way through this information age.

When dealing with computer hardware and software, keep the following tips in mind:

- Don't be intimidated. It's just a machine, nothing more.

- Don't think the students know more than you do. They do not. They are learning as they go along, just like you. The only difference is that they have never known a world without computers; they aren't afraid of them.

- Do look through manuals. You don't need to read them cover to cover, but you need to be familiar with their contents. When faced with a problem, you'll be surprised how many times you remember that there are pages in the manual addressing the issues you are facing.

- Do play around with the computer and softwares at your school. Give yourself assignments. Learn how to connect and disconnect the machine and all its peripherals. Challenge yourself to create your budget using a spreadsheet this year so you learn how to use Microsoft Excel.

- Do recognize common skill sets and transfer them when learning new applications. You'll be surprised how many times you are able to learn a new program quickly when you are able to recognize that parts of it require you to do the same things as a program you already know.

- Perhaps most importantly, nurture relationships with your school's technical staff. They will teach you and help you. They are your partners in acquiring and maintaining the technology at your school. You need your school technology support person on your side.

Computer Software

Media specialists use a variety of computer softwares and, as with computer hardware, it is impossible to know everything about all the programs available in your school. With time and patience, however, you can become knowledgeable enough to work through many problems. Teachers and students will turn to you for advice on using different computer programs, so you will want to learn how to work with common computer applications used in your school and district.

Many districts offer in-service training opportunities for staff who want to improve their technical skills; sign up for classes if they are available in your area. If it is not possible to attend a training course, check your local library or bookstore for an easy to follow guide to your software. Several excellent series on the market offer clear concise directions and hints for using many common computer softwares. One of the easiest ways to learn new software is, quite simply, to use it. Create small assignments for yourself and complete them. You will be an advanced user in no time.

Perhaps the most important program for most media specialists today is their media management software. This application allows you to do your job. You will use it to circulate books, audiovisuals, and equipment; organize and maintain records of the collection; and to keep track of your patrons. There are many different management softwares available on the market today, and the qualities of a good management software program are discussed at length in chapter 4. If you are a new media specialist who is not familiar with the management software at your school, it is important to immediately spend time learning about it. Check to be sure that your support agreements are up to date. Good tech support will be a lifeline for you as you become familiar with this vital media center tool. Network with other media specialists in your area who use the same software—experienced media specialists are usually happy to share their knowledge and expertise with newcomers to the field. Locate the Web site for your software online and become familiar with it. You will find a wealth of information about your management system on the company's Web pages. Locate the software manual that came with the program and keep it handy. Even if the product has been updated, the manual will still provide valuable insights into how to do everything from adding patrons and books to printing circulation reports and overdue notices.

Finally, don't be intimidated by the many types of software you are called upon to use as a media specialist. In time, you will master the many programs you need to use each day. In fact, you will find that embracing the many software programs you use each day can be a fun challenge. Your peers will respect your attitude and recognize that you are involved in a time of learning and skill development. They will support your efforts and may even offer some of their own expertise to help you hone your abilities. Before long, you will realize your role has changed as people perceive you to be the expert and go-to person for computer technology information.

Online Resources

Online resources are increasingly important in school library programs. They extend the library beyond its immediate walls by allowing your patrons to access information from the classroom, home, or any computer in the world connected to the Internet. They are also big business, and as a media specialist, you will find yourself deciding which of these resources are worth your precious dollars. New media specialists need to be aware of what these resources are, how they work, and how they relate to your curriculum before signing up for these often costly products.

Online database resources are programs accessed via the Internet by students or staff using a log-on ID and password. Once the user logs onto the program, they are able to research a variety of topics using the information stored in the database files. These programs can be broad in their information coverage—*World Book* or *Encyclopedia Britannica* online, for example. They can also be specialized, focusing on one particular topic. For instance, *Choices Explorer* is a database that provides career information for students. Several of these database programs focus on current events information by contracting with news sources. They allow users to access and reprint articles from newspapers and magazines around the world. These databases take the place of the *Reader's Guide to Periodical Literature* and make searching for current event topics much easier. Popular online newspaper and magazine indexes include *EBSCO* and Gale Publisher's *InfoTrac*. Most of these programs have multimedia content offering pictures, audio, and video. Some offer products specific to elementary or secondary grades. Others offer the ability to scale the information to your student's age group by limiting search ability to particular reading levels. A few of these online database resources charge a flat fee for an annual subscription. Most charge based on your school population, so larger schools will pay more for the service than schools with fewer students.

Each of these online resources operates in a way that is specific to the program. Most usually have general and advanced search options similar to any good Internet search engine. Increasingly, these products are offering graphic interfaces that make it easier for users to navigate the options available to them. Users will also find links taking them to additional information in the database or on the World Wide Web that relates to the topic they are researching. Bibliographic citation information is normally imbedded in the articles students use, and frequently the services come with copyright permission to cut and paste photographs into projects. Perhaps the most difficult part of using these online database resources is getting students, who are used to random Internet searching, to buy into the rationale for using these services. Media specialists need to work diligently, publicizing the availability of these resources to students, staff, and parents. Provide examples demonstrating the improved quality of information located using the database. Incorporate timed searches into presentations to show the speed of information location using your online resources. Offer staff trainings and convince teachers to make the use of these programs mandatory for students when completing projects and assignments. Making all your stakeholders aware of these valuable resources will increase their use and guarantee improved research processes to support student learning in your school.

Because online database resources can use a large percentage of your budget, media specialists need to carefully consider the advantages and disadvantages of each service before signing a contract. Most services are glad to arrange a free-trial period for your school to evaluate their product. When your school has one of these trials, try to enlist teachers and students to use the product, and then be sure to survey them for their reactions to the database. Another way to preview online resources is

Sidebar 16.03 Rationale Supporting the Use of Online Subscription Resources

If your administrator wants to know why you need funding for online resources, consider some of the following reasons as you form your case supporting your funding request. Resources guarantee the accuracy and reliability of their information.

- They provide screening for Web links to assist students in locating valid sites on the Internet.
- They allow students to use resources most schools could not afford to provide in print, such as international newspapers and hundreds of magazines and professional journals.
- The multimedia capabilities of many online resources allow teachers and students to grasp difficult concepts and ideas quickly and with greater understanding.
- They provide quick easy access to current information.
- Searching is generally easy and results appear in seconds.
- Links to related information allow students to explore topics, improving background knowledge and developing a greater understanding of the topic.

to attend technology conferences. Suppliers of online content attend all major conferences. At these events, you will be able to try products and attend demonstrations and concurrent sessions to see the products in action. Conferences also provide opportunities to network with other attendees who will often candidly offer their opinions about the various available resources. Survey your local public library to find out which online resources they offer. This will allow you to explore additional products and to consider additional options since you can refer students to the public library's online resources as well as those purchased by your school. Many school districts and some state education departments and state libraries supply online resources for all schools in their area. If you are not aware of any programs offered by your district, check with your district support personnel to be sure they are not already offering or considering such programs. You do not want to duplicate resources and waste dollars that could be used elsewhere.

Examine your school curriculum and computer availability. Ask your faculty what types of online resources they would like to see available and investigate them. Think about how your teachers approach research projects. How do the different online resources correlate to your school's programs? Elementary school programs may find that a good generalized encyclopedia database and several targeted resources are a perfect fit for your students. Middle school programs may require the above with the addition of a few online resources targeting current events and science or social studies topics. High schools may require multiple focused data resources because their students are in unique magnet programs requiring specialized research. Does your school have enough computers with Internet access to make spending money on online programs practical? What about your students? Can they connect to your online resources at their homes? There is much to consider when analyzing online database resources. Be sure to consider every possible angle when making your choices.

Finances are often the most important consideration when making selections for your school, and online resources are no exception to this rule. When planning your annual budget, be sure to include them in your proposal so your principal is aware of their costs. Consider approaching sources like your SAC or PTA for funding. Since online resources are available for all students in the school, they are often willing to provide full or partial funding for these resources. Some principals are willing to use textbook funds for online resources since many teachers use them in their day-to-day curriculum. A wise media specialist will carefully consider the needs for online resources, analyze available products, compare costs, and then propose a slate of online databases that will be useful to all students, staff, and the larger school community.

Multimedia Projectors

One of the most in demand pieces of equipment in our schools is the multimedia projector. This versatile unit allows the user to project from a variety of sources, typically a computer, DVD/VCR, and a visual presenter. With the touch of a button, teachers can switch back and forth, displaying a Web site one minute, a video segment the next, and then a page from the textbook to summarize what students have seen.

Many new schools feature smart classrooms. In this approach, there is no television set in the room. A multimedia projector hangs from the ceiling. Wiring is in place to connect the projector with the other equipment assigned to the room. This classroom of the future is rapidly becoming a reality across the nation as new schools are constructed and districts retrofit old schools to bring them up to date. In fact, it is easy to imagine a time in the not so distant future when students will laugh at the old-fashioned classroom setup they see in old photos showing children watching a TV in class.

In the meantime, the media specialist is expected to be an instant expert, purchasing and managing a growing collection of these projectors. Here are a few tips for purchasing multimedia projectors for your

Notice the connection ports on the side of this multimedia projector. Typically, users connect computers, document cameras, and video/DVD players to this versatile machine to enhance presentations with a variety of media formats.

school. Hopefully this information will guide your purchases of this high-demand machine and increase the number of these units available to your school community.

Purchasing Tips

First, become familiar with the vocabulary of multimedia projectors. Below is a short list of some common terms you'll hear when discussing these units.

- *Lumens*: This is a measure of a projector's brightness. A unit with 2,000 lumens will be twice as bright as a unit with only 1,000.
- *LCD*: Liquid crystal display units use three glass panels inside the projector separating the color spectrum into red, green, and blue. The light passes through these panels and creates the image on the screen.
- *DLP*: Digital light processing takes the light from the lamp and reflects it off spinning mirrors, then through a color wheel, which makes up the image.
- *SVGA and XGA*: These terms refer to the scaling used by the machine when projecting the image. SVGA scales a picture to 600 lines; XGA scales to 768 lines of resolution. The concern here is how the projector will be used. If your machines will be used for video projection, an XGA projector, because of its higher resolution, will give a better picture. If the projector will be used mostly for PowerPoint, SVGA should be fine.

Next, consider the spaces where the projectors will be used. Can the rooms be darkened? If not, you will need to purchase units with higher lumens to compensate for the lighting. Study room size. Larger spaces such as an auditorium will require projectors capable of handling the distance between the machine and screen while still delivering a sharply focused image. Be prepared to address these issues with your sales person.

Decide if you need LCD or DLP projectors. Both types of projectors have advantages and disadvantages. Generally, LCD models work well for the classroom, where their larger size is not an issue. The

LCD models also project video with more clarity and color intensity. DLP projectors are usually smaller and more easily transported for doing presentations at conferences; however, this lighter weight comes with a few trade-offs that usually include poorer color quality and sometimes a slight shadow around the edges of the projected image. These problems are often not discernable by the average person, but may be an issue for some.

What are your sound needs? If your projectors will be used for video, you need quality sound. Some projectors have limited sound output, but you would still want external sound output jacks to connect speakers for a classroom setting. Be sure these jacks are on your unit and are easy to access.

Does the model you are considering come with a lock mechanism or have a built-in place for some sort of antitheft lock? Even the larger LCD model projectors can be easily slipped into a backpack and stolen. Ask your salesperson about securing your projectors. The additional expense will be worth the price.

Finally, consider what you really need from the projector. These machines now come with a variety of features. While these extra features are nice, they are also frequently unnecessary and drive up the price. Study the models your sales representative shows you, ask questions, and seek out simpler, pared down versions of the machine. By doing this, you will also pare down the price and possibly stretch your budget to include additional machines.

Take your time when shopping for multimedia projectors. Compare prices and ask vendors if they provide postsale services like training or repairs. Look up the models you like on the Internet and study their features. Ask about warranties and the cost of replacement lamps. Does the projector manufacturer provide tech support? Find out if there are authorized repair centers in your area. Since these units will be part of your collection for years, it is worth your time to gather as much information as possible before making your choice.

Visual Presenters

Visual presenters, also commonly called document cameras, take the place of the old-fashioned opaque projector that was designed to project an image from the printed page onto a screen. The opaque projector required a dark room to be effective and was big, bulky, and noisy. Visual presenters take advantage of video technology by mounting a small camera over a stage area. The unit is then connected to a television set or multimedia projector, allowing the class to see what is placed on the unit's stage area. Users can place a solid sheet of paper on the stage. The camera will photograph whatever is written or drawn on the paper for projection. Document cameras can also display small objects such as insects, flowers, leaves, coins, and watches. The zoom feature on the camera allows for close-up viewing and study of these objects. Visual presenters differ from standard overhead projectors, which cannot project from a solid sheet of paper. Overhead projectors must have the desired content copied onto a clear acetate transparency for projection and cannot project solid objects.

Small visual presenters are relatively inexpensive. They work well in most classrooms. Some units fold up to the size of a large book for easy storage and are simple to connect. Larger, more expensive models contain side-mounted lights to help illuminate objects on the stage area. It is helpful to have some of each in your media center. Teachers will love the small models since they do not take up much room. The larger units will be useful in your school television studio to transmit flyers and other printed announcements into the school's closed-circuit system for broadcast. You will also find them helpful at faculty meetings and professional development sessions, which often require the projection of charts and data to large groups in a bigger setting such as an auditorium or cafeteria. The larger units are more effective in these settings because they possess a better zoom capacity and superior focusing ability.

There is one final consideration when purchasing visual presenters. By themselves, document cameras cannot project. Teachers using visual presenters will need to connect them to another piece of equipment

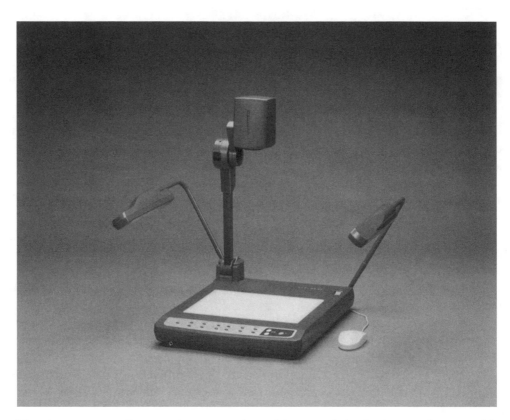

Visual presenters allow teachers to project objects and single sheets of paper with text onto a screen or television. Photo courtesy of Elmo USA.

so that students can see what is on the stage area. Commonly, they are connected to either a televisions set or multimedia projector. If you plan to use your document camera with a television set, be sure the monitor will accept the presenter's signal input for display before purchasing the presenter unit. You may also need to purchase a longer RCA cable to make the connection since the one that comes with the projector will only be a few feet long. When using the visual presenter with a multimedia projector, you will need to adjust the input on the projector until you see the signal from your document camera. Typically, most multimedia projectors take three inputs. Read the multimedia projector's instruction manual if you have difficulty viewing the document camera image.

Interactive White Boards

Interactive white boards are exciting presentation tools that allow users to interface between a computer and the white board. Using a multimedia projector, images from the computer are displayed on the white board. It is possible for the speaker to manipulate the image using a special pen, or stylus, on the board or by moving a finger and tapping on the board's surface. It is also possible for the person operating the computer to present information on the board surface, adding to the presentation's content. Finally, the computer can capture any writings or drawings on the board and convert them to typed text, which can then be saved or printed. This feature makes interactive white boards great for brain storming sessions or class lessons since it is easy to capture and print the material covered for future use.

When purchasing an interactive white board, consider all options. Some small portable devices will convert regular white boards into interactive surfaces. These work well for most applications, but may

Interactive white boards can be mounted on the wall or on a rolling stand. They are used to interface between the user and a computer. Note, you must also have a multimedia projector to use an interactive white board. Photo courtesy of Smart Technologies.

not deliver all the services you desire. Larger mounted boards are more expensive, but have more software options. Consider the size, weight, and portability of the white boards you need. Will there be enough room for them in your classrooms? Is it possible to move a mounted white board around your school with ease? Another important question to ask yourself is this: do you have any students with disabilities that may use the interactive white board? If you do, you will need to consider how to position the board so that students with some disabilities can use it. A typical board mounted on a stand will probably be too tall for the average wheelchair-bound student.

Keep in mind that interactive white boards do not operate in isolation. You must also have compatible computer equipment to use with the board. Consult with your school technology staff to be sure your computers meet the specifications required by the manufacturer of the board that you are interested in purchasing. You will also need a multimedia projector to show the computer display on the board. Most schools will have computers that are compatible with the white boards, but if you do not have a multimedia projector or enough projectors to dedicate one to the interactive white board setup, you may need to include the cost of an additional machine in your budget.

Scanners

Scanning devices come in all shapes and sizes. A standard flatbed scanner will work for most school applications, but before purchasing one, it is best to consider how it will be used in your media center. Will students be using the machine? Will it be used primarily for scanning text or photos? Investigate your district requirements for purchasing scanners to be sure your purchase will conform to district regulations and computer networks. Since a scanner must be connected to a computer, it is also wise to be sure the computer you plan to use with the scanner will be compatible with the new device. Generally, one scanner located somewhere in the media center is sufficient for most needs. Due to copyright concerns, many media specialists place the scanner away from easy student access. Policies must then be in place to allow students to use the machine when appropriate.

A variation on the standard scanner is a machine that makes posters. Poster makers scan documents printed on regular sized paper and blow them up into poster-sized printouts using special paper. Typically, the paper comes in 17-, 23-, and 36-inch widths. Depending on the model of poster maker your school owns, posters may be monotone or color. Poster maker machines and the special paper they require to make the posters are expensive; however, they produce a useful product that is easy to read from a distance. School staff like the posters and use them for everything from posting rules and schedules to curriculum-related topics and assignment requirements. If your school does not own a poster maker, you may want to investigate the cost and add it to your technology plan for future purchase.

Digital Cameras and Camcorders

Teachers and students use digital cameras and camcorders to document, illustrate, and create many different things around the school. Most media centers will need to have multiple units of each available for checkout at all times. Be sure to look at the specification sheets for any digital camera or camcorder you are considering for purchase. There are several important things you may need to consider such as:

- What type of storage media does this unit use? Digital cameras might use memory cards or sticks, floppy disks, or internal memory. Camcorders using traditional VHS are being phased out and replaced by several types of digital media. Whether you are buying a camera or camcorder, ask what type of media it uses to store images, how the images can be retrieved or played back, and what cost is involved in purchasing the media. You will also need to decide if you will provide these storage devices for teachers or expect them to provide their own and communicate this policy to the faculty at your school.
- Batteries are another important consideration. Most camcorders have a special rechargeable battery pack. Investigate the cost of replacement batteries and consider purchasing more than one for each camcorder so users have a spare available to them. When considering digital cameras, find out what type of battery is used by the cameras you might purchase. Find out if the battery is rechargeable, how much it costs, and if it is readily available. Since the portability of cameras and camcorders is one of their most desirable traits, good batteries are essential. Take time to investigate and choose equipment with easily supplied batteries to keep all your cameras and camcorders running.
- Unique to camcorders is the issue of a microphone input. The microphone mounted on the camera is designed to pick up all the ambient sound in an area. However, many teachers and students require the ability to connect an exterior microphone to record specific sounds. If you know

good audio is important for the end user, you will need at least one camcorder with an external microphone input jack. Be sure to ask your salesperson about this and examine the camcorder specification sheet for this important information.

- Since many new camcorders are digital, a special VCR might also be useful for your media center. The new digital videotapes are smaller than traditional VHS tapes and will not play on the VCRs in most classrooms. You may need to purchase a digital video to VHS machine. Besides being able to play back digital videotapes, these special units are able to duplicate copies from digital tapes onto VHS. These special VCRs are available from several manufacturers, so be sure to compare prices.

CD, Tape, and MP3 Players

CD and tape player/recorder units are still needed in school classrooms. Make sure your media center is stocked with these. CD players are increasingly popular as textbook publishers supply audio CDs of texts for students to use. Many media centers are also stocking audio books, which are now commonly available on compact disc. Old-fashioned cassette tapes are still used as well for audio books, music recordings, and other curriculum related needs. Be sure to have some cassette recorders, not just players, in your equipment collection. CD recorders are not yet commonplace and are costly. Stay alert to technology pricing, however, because CD recorders will eventually become more affordable, and when that happens, you will want to upgrade your collection to include them. In the meantime, cassette tape recording is used in a variety of ways to help students learn, document progress, and produce products to document their accomplishments.

When considering CD and tape player/recorders, you may want to stock up with some of the following styles:

- Larger players that allow users to plug in headphones and become listening stations for individual or group work.
- Smaller individual portable players for students to use in the class or media center with headphones to listen to audio books.
- Boom box–style players for classroom use. Many teachers will appreciate these models as they play music or audio books for their classes.
- Some dual-purpose units allow users to copy a CD onto a tape. While it is important to be aware of copyright laws when using this feature, it is helpful for many purposes around a school. For example, a chorus or band teacher may duplicate selected parts of a musical piece for students to take home for practice.

Along with your CD/tape player units, you will also need to stock headphones for students to listen to tapes. Many different brands of headsets are on the market, and most are inexpensive. You will probably want to purchase both larger headphones and smaller Walkman-style headsets. Since most headphone units are generally inexpensive, they are not usually worth the cost of repair. Therefore, it is usually wise to order more than you need so that you have extras on hand for instant replacement when you determine that a pair is not working. Check to see how these units plug into your player/recorder units. Adapters are sometimes needed to enable the headset to fit into the player/recorder unit. These adaptors are commonly available at most electronic stores and from a variety of catalog and online vendors. Wise media specialists keep a stock of these adaptors on hand since they are easily lost.

MP3 players are increasingly popular with students and teachers who download music and audio books in digital format from the Internet. Individual audio books on MP3 players are now available in bookstores, signaling the rise of this new format for libraries. These MP3 devices contain one book that can be replayed an unlimited number of times and are competitively priced with traditional books on tape or CD. Some vendors who supply schools with audio books now offer this format. Media specialists unfamiliar with MP3 players need to learn about them and imagine ways to incorporate them into media programs. Media specialists can lead the way by assisting teachers who want to incorporate this emerging technology into their classrooms.

Portable Keyboard Units

Portable keyboard units are relatively inexpensive when compared with the cost of portable laptop computers. This makes them very attractive to many schools seeking to maximize technology dollars. Since these units are mostly limited to word processing, students often use them to type rough drafts of projects that they then download onto a computer for editing. Students with learning disabilities are able to use them more successfully for class work than traditional pen and paper, and they also come in handy for students who do not have computers at home. Portable keyboards make it easy for these students to type and present projects in the same way as their peers. Having one or two of these units available in the media center for checkout is a nice plus. Teachers may also want to use them, and a policy may need to be developed for checking them out to individual students. Some schools purchase class sets of these units

A portable keyboard unit, such as the one shown above, runs on batteries and can be used anywhere for word processing and other things. When the user finishes typing, the unit is connected to a computer and the files are downloaded directly into common software applications for use.

that can be rolled to classrooms for student use. Consider investing in one or two portable keyboards if your school does not own any. You may need to spend a little time promoting them, but once your faculty and students see what they can do, they will not be sitting idly on the shelf.

Video Playback Machines

Contemporary media centers still need video playback machines, but it is recommended that all purchases be combined (DVD/VCR) units. While DVDs are increasingly common in the educational media market, there are still items available only on VHS, plus most schools will not be able to pay the costs associated with converting collections to the DVD format at one time. There is likely to be an extended period during which most schools will be using both formats, hence the need for combined unit purchases. Many schools commonly installed VCRs in all classrooms. If this is the case in your school, purchase a few DVD players for checkout as you begin to purchase video discs for the collection. Make a plan to begin replacing the existing VCRs with combined DVD/VCR units as soon as possible. It is always advisable to have a few extra video player units in the media center. They will be useful as temporary replacements when units break and need to go for repair or for special events that require video playback in an unusual place.

AV Carts

Audiovisual carts come in a variety of sizes. Commonly, most school media centers need several larger carts to hold television monitors and video playback units. It is important to be sure these carts have a safety strap properly secured to the cart to hold the television monitor in place. In addition, you will need smaller standard audiovisual carts that typically stand about waist high and contain three shelves. The number of carts needed by the media center is determined by the size of the school community. Finances usually make it impossible to supply one cart per teacher, so the media specialist will have to establish priorities, for example, floating teachers truly need to have a cart. Always keep a certain number of carts in the media center for moving things around the school and limited checkout as needed by teachers and staff.

Be sure to ask your vendor when pricing the carts whether electrical cords and outlets are included with the carts you are purchasing. Electrical outlets for both the cart types described above are worth the extra money. The convenience they provide becomes a necessity when trying to connect a television, DVD/VCR unit, or any other electronic device in a classroom setting. The electrical cords on these units are never long enough, so the safety provided by the extra cord on the cart is important.

Overhead Projectors

Overhead projectors have been a standard piece of technology in classrooms for decades, and while newer machines like multimedia projectors are replacing them, they are not likely to disappear from the educational scene for several reasons. First, they are economical. A good overhead projector costs less than $200. The replacement lamps are also more economical than the lamps used in multimedia projectors. Secondly, they can be used alone. You do not need a computer or other peripheral device, just transparency acetates and water-soluble marker pens. Finally, they are easy to use—just plug it in and turn it on. They do not require special wiring or cable connections, making them much less intimidating to many teachers. They may be old, but this workhorse of the classroom is not going away anytime soon, so be sure to stock up your media center with enough of these units to provide for instructional use in the classrooms and for special needs that come up from time to time.

When purchasing overhead projectors, consider the following:

- You will want to stock up on replacement lamps for the projectors, so find out what type of lamp the unit you may buy uses. Is it compatible with your current projector bulbs? What is the cost and availability of the projector lamp in question?
- Some teachers may want a roller attachment for the overhead that takes a spool of clear acetate and allows it to be moved back and forth over the stage area. If this is the case, be aware that you will probably have to purchase a more expensive projector model. Less expensive machines do not usually allow the rollers to be attached to the unit.
- Overheads generally take a lot of abuse. People tend to carry them by the arm that holds the projector eye instead of handling them by holding the unit's base. Focusing mechanisms become stripped as teachers and students play with them excessively. Teachers without transparencies will

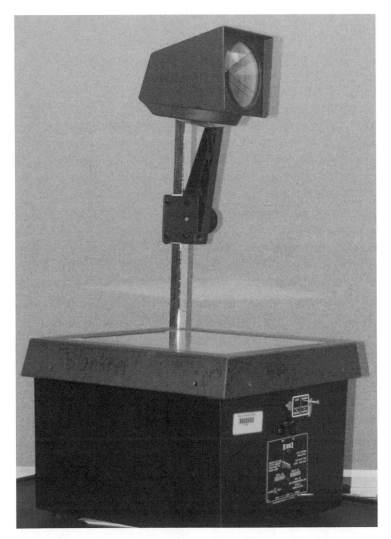

The overhead projector remains popular with teachers because it is easy to use. Media specialists like them because their low cost doesn't eat up valuable budget money.

write directly on the glass stage then spray water on it to clean the surface. Since overheads are electrical devices, cleaning them with water is not a good idea. The use of water in this capacity can cause the unit to short out and become unusable. Given these situations and more, it is a good idea to have a few spare overheads available for classroom replacements should a unit need to be repaired. You also may consider buying a more expensive model because of sturdier design. Finally, it is important to schedule annual maintenance for your overheads. A quick cleaning of the inside, exterior, and lenses of each unit once a year will increase the unit's lifespan.

The equipment listed above encompasses most of the audiovisual needs of modern school libraries. When you inherit a media center, take time to inventory the equipment you have. You may inherit some old dinosaurs like filmstrip projectors, 16mm movie projectors, laser disc players, and microfiche readers. Before you begin throwing these things away, take time to survey your collection and teachers. Perhaps you have someone still using some of these old formats for legitimate reasons (maybe your school owns a rare old movie not converted to video or DVD), or there may be budgetary concerns causing the maintenance of older technologies. You may have to build a case with your principal and school community for weeding both the older technologies and media. Be sure you develop a plan for replacement and updating of the collection to make all the school stakeholders feel secure in the knowledge that you are looking out for their curriculum and student needs. Then, begin updating the equipment collection as soon as possible.

Managing Your Equipment Collection

As media specialists, we are "keepers of the stuff," and there is a lot of it, especially when we start talking about keeping track of our equipment collections. It is also crucial that we do this part of our jobs well since many of our most coveted pieces of equipment are extremely expensive and not easily replaced. This same equipment can be rendered useless by the loss of cables and other things needed to properly connect them and allow for maximum usage. Fortunately, the advent of modern media management software has made it easier to keep track of who has a particular piece of equipment, since most media specialists now bar code equipment and check it out using the computer. The real issue now is keeping track of all the pieces belonging to a particular item.

In the past, audiovisual equipment, for the most part, came in one piece with an electrical cord attached. Now things come with many different parts that are necessary to use the equipment. Keeping track of all these parts can be a daunting task. As an example, imagine opening the box of a new multimedia projector. As soon as you begin unpacking the new projector, you will begin to wonder, "How can I check this out to someone? There are so many pieces!" These parts can include video cables, several computer cables, remote controls, batteries, software disks, and more. Multimedia projectors are not an isolated case; digital cameras, camcorders, and document cameras all have the same issue. How will you manage these machines and all their parts so that they can continue to be used for years to come? It is important to develop an organized plan and stick to it in order to keep track of the equipment in your school collection.

Here are a few simple suggestions for managing your audiovisual equipment collection, Look them over and consider how they can be adapted for your workplace.

- When opening new equipment, look through the instruction manual to gain a perspective on how the machine is connected and works. Look for an inventory page that identifies all the parts, connection instructions, and troubleshooting tips. It is not important to memorize the manual at this point, but you do want to get a feel for the machine and all its parts so you can begin organizing everything for circulation. Decide if you will circulate the manual with the equipment.

Sidebar 16.04 Voice of Experience from Claire

EQUIPMENT MANAGEMENT REQUIRES TOOLS AND ORGANIZATION!

Over the years, I've learned that managing your equipment collection and your media center will require some tools. I'm not speaking metaphorically here—I mean literal tools. Get yourself a small toolbox and some basic tools like a hammer, flat and Phillips head screwdrivers in a variety of sizes, pliers, and so forth. You'll also need some organizers for things like batteries, cable connectors, and electrical tape. You'll be surprised how often these things are used, and you'll find yourself adding to them each year.

A small collection of tools and some things to keep your equipment room organized will be invaluable.

You may want to keep one or two copies of the entire manual in a file and only include copied pages showing set up steps and other relevant information with your circulating machines.

- Identify all the parts and decide if they are really needed for most classroom applications. If a part is not needed, eliminate it from the circulating unit. For example, some things now come with European style electrical cables, which will not be used in America. These power cords can be thrown away.

- You may want to bar code some parts individually. An example of this may be the remote controls that come with DVD/VCR units. Remotes are frequently misplaced or lost. By attaching a bar code to each remote and scanning it out to the teacher using it, much confusion can be eliminated. Study the equipment manual and consider your staff that will be using the equipment and your ability to store whatever you bar code separately from the main piece of equipment it supports before you make the decision to break up equipment sets.

- After identifying all the necessary parts for day-to-day machine use, create an inventory list for each machine. Use this list to be sure you have all the parts with the machine whenever it is checked out and, even more importantly, when it is returned. Attach a copy of the inventory list to each unit to assist clerical staff when they work with the equipment. Take a hard line with teachers who return units missing a part. Nicely, but firmly, insist they locate the missing piece. If the teacher is offended, point out that the next person will not be able to use the machine without the missing part.

- If your machines do not have carrying cases, decide how to keep the unit and all its parts together. Often a small- to medium-sized plastic bin with a lid can hold all the parts and the machine. These bins make it easy to keep the equipment and all its parts together as a set and can be stacked for

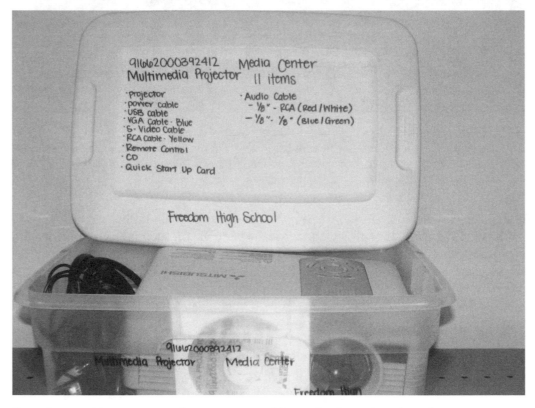

Store items with many parts in easy to carry bins or baskets. Attach an inventory tag or write it on the storage bin. Train your staff to inventory the item each time it is checked out or in.

easy storage. Using a waterproof marker, write the bar code number for the machine on the bin. Write the inventory list for the machine directly on the lid. If a machine does have a carrying case, you can write all the identifying information on the container. Whether the projector is in a case or plastic bin, the unit and all parts become a set checked in and out under one bar code number.

Decide how you will process your equipment with the required property information and consistently mark each piece of equipment. This multimedia projector is marked with a district-required fixed asset number and property inventory bar code.

- Examine each machine. Decide where to put your bar code and other identifying information. Examine all the parts. Is it possible to write the bar code on each piece in some way? This will help keep sets together when pieces are inevitably returned in a piecemeal fashion.
- Record each serial number and bar code. This is important information for repair orders and very important in the event of theft. Many media management systems make it possible to record this information on the computer in some fashion. If your media management software does not have this feature, be sure to make multiple copies of this list and place them in logical places so you can locate the information when it is needed.
- The last thing you must do before circulating your new equipment is to practice setting it up and taking it down yourself. This will prepare you to handle the questions teachers ask and be aware of problems they may encounter. Be sure to train your staff on how to use the new audiovisual equipment, too, since teachers will ask them questions about the equipment when you are busy. Consider offering an in-service session to teachers, training them to use the new projectors. Teachers who attend the session could have first priority for using one in their classroom.

Audiovisual equipment is indispensable in the classroom. Whether your school has a lot of equipment or a few workhorse machines, it is likely that you will be purchasing and using new pieces of equipment in the future. Don't let modern technology intimidate you. Remember, with some basic knowledge and research, you can easily make good and wise purchases for your school, providing your faculty and students with the ability to incorporate multiple forms of technology into their lessons and projects for years to come.

Bibliography

AVParnter.com. *Tips and Tricks: Projector Buying Tips*. Available at: http://www.avpartner.com/Tips_tricks/ tips_buying.htm (accessed October 9, 2005).

AV Presentations, Inc. *Intro to Home Theatre: LCD vs. DLP*. Available at: http://www.avphometheatre.com/ IntroMain.htm# (accessed October 9, 2005).

Education World. *Speaking of Electronic Whiteboards...* Available at: http://www.educationworld.com/a_tech/ tech/tech206.shtml (accessed February 28, 2006).

Life Tips, 2005. *Life Tips, The Online Owners Manuel for Your Life: Projector Tips*. Available at: http://projector. lifetips.com/cat/59699/tips-for-choosing-a-classroom-projector (accessed October 9, 2005).

Wedgewood IT Group. *Document Cameras and Visualizers*. Available at: http://www.wedgwood-group.com/ document_cameras_and_visualisers.htm (accessed February 28, 2006).

Whiteboards Review. Available at: http://acitt.digitalbrain.com/acitt/web/resources/pubs/Journal%2002/ whiteboards2.htm (accessed February 27, 2006).

Appendixes

National Level Professional Organizations

These national and international organizations will be useful for new school library personnel. Included with each organization is a brief description and Web address for further information.

American Association of School Librarians (AASL)—A division of ALA, AASL exists to promote excellence in school librarianship. AASL has worked tirelessly to advocate for school library standards and authored important philosophical works, such as *Information Power*, which have influenced school library programs around the world. Web site: http://www.ala.org/ala/aasl/aaslindex.htm.

American Library Association (ALA)—The professional organization for professional librarianship in the United States, ALA has several divisions of interest to school library/media professionals, including the AASL and the Association for Library Service to Children. Web site: http://www.ala.org.

Association for Educational Communications and Technology (AECT)—This group has collaborated with AASL to help create guidelines for school media programs. They exist to promote scholarship and best practices for technology use in schools. Web site: http://www.aect.org/default.asp.

Association for Library Service to Children (ALSC)—A division of ALA, this group focuses on developing quality programs to service children through library programs. Web site: http://www.ala.org/ALSCTemplate.cfm?Section=alsc.

International Reading Association (IRA)—This professional organization is for people involved in the teaching of reading. Web site: http://www.ira.org/.

International Society for Technology in Education (ISTE)—This nonprofit organization seeks to advance the effective use of technology and teacher education in schools. ISTE sponsors the National Education Computing Conference (NECC), the largest conference of its type, and has authored national education technology standards for schools. Web site: http://www.iste.org.

Young Adult Library Services Association (YALSA)—Another ALA division, YALSA's focus on programs and literature for teens makes it a great choice for those working in secondary education. Web site: http://www.ala.org/yalsaTemplate.cfm?Section=yalsa.

State Professional Organizations

These state organizations will be helpful for new school library media specialists seeking to network with other nearby professionals. In addition to these statewide professional groups, seek out local level organizations supported by your district or county.

Alabama

Alabama Instructional Media Association—Web site: http://www.fayette.k12.al.us/fes/aima/
Alabama Library Association—Web site: http://allanet.org/.

Alaska

Alaska Association of School Librarians—Web site: http://www.akla.org/akasl.

Arizona

Arizona Library Association—Web site: http://www.azla.org/.

Arkansas

Arkansas Association of School Librarians—Web site: http://www.arlib.org/AASL/index.htm.

California

California School Library Association—Web site: http://www.schoolibrary.org.

Colorado

Colorado Association of School Libraries—Web site: http://www.cal-webs.org.

Connecticut

Connecticut Educational Media Association—Web site: http://www.ctcema.org.

Delaware

Delaware School Library Media Association—Web site: http://www.udel.edu/erc/dslma/.

District of Columbia

District of Columbia Library Association—Web site: http://www.dcla.org.

Florida

Florida Association for Media in Education—Web site: http://www.floridamedia.org.

Georgia

Georgia Library Media Association—Web site: http://www.glma-inc.org.

Hawaii

Hawaii Association of School Librarians—Web site: http://hasl.ws/.
Hawaii Library Association—Web site: http://www.hlaweb.org/index.html.

Idaho

Idaho Library Association Educational Media Division—Web site: http://www.idaholibraries.org/
    divisions/ed-media/index.htm.

Illinois

Illinois School Library Media Association—Web site: http://www.islma.org/.

Indiana

Association for Indiana Media Educators—Web site: http://www.ilfonline.org/AIME/index.htm.

Iowa

Iowa Association of School Librarians—Web site: http://www.iasl-ia.org.

Kansas

Kansas Association of School Librarians—Web site: http://skyways.lib.ks.us/kasl/.
Kansas Library Association (Children's and School Libraries Section)—Web site: http://skyways.lib.
    ks.us/kansas/KLA/divisions/csls/.

Kentucky

Kentucky School Media Association—Web site: http://www.kysma.org/.

Louisiana

Louisiana Association of School Librarians—Web site: http://www.llaonline.org/sig/lasl/.

Maine

Maine Association of School Librarians—Web site: http://www.maslibraries.org.

Maryland

Maryland Educational Media Organization—Web site: http://mdedmedia.org.

Massachusetts

Massachusetts School Library Association—Web site: http://www.maschoolibraries.org/.

Michigan

Michigan Association for Media in Education (MAME)—Web site: http://www.mame.gen.mi.us.

Minnesota

Minnesota Educational Media Organization (MEMO)—Web site: http://www.memoweb.org/.

Mississippi

Mississippi Library Association—Web site: http://www.misslib.org/index.php.
Mississippi Library and Media Professionals (LAMP)—Web site: http://www.lampworkshop.org/.

Missouri

Missouri Association of School Librarians (MASL)—Web site: http://www.maslonline.org.

Montana

Montana Library Association School and Library Media Division—Web site: http://www.mtlib.org/.

Nebraska

Nebraska Educational Media Association—Web site: http://nema.k12.ne.us.

Nevada

Nevada Library Association—Web site: http://www.nevadalibraries.org/index.html.

New Hampshire

New Hampshire Educational Media Association—Web site: http://www.nhema.net/.

New Jersey

New Jersey Association of School Librarians—Web site: http://www.emanj.org.

New Mexico

New Mexico Library Association—Web site: http://www.nmla.org/home.html.

New York

School Library Media Section of the New York Library Association—Web site: http://www.nyla.org/index.php?page_id=52.

North Carolina

North Carolina Association of School Librarians (NCASL)—Web site: http://www.nclaonline.org/ncasl/.

North Dakota

North Dakota Library Association—Web site: http://www.ndla.info.

Ohio

Ohio Educational Library Media Association (OELMA)—Web site: http://www.oelma.org/.

Oklahoma

Oklahoma Association of School Library Media Specialists—Web site: http://www.oklibs.org/~oaslms/.

Oregon

Oregon Educational Media Association (OEMA)—Web site: http://www.oema.net/.

Pennsylvania

Pennsylvania School Librarians Association—Web site: http://www.psla.org.

Rhode Island

Rhode Island Educational Media Association—Web site: http://www.ri.net/RIEMA/index.html.

South Carolina

South Carolina Association of School Librarians—Web site: http://www.scasl.net/.

South Dakota

South Dakota Library Association—Web site: http://www.usd.edu/sdla/.

Tennessee

Tennessee Association of School Librarians—Web site: http://www.discoveret.org/tasl/.

Texas

Texas Association of School Librarians (TASL)—Web site: http://www.txla.org/groups/tasl/.

Utah

Utah Educational Library Media Association—Web site: http://www.uelma.org.

Vermont

Vermont Educational Media Association—Web site: http://homepage.mac.com/crowleyvt/vema.

Virginia

Virginia Educational Media Association—Web site: http://www.vema.gen.va.us/.

Washington

Washington Library Media Association—Web site: http://www.wlma.org.

West Virginia

School Library Division of the West Virginia Library Association—Web site: http://www.wvla.org/.

Wisconsin

Wisconsin Educational Media Association—Web site: http://www.wemaonline.org/ab.main.cfm.

Wyoming

School Library Media Personnel Section of the Wyoming Library Association—Web site: http://www.wyla.org/schools/index.shtml.

Helpful Resources

The following resources can be helpful to school library professionals. Take time to investigate them as you learn more about the profession.

The Children's Author Network is a group of authors who work to promote literacy and excitement about children's books through school visits. For more information, refer to http://childrensauthorsnetwork.com/.

The Children's Book Council is the nonprofit trade association of publishers and packagers of trade books and related materials for children and young adults. The council seeks to promote reading and literacy for American children and young adults. They sponsor Children's Book Week each year. For more information, refer to http://www.cbcbooks.org.

The Children's Literature Association promotes study and scholarship in children's literature. For more information, refer to http://chla.wikispaces.com/Home.

The Horn Book is a publisher of professional journals about books for children and young adults, including *Horn Book Magazine* and *Horn Book Guide.* They also sponsor book awards and other reading promotional events. For more information, refer to http://www.hbook.com.

The Laura Bush Foundation for America's Libraries promotes reading and literacy by providing grants to school libraries for the purchase of books. For more information, refer to http://www.laurabushfoundation.org.

The National Book Foundation seeks to increase cultural awareness of great writing in America. They sponsor the National Book Awards each year, including an award recognizing excellence in writing for children and young adults. For more information, refer to http://www.nationalbook.org.

Read across America Day is sponsored each year by the National Education Association and held on March second, the birthday of the beloved children's author Dr. Seuss. This popular event has grown over the past 10 years into a nationwide celebration of reading. For more information, refer to http://www.nea.org/readacross/index.html.

The Society for Children's Book Writers and Illustrators (SCBWI) is a professional organization for writers and illustrators of children's books. SCBWI has grown into an international group working to improve the art and craft of children's writing and publishing. They also sponsor annual awards recognizing new authors and illustrators. For more information, refer to http://www.scbwi.org.

Awards and Prizes
and Books . . . Oh My!

Book Award Information on the Web

Book awards can be an excellent resource for collection development. Below, you will find links to general and specific award sites.

1. General Award Links (Bookmark these!)

ALSC Awards and Grants: http://www.ala.org/ala/alsc/awardsscholarships/literaryawds/literaryrelated. htm.

> This page offers links to all the American Library Association award sites. It also includes ALA notable books and others.

Children's Book Awards—sponsored by the Children's Literature Web Guide: http://www.acs.ucalgary. ca/~dkbrown/awards.html.

> This site contains links to information and lists for many different awards (includes international and nonmainstream). Its weakness is that some of the background information is sketchy, and many of the award lists are just that—lists with no bibliographic or content information.

2. Specific Award Sites

Ben Franklin Awards: http://www.pma-online.org/benfrank.cfm.

> Sponsored by the Publishers Marketing Association, this award recognizes excellence in independent publishing. The awards are given based on book genre and judged by editorial and design merit. There are a variety of different genre or categories that apply to educational libraries and many that do not. Please check the winning category before ordering based on this award.

Boston Horn Book Awards: http://www.hbook.com/awards/default.asp.

> Recognizes excellence in literature for children and young adults in three categories: fiction and poetry, picture books, and nonfiction.

Caldecott Medal: http://www.ala.org/ala/alsc/awardsscholarships/literaryawds/caldecottmedal/
caldecottmedal.htm.

Named in honor of nineteenth-century English illustrator Randolph Caldecott, this award
is given annually by ALSC to the artist of the most distinguished American picture book
for children in the preceding year.

Charlotte Zolotow Award: http://www.education.wisc.edu/ccbc/books/zolotow.asp.

Honors the best picture book *text*. The award is administered by the Cooperative Children's
Book Center, a children's literature library of the School of Education, University of Wisconsin–Madison, and honors the work of Charlotte Zolotow, a distinguished children's book
editor for 38 years with Harper Junior Books and author of more than 65 picture books.

Coretta Scott King Book Award: http://www.ala.org/ala/emiert/corettascottkingbookawards/
corettascott.htm.

Given to an African American author and illustrator for an outstanding contribution to children's and YA literature, the Coretta Scott King Award seeks to promote understanding
and appreciation of all peoples and their contribution to the realization of the American
dream.

Giverny Award: http://www.15degreelab.com/award.html.

Specifically honors picture books that teach scientific concepts.

Henry Bergh Award: http://www.aspca.org/site/PageServer?pagename=edu_bookaward.

The award was established by the ASPCA to honor books that promote the humane ethic of
compassion and respect for all living things. The award is named in honor of the ASPCA
founder, Henry Bergh. Given in several different categories, the award is presented each
year at the ALA conference. Check the book level and appropriateness for your school
level when ordering for this award. Most titles seem to be suitable to elementary and
middle grades.

Laura Ingalls Wilder Award: http://www.ala.org/ala/alsc/awardsscholarships/literaryawds/
wildermedal/wildermedal.htm.

This award honors an author or illustrator whose books, published in the United States, have
made a substantial and lasting contribution to literature for children over the years.

The Man Booker Prize: http://www.themanbookerprize.com

Awarded annually, the Man Booker Prize recognizes the best fiction writing by a citizen
of the Commonwealth or the Republic of Ireland. Winners of this prestigious award
become international best-sellers. High school media specialists may want to consider
adding these prizewinners to their collections.

Michael L. Printz Award for Excellence in Young Adult Literature: http://www.ala.org/ala/yalsa/
booklistsawards/printzaward/Printz,_Michael_L__Award.htm.

The Printz Award recognizes excellence in writing for young adults and is administered by YALSA, a division of ALA, and sponsored by *Booklist*, a publication of ALA.

Mildred Batchelder Award: http://www.ala.org/ala/alsc/awardsscholarships/literaryawds/ batchelderaward/batchelderaward.htm

The Batchelder Award recognizes an American publisher for a children's book originally published in another country and then translated into English for publication in the United States. The award seeks to encourage publishers to promote communication among the peoples of the world. This award is also sponsored by ALSC.

National Book Awards: http://www.nationalbook.org/nba.html.

Recognizes excellence in literature in four categories including children's literature. Award is administered by the National Book foundation.

Newbery Award: http://www.ala.org/ala/alsc/awardsscholarships/literaryawds/newberymedal/ newberymedal.htm.

Awarded annually by ALSC to the author of the most distinguished contribution to American literature for children in the preceding year.

Orbis Pictus Award (NCTE): http://www.ncte.org/about/awards/sect/elem/106877.htm.

Given by the National Council of Teachers of English, the Orbis Pictus Award recognizes outstanding nonfiction publications for children.

Parent's Choice Awards: http://www.parents-choice.org/get_direct.cfm?cat=p_boo.

The Parent's Choice Foundation seeks to identify the best products for children of different ages, backgrounds, skills, and interests.

The Pulitzer Prize: http://www.pulitzer.org.

Named to honor Hungarian-born American journalist Joseph Pulitzer, this award is considered the highest national honor for achievement in American journalism, literary works, and musical composition. The Pulitzer Price board administers the award, which is housed at Columbia University in New York City. High school media specialists may want to consider adding the Pulitzer winners each year.

Pura Belpré Award: http://www.ala.org/ala/alsc/awardsscholarships/literaryawds/belpremedal/ belprmedal.htm.

This award is presented to a Latino/Latina writer and illustrator whose work portrays, affirms, and celebrates the Latino cultural experience in an outstanding work of literature for children and youth. It is cosponsored by ALSC and REFORMA, the National Association to Promote Library and Information Services to Latinos and the Spanish-Speaking, an ALA Affiliate.

Robert F. Sibert Informational Book Medal: http://www.ala.org/ala/alsc/awardsscholarships/ literaryawds/sibertmedal/Sibert_Medal.htm.

The Sibert Award is awarded annually to the most distinguished informational book published in English during the preceding year.

Schneider Family Book Awards: http://www.ala.org/Template.cfm?Section=awards&template&#x00 3D;/ContentManagement/ContentDisplay.cfm&ContentID=115041.

This award honors an author or illustrator for a book that offers a creative look at the disability experience for child and adolescent audiences.

Scott Odell Historical Fiction Award: http://www.scottodell.com/odellaward.html

Established in 1981 by Scott O'Dell, the Scott O'Dell Historical Fiction Award is an annual award presented for a work of historical fiction for children or young adults published by a U.S. publisher and set in the New World.

Theodore Seuss Geisel Award: http://www.ala.org/ala/alsc/awardsscholarships/literaryawds/ geiselaward/GeiselAward.htm.

This new award is named in honor of beloved children's book author Dr. Seuss and is given to honor writers and illustrators of beginning reader books.

Library 101 Vocabulary: A Glossary of Library Terms

Like any profession, school librarians have unique words they use when communicating with each other. Understanding these terms and acronyms will help new school personnel cut through the jargon and better communicate with their peers and staff. Note: this glossary is not based on academic definitions of these terms; rather, we developed it according to our daily practice as school media specialists.

AACRII: Anglo-American Cataloging Rules, second edition. The standard set of rules for cataloging. These rules describe how to handle multiple authors, alternate titles, and so forth. In other words, they provide a framework for handling the presentation of information in a catalog record. AARCII is specific; it details the information required to catalog completely and correctly.

AASL: The American Association of School Librarians. AASL is a division of the ALA.

Abstract: A brief description of a work, which summarizes its major points. See also "annotation."

Academic Library: A school library organized to meet the information needs of students, faculty, and affiliated staff.

Access: The availability of the library to its patrons. Access also is used to describe the ability of patrons to utilize specific sources of information in a library.

Accession Number: Not commonly used anymore in school libraries, the accession number refers to a consecutive number assigned to each item as it is added to a collection. Accession numbers provided a way to identify things in a collection in the order they were purchased.

Accredited Library School: A college or university offering a library education program meeting standards of the ALA. For those desiring to be school library media specialists, some colleges and universities offer programs meeting the standards of the National Council for Accreditation of Teacher Education (NCATE). Most states accept school librarians for certification that attended an ALA or an NCATE accredited school.

Acquisitions: The actions taken to obtain library resources. Acquisitions can involve purchasing, seeking donations, grant writing, or other means of getting materials.

ALA: American Library Association. A large, national-level association that serves all sorts of libraries. ALA contains many divisions, including AASL.

Annotation: A brief summary of a book usually found in a note on the MARC record. See also "abstract."

Bibliographic Records: Cataloging information used to describe an item. Modern libraries use computerized bibliographic records known as MARC records. Libraries that are not automated use card catalogs; in this case, each catalog card is an example of a bibliographic record. Patrons access resources by searching the bibliographic records in the library catalog.

Bibliography: A resource list identifying items that have something in common. A bibliography might list books on a common subject or theme, for example, holiday books or books by a particular author. Students are often required to compile bibliographies of the works used to research a paper or project.

BIP or Books in Print: A listing of titles available in print. BIP was originally a multivolume book set, but is now available online from several different vendors.

Boolean Searches: A computer search using various terms linked by the words *and, or*, or *not* to narrow or expand the search. Boolean searches are commonly used when searching the Internet. The term comes from Boolean algebra, a branch of mathematics founded by George Boole in the 1800s.

Call Number: The classification number on library materials used to designate the item's place on the shelf. The Dewey Decimal and the Library of Congress are two classification systems. Call numbers should place books together with other titles of similar subject matter. The call number of a book is typically found on the spine label.

Card Catalog: A rapidly disappearing library resource. The card catalog was a piece of furniture that contained multiple small file drawers. Cards were placed in the drawers containing the identifying information about a book. Patrons looking for resources would browse the card catalog, writing down the call number and title of books they wanted from the book stacks. Computerized cataloging and online catalogs have largely replaced the card catalog.

Catalog: A file of bibliographic records that describe the materials in a collection. Modern catalogs are usually online. Schools that are not yet automated probably have an old-fashioned card catalog.

Cataloging: The process of physically describing library materials so that they can be listed in a catalog and located on a shelf for use by patrons.

CIP or Cataloging in Publication: A book's bibliographic record, usually found on the back of the title page.

Circulation: The checking in and out of library materials. When items in a library are checked out, they are referred to as circulating. School librarians frequently create circulation statistic reports showing use of the library by a count of materials checked out.

Circulation System: In a newer sense, this term refers to the computer media management system used by a library media center. Traditionally, it referred to the policies and procedures used in a library for lending materials to users and keeping checkout records

Citation: The identifying information for a source written in a strictly prescribed fashion (for example, the American Psychiatric Association [APA] or the Modern Language Association [MLA] formats). Citations are usually at the end of a report or article to give credit to the resource.

Classification System: A system for arranging library materials according to subject or form. The system most commonly used by school and public libraries is the Dewey Decimal System.

Collection: The library's holdings—the books, films, tapes, pictures, and so forth. that make up the materials the library offers its patrons for use. A special collection refers to an area of specialization, for example, many school libraries pull out Newbery Award books or career books into a separate section so it will be easier for students to locate them.

Collection Development: A broad term that covers the activities involved in building a library collection. Collection development in school library media centers includes defining selection policy, assessing user and curriculum needs, studying collection use, selecting materials, maintaining the collection, weeding, and so forth.

Copyright: The laws governing the exclusive rights granted by the government to an author, composer, artist, publisher, and so forth. for publishing and selling a work. All libraries are responsible for abiding within the law and district policies related to purchasing, copying, showing, and distributing copyrighted materials such as books, videos, audiotapes, and online content.

CPU or Central Processing Unit: The box or tower that contains the main hardware or circuitry of a computer system. The CPU is the brains of a computer system.

Cross Reference: A listing directing researchers from one heading to another or to related subject matter. For example, when looking up cars, a student might find the following: "Cars see Automobiles." Another common cross reference term is "see also." A researcher looking for penguins might find the following: "Penguins see also Birds."

Cutter Number: Developed by C.A. Cutter to help further organize books on a shelf, cutter numbers actually combine letters from an author's name and numbers assigned from a classification system to form a book's call number. In practice, the cutter numbers are the letters located on a spine label under the Dewey Decimal number. Usually the first three letters of the author's last name are used. When shelving, books are grouped in order first by the Dewey numbers, then arranged alphabetically according to the cutter numbers.

Dewey Decimal System: The system developed by Melvil Dewey to organize all the materials in a library based on common subject matter.

ERIC: This acronym stands for Educational Research Information Clearinghouse. ERIC is a project of the U.S. Department of Education that indexes information about education and teaching. The information is available through various online resources.

Folio: An oversized book.

Full Text: When an article accessed through an online database is presented in its entirety.

Holdings: The materials owned by a library or media center. See also "collection."

Index: Traditionally at the back of a book, the index is a guide to locating specific topics inside the resource. Usually an index is organized alphabetically, but it is not uncommon to find chronological or numerical organization. There are also some books that are indexes; these resources list specific things, for example, a short story index helps locate specific books containing particular short stories.

Information Literate: A person is information literate when he or she knows how to access quality information, extract accurate data, and correctly use the found information to meet his or her needs.

Interlibrary Loan: Sharing resources between libraries. If one media center does not own a certain book, they might request it from another library.

Inventory: The holdings of a media center are referred to as its inventory. In addition, the act of checking the collection against the recorded holdings is referred to as doing the inventory. Inventorying the collection is usually done once each year and is important to assure what holdings are accounted for and what may be lost or missing.

ISBN: International Standard Book Number, a unique identification number for books and other media such as magazines and recordings. Traditionally, ISBN numbers have been 10-digits long, but are being changed to 13 digits.

ISSN: International Standard Serial Number, the unique number assigned to each magazine or periodical that is published.

Jobber: A company that supplies books and other resources from different publishers to libraries and retailers. Common jobbers are Brodart, Baker and Taylor, Follett, and Mackin.

Journal: An academic or professional magazine published at consistent intervals.

Key Word: A term used to search for information in a bibliographic record. A keyword search looks for the term anywhere in the bibliographic record not just in the subject listings.

Library of Congress: The library in Washington, DC, which serves the U.S. Congress and other libraries. The LOC also works with the publishing industry and libraries to assist in developing rules for classification and cataloging of materials. For more information, refer to their Web site: http://www.loc.gov.

Library of Congress Classification System—A classification system for libraries devised by the LOC. Unlike the Dewey Decimal System, the LOC classifies information into 21 subject areas and uses a combination of letters and numbers for organization. Library of Congress classification is used mostly in college-level libraries.

MARC: Machine-Readable Cataloging. A standard arrangement of bibliographic information that allows for computer manipulation of the data.

Monograph: A term sometimes used in cataloging, it refers to a publication that is not a serial.

Nonprint Materials: Audiovisuals, computer software, videos, and so forth. that make up media center holdings but are not books or other printed materials.

Online Search: A search of databases through a computer.

Out of Print: An item falls out of print when its publisher no longer stocks it and does not intend to reprint additional copies.

OPAC: Online Public Access Catalog, the computerized catalog used by modern library patrons to search MARC records for resources.

Periodical: A regularly published magazine.

Periodical Index: A guide to assist in locating information published in periodicals (magazines). The *Reader's Guide to Periodical Literature* is the most common example of a periodical index. Traditional periodical indexes are being replaced by online databases that catalog magazines and newspapers and allow for computerized searches. *Children's Magazine Guide* is a periodical listing for children's magazines.

Processing: The act of preparing an item for circulation. Processing can include stamping an item with an identifying stamp, barcoding, and so forth.

Primary Source: An artifact from a particular period, which shows first-hand knowledge of an event.

Reading the Shelves: This refers to checking shelf order, usually with the help of a shelf list, to be sure all materials are in the correct order.

Retrospective Conversion: A school that has not yet been automated will have to go through a retrospective conversion process. This process converts the information found in the traditional card catalog to electronic or MARC format.

Sears List of Subject Headings: A standard reference source, published by H. W. Wilson, that is commonly used by school media specialists to determine correct subject headings when doing original cataloging.

Serial: Any publication (periodicals, newspapers, annuals, journals, transactions of societies, numbered monographic series, and all other publications in any medium) issued in successive parts and bearing numerical or chronological descriptions.

Series: A group of individual books, DVDs, or other media that are related by common subjects, characters, or themes. Series are usually not issued at the same time, but they do share a common title. Good examples from school library collections include *The Magic School Bus* series, *Goosebumps* books, and the four-book *Sisterhood of the Traveling Pants* series.

Shelf List: A correctly ordered listing of a collection's holdings. Now the shelf list is usually done by printing a report from the media management software.

Shelf Ready: Materials that are correctly processed and ready to go on the shelf. Some vendors advertise that their books will arrive shelf ready; however, in practice, there is usually some processing that needs to be done at the school site.

Special Collection: A group of materials that are housed separately from the rest of the collection because of a particular theme. In school libraries, special collections often include the Newberry or Caldecott Award books.

Spine Label: An identification sticker placed near the bottom of a book's spine that contains the book's call number. The spine label designates the book's address on the shelf.

Stacks: Areas of shelving in the media center set up to house collection holdings. Media specialists often refer to the book stacks as the area of the room where books are stored for patron access.

Subject Heading: A word or phrase used to indicate the topic, theme, or focus of a work. Subject headings are incorporated into MARC records and patrons can search for them using the OPAC to find materials.

Title Page: A page near the front of a book that identifies the book's title, author, and publishing information.

Tracings: An old term used to refer to the listing of all the subject headings a book could be found under in a card catalog. The tracings were on the book's shelf list card and were especially important if an item was weeded from the collection. Library staff would use the tracings on the shelf list card to pull all cards referring to the work from the catalog.

Union Catalog: A listing of the holdings from several different libraries that have agreed to share resources. With the advent of computerized cataloging, union catalogs have become much easier to create and maintain. They are also increasingly popular because they enable school and public libraries to stretch budget dollars through interlibrary loans.

Vertical File: An old term referring to a file cabinet containing newspaper and magazine clippings, photographs, pictures, and other documents deemed noteworthy for reference purposes. Many contemporary libraries have eliminated the vertical file because modern online databases make it possible to retrieve old newspaper and magazine articles quickly and easily.

Weeding: Removing old or damaged works from the collection. Items may be pulled because of age, damage, out-of-date information, and so forth. Weeding is an important and ongoing process in a healthy media center. It helps to keep the collection usable and up to date.

YA or Young Adult: A genre of books written for teens and young adults.

Index

About the Authors

CLAIRE GATRELL STEPHENS is a National Board Certified school library media specialist and works as a high school librarian in the Orange County Public Schools in Orlando, Florida. Claire has written two previous books with Libraries Unlimited, *Coretta Scott King Award Books: Using Great Literature with Children and Young Adults* (2000) and *Picture This! Using Picture Story Books for Character Education in the Classroom* (2003).

PATRICIA FRANKLIN is a National Board Certified school library media specialist and a high school librarian in the Orange County Public Schools in Orlando, Florida.